RADICAL STAGES

Recent Titles in
Contributions in Drama and Theatre Studies

RADICAL STAGES

Alternative History in Modern British Drama

D. Keith Peacock

Contributions in Drama and Theatre Studies, Number 43

Greenwood Press
New York · Westport, Connecticut · London

Library of Congress Cataloging-in-Publication Data

Peacock, D. Keith.
    Radical stages: alternative history in modern British drama /
D. Keith Peacock.
        p.   cm.—(Contributions in drama and theatre studies, ISSN
0163–3821; no. 43)
    Includes bibliographical references and index.
    ISBN 0–313–27888–1 (alk. paper)
    1. English drama—20th century—History and criticism.
2. Historical drama, English—History and criticism. 3. Social
problems in literature. 4. Radicalism in literature.   I. Title.
II. Series.
PR739.H5P4   1991
882′.91409—dc20   91–17119

British Library Cataloguing in Publication Data is available.

Library of Congress Catalog Card Number: 91–17119
ISBN: 0–313–27888–1
ISSN: 0163–3821

First published in 1991

Greenwood Press, 88 Post Road West, Westport, CT 06881
An imprint of Greenwood Publishing Group, Inc.

Printed in the United States of America

The paper used in this book complies with the Permanent Paper Standard issued by
the National Information Standards Organization (Z.39.48–1984).

10 9 8 7 6 5 4 3 2 1

Contents

Introduction

⟨

In 1956, in the play that inaugurated the New British Theatre, John Osborne's Jimmy Porter looked back in anger at what he considered to be his country's spiritual decline. In the years that followed, many British dramatists were also to reveal an acute consciousness of history, particularly of English history, and were repeatedly to exhibit an almost reflexive tendency to evoke the past in their dramatic exploration of hitherto neglected areas in the social and political life of their country. As Edward Bond has written, "Our age, like every age, needs to reinterpret the past as part of learning to understand itself, so that we can know what we are and what we should do."[1] Indeed, in a theatre that was attempting to chart the kind of new territory referred to above and was to associate itself predominantly with those ideals of social democracy which marked the early years of the post-war period, the examination and use of the past was to become as important as the analysis of the present. Most significantly, in the 1960s historical drama increasingly began to reflect the aspirations and activities of ordinary people rather than the lives and achievements of their rulers and in the 1970s was to become closely associated with the political aspirations of the New Left. It is with the nature and evolution of this radical British historical drama over three decades that this book is concerned.

It must be admitted from the outset that the post-1956 dramatisation of history has in many cases proved controversial. As might be expected from a theatre born in a period of social protest and associated with youthful rebellion, its opposition to the values and assumptions of the previous generation was also to extend to the re-evaluation and even outright rejection of that generation's perception of the past. A nation's history is not simply a record of events but is an agreed version of the past which embodies present values. As such it is a facet of what Marxists have described as that "ideological superstructure" which encompasses other art-forms, the communication media and the education system and is employed by the ruling group to perpetuate its power and dominance. To question or to attack that mythic history is, therefore, according to one's political viewpoint, tantamount either to mounting a revolutionary assault upon a bastion of the establishment or to committing an act of treason. Any variation from that myth—or, worse still, any intentionally alternative interpretation—may in consequence provoke a quite inordinate and even hysterical degree of censure from whichever interest group perceives its values to be threatened. In 1987, for example, Jim Allen's *Perdition* was to provoke accusations from Zionist organisations of prejudice and factual distortion. In response Max Stafford-Clark, the artistic director of the Royal Court Theatre where the play was scheduled for performance, took the decision shortly before its opening night to cancel the production. There was some irony in the fact that, as a director of the Joint Stock Theatre Company, Stafford-Clark had during the 1970s been one of the foremost promoters of plays that offered an "alternative" view of history.

The problem with Jim Allen's play was that it suggested that, with the aim of building up a case for the establishment of the new state of Israel, Hungarian Zionists had collaborated with the Nazis in sending Jews to the gas-chambers. In spite of attempts by Allen to draw a distinction between Judaism and Zionism, there were accusations from the Jewish lobby of "anti-semitism" and the dramatist was accused of employing factual inaccuracies and out-of-context quotations in an attempt to mount an ideological attack. While disputing the validity of such accusations, Allen was prepared to admit that his socialist sympathies for the oppressed had indeed in this instance led him to sympathise not with the Zionists but with the dispossessed Palestinians. In common with many left-wing dramatists during the previous thirty years, Allen had himself come face to face with that sacred cow, *agreed* history, assault upon which would, apparently inevitably, always be taken as an attack upon a whole culture.

Edward Bond, more than any other recent dramatist, has repeatedly attracted the kind of criticism heaped upon the unfortunate Allen. His iconoclastic portrayal of the Royal Family, politicians and other national figures of the Victorian era in his nightmarish historical fantasy, *Early Morning* (1968), and of Britain's most revered national dramatist, William Shakespeare, in *Bingo* (1974), in fictional contexts that were clearly pertinent to Britain's political and cultural present, provoked more than their fair share of critical resentment. Indeed Gareth Lloyd Evans, in his introduction to his collection of journalistic theatre criticism, *Plays in Review 1956–1980*, deemed it necessary to devote some time to illustrating and attacking Bond's treatment of history in general and of Shakespeare in particular. He claimed that

Any consideration of Bond's plays drops us bang in the middle of the whirlpools aroused by the dramatic use of history, the uncertain eddies it creates between fact and fiction and the critical assessment of them. Bond is a notable example of the buccaneer's way with history. He doesn't ignore it, but he makes it walk the plank of concepts, values, shibboleths, opinions—of which those contemporary with the events knew nothing, or knew them in forms very different from the modern shape he gives them.[2]

While allowing that dramatists have always exhibited a normally tolerable "beguiling waywardness with historical record", Lloyd Evans nevertheless considered that Bond had gone too far in wanting "both to have his cake and eat it, to use history as the handmaid of modern ideology, while at the same time claiming a sort of objective truth for his visions".[3] This is not the moment to argue whether Bond, in the preface to *Bingo* to which Lloyd Evans is referring, was in fact claiming to present "objective historical truth" or even whether "visions" may be considered to be expressions of anything so concrete, but it is certainly worth noting that, particularly during the 1970s, Bond was not the only dramatist to employ what might be considered to be "a beguiling waywardness with historical record" in that many others could likewise be accused of quite calculatedly and perversely offering "at best" an *alternative* and "at worst" an *iconoclastic* interpretation of history.

Let us not run away with the idea that it is only the Establishment which seeks to maintain and if necessary defend its own version of history. As Trevor Griffiths was to discover from the critical responses to his own play, *Occupations* (1970), those who are opposed to the Establishment are as keen to maintain their own mythic history as they are to deconstruct that of their political opponents. In the wake of the Royal Shakespeare Company's production of Griffiths' play at The Place in London in 1971, in an article in *7 Days* Tom Nairn criticised its portrayal of the Italian Marxist, Gramsci, and its dramatisation of the potentially revolutionary factory occupations that took place in Italy in 1920. Griffiths' letter of response to Nairn is appended to the published text of the play. As in most other debates concerning historical drama, the argument centred upon the play's historical accuracy and/or its "symbolic" representation of the historical forces at work within the events. The opening paragraph of Griffiths' response, itself prefiguring arguments that were to be aired again in the case of Jim Allen's *Perdition*, clearly outlines the nature of that controversy which is so often, and sometimes intentionally, provoked by historical drama. Griffiths wrote:

It's important to respond to historical plays as art-works, not as selected documentary accumulations containing historic-political speculations evaluable largely in terms of "known" historical and political reality. And we must learn to look for "historicity" more as Lukacs finds it in the histories of Shakespeare. As for example when Lukacs says: "Shakespeare states every conflict, even those of English history with which he is most familiar, in terms of typical-human opposites; and these are historical only in so far as Shakespeare fully and directly assimilates into each individual type the most characteristic and central features of a social crisis." Nairn's it's-either-his-torically-"accurate"-or-it's-purely-and-only-"symbolic" is just too crude and unfruitful a measure of the value of a play (or, indeed, of anything else).[4]

Although of major importance, discussion of the significance for the modern historical dramatist of such concepts as "typicality", "historicity" and "symbolism" will be deferred to the more appropriate and expansive context of later chapters.

If then there is disagreement amongst critics of all political persuasions about *how* history should be represented, such disagreement is only exacerbated by the vagueness that obscures even the term "historical drama" itself. What is, in fact, fascinating about the genre is that its form and emphases alter with the social and political changes that are themselves the constituents of history itself. Indeed the very aim of this book will be to interpret one in terms of the other. But to return to the problem of definition. At the most fundamental level the settings of *all* plays will, of course, inevitably become *historic* in the eyes of succeeding generations simply in consequence of the normal passage of time. Each and every play would, however, even in the loosest application of the term hardly qualify as historical drama simply because its previously contemporary setting had now been superseded. Even a play set in a period earlier than that in which it was written may not, however, be considered to merit the description of historical drama for, normally, such drama is expected not only to be set in times past but also to resurrect actual historical personages or reconstruct actual historical events. It is also assumed that the dramatist will approach the facts concerning the recreated period or figure in a spirit of "serious scholarship". It is nevertheless usually considered too prescriptive for even the most scholarly of critics to demand that historical drama should confine itself only to the dramatisation of those characters known historically to have taken part in the events described. Were such prescription to be enforced, the portrayal of the lowliest orders of society for which there is normally precious little historical evidence available would be banished from the stage, as indeed it has in some periods of historical drama, other than as bearers of either messages or spears. Perhaps, then, all that can be agreed upon about historical drama is the requirement of historical factuality in either or both character and event. It is therefore not surprising that historical dramatists have so often found themselves the target of censure when, owing to the very insubstantiality of the genre, almost limitless areas of potential disagreement are made available to the critic.

So comprehensive has been the reference to history in the post-1956 British theatre that to examine the historical drama of the period is at once to take into account plays by many of Britain's leading contemporary dramatists, to recognise the influence of the fringe, mainstream and national theatre companies, and to refer to the work of theatre groups motivated by politics, community issues, education and, to a lesser extent, feminism. A high level of historical consciousness may indeed be seen as one of the precious few common factors detectable within a theatre whose claim to novelty was its aim to reflect social change and to explain, if not Britain to the British, at least England to the English.

In setting out on such an examination I am therefore only too conscious of the potential vastness of the enterprise. Although my concern is primarily to identify the peculiar nature of the historical drama which emerged in Britain after 1956, in order to illustrate what changes have taken place I must inevitably offer an appropriate context by discussing both the nature of historical drama as a genre and by illustrating how, why and from what the new drama developed. Immediately it becomes necessary to establish boundaries, to decide, for example, how far to venture into the history of drama itself without in consequence losing sight of the particularities of the period under examination. I have, therefore, attempted as far as possible to be present-minded in my approach and to refer to the historical drama of the past only in so far as it can be used, through contrast or comparison, either to illustrate aspects of the present form or to establish its immediate antecedents.

I have also been consciously selective in the choice of plays employed to describe the progress of the drama and to support various contentions. This selectiveness has meant that I have confined myself to those dramatists who have exhibited something more than a passing interest in history. In relation to the wide range of historical drama which characterises the period, I have therefore been able to refer in detail only to a relatively small number of plays. My selection of such plays has been governed primarily by my perception of their typicality rather than purely of their aesthetic merit, and I have no doubt that readers will be able to supplement or even replace them by others applicable to my argument. I am sure that this is unavoidable. Nevertheless, if the reader is able to accept the basic premise that the cited illustration is intended to support we must otherwise agree to differ over the precise choice of plays.

My particular aim in the following chapters is to outline the distinguishing features of the historical drama which emerged, at first unsurely, within the new British theatre of the late 1950s and early 1960s. By the 1970, it had absorbed and modified influences as various as the historical drama of George Bernard Shaw, the formal devices of the Living Newspaper and the work of Bertolt Brecht, had been fuelled by the rise in extra-parliamentary left-wing political activity and, by the middle of the decade, had successfully established its presence both in the "fringe" and in the "institutional" theatres. In an attempt to find a point of focus and to do justice to a very complex topic, I shall centre upon what would appear to have been its unifying elements, a concern with ordinary people rather than their rulers and its associated attempt to shift the emphasis from an essentially individualistic view of history to one that would illustrate the inter-relationship between private and public experience. Guided by the increasingly political tone of the historical drama of the period I shall also attempt to set my examination of the plays within their peculiar theatrical, social, political and aesthetic context.

For the sake of clarity and mindful that some readers may not already be acquainted with the overall development of the British theatre of the period, I shall, as far as possible, work chronologically, dividing the book into two parts. The first is concerned with the antecedents and evolution of the post-1956 historical drama up to 1968; the second, with the years of its consolidation during the 1970s, concluding with a reflective glance at the 1980s. Firstly, however, to the modern British theatre's interpretation of the genre itself.

PART I

1

Historical Drama

In his influential book, *What Is History?* (1961), E. H. Carr asserts unequivocally a view of history and of the role of the academic historian which has gained so much credence amongst contemporary historians since the late 1950s that it may now be regarded as a truism. "History", he writes, "means interpretation."[1] Furthermore, suggests Carr, the nineteenth-century "Positivist" belief in the objectivity and unassailability of facts—that they could be left to speak for themselves and that history could be told "as it was"—has also since the First World War gradually given way to a general recognition of the validity of Benedetto Croce's (1866–1952) famous assertion that "all history is contemporary history", that history written during a given period will reflect, in addition to the individual concerns of its author, the beliefs, social structure, aspirations and myths of its society. As Carr also points out, even the primary factual information available to the historian (or dramatist) will have already been pre-selected on the basis of the partisan interests, needs and prejudices of those who were responsible for its collection, or may simply be incomplete owing to unintentional loss or destruction. Most early documentary evidence is, for example, related to some facet of government. It is therefore limited to those areas of life that were considered by those in power to be open to, or in need of, some form of regulation—most probably for the purposes of taxation or public order—and is consequently restricted by the imperatives, values, interests and concerns of a specific social group. Faced with such incompleteness, the historian is left with no alternative but to attempt to judge the veracity of the available facts and to offer personal conjecture concerning their importance or typicality. These facts themselves will generally also be received by the historian as a haphazard collection from which he or she must select in order to construct a pattern that will reveal their nature and significance.

The outcome of this process may be claimed to be historical truth but the conception of what actually constitutes that truth will vary according to the values of the interpreter or the recipient. "By and large", claims Carr, "the historian will get the kind of facts he wants."[2] Truth, however, "is not merely a statement of fact and not merely a value judgement, but embraces both elements."[3] As Gareth Lloyd Evans concedes, however, in *Plays in Review*, unlike academic historians, dramatists have normally been expected to take liberties with historical fact not only in consequence of their personal ideologies, but also as a result of the peculiar aesthetic demands of the medium of drama. This therefore leaves them even more open to potential criticism than the academic historian. It was surely to incite a reaction and to provoke awareness and discussion of the question of what constitutes historical truth that Edward Bond was to claim contentiously in his introduction to his grotesque deconstruction of the accepted historical view of Victorian values, *Early Morning* (1968), that "the events of this play are true".[4] The "truth" revealed in the play, however, proves strange and shocking to behold! Queen Victoria, who in life reputedly resisted legislation to make lesbianism illegal, believing that women could not behave in such a manner, is pursuing a lesbian relationship with Florence Nightingale. Meanwhile Disraeli and Prince Albert are plotting a coup d'état during which they intend to murder Queen Victoria and to enthrone, not the Prince of Wales—here called George—but his still-attached siamese twin, Prince Arthur! Not only in terms of character but also of plot does the play's "truth" depart radically from historical fact. The fictional coup fails when Prince Albert dies, poisoned by champagne drunk from Florence's slipper. In consequence of a subsequent plot, this time hatched by Arthur, involving a tug-of-war on Dover Cliff, the Royal Family and its subjects are transported to heaven. There, with extreme relish, they perpetuate that cannibalism which had been a feature of their society on earth but which is now made eternal by the constant regeneration of those parts of the body which have been devoured. The play is undoubtedly intended as a vision of a *deeper* historical truth than either accepted history or a mere recapitulation of the events of the period would reveal. By employing a combination of anachronism and surrealistic imagery Bond suggests that not only Victorian capitalism but also its apparently more benevolent modern manifestation depend for their survival upon the selfish exploitation or "devouring" of one social group by another. The mode of expression is indeed intensely subjective, and the play's assault upon history in the pursuance of a deeper truth is a reflection of Bond's extreme moral indignation at what he considered to be not only an unjust but also a cruel and inhumane system.

One of the most awe-inspiring and, in the opinion of some, dangerous features of the theatre lies in its almost magical power of resurrecting historical personages from their graves. The historical dramatist is therefore able to make a much greater impact with the re-creation of such characters than is the literary biographer or novelist for, subject only to historical actuality and behavioural plausibility, historical figures may be reincarnated there, on the stage, before the audience. Like a Dr. Frankenstein, the dramatist's task is ostensibly to reassemble the character from the available information in order to produce a plausibly consistent combination of physique and personality. Naturally, the less the audience knows about either the historical period or the figure concerned, the more the dramatist is able to intrude his or her own conceptions into the creation of the character. The need to "fill in" and "flesh out" historical record is, of course, also increased in proportion to the play's greater proximity to Naturalism, which presents not the private but representative individuals of Realism and the Epic but characters conceived of essentially in personal, idiosyncratic and usually psychological terms. Such divergences in aesthetic approach are particularly meaningful in historical drama where they stand as a clear reflection of the dramatist's and/or society's ideological assumptions concerning the role and influence of the individual within the historical process. Indeed, the individual's part in historical processes may be portrayed in a variety of ways. He or she may be presented, at one end of the scale, as merely a puppet whose destiny is predetermined by the gods, fate, genetics or economics or, at the other extreme, as a supreme individualist who, like Marlowe's Tamburlaine the Great, appears to "hold the Fates bound fast in iron chains, and with my hand turn Fortune's wheel about" and who is able heroically to imprint history with his or her own will. In order to imbue their plays with real conflict and suspense, dramatists have generally acknowledged the part played both by individual will and by external forces. Bearing such influences in mind, it becomes clear that, no matter how assiduous is the collection of historical facts or how objective the dramatist may set out to be, in historical drama the past will always in some measure be refracted by the present.

When it is strongly motivated by moral or political sentiment, the dramatic re-creation of an historical figure can undoubtedly shape an

audience's perception of the person portrayed. Writing of the controversy provoked by productions of Rolf Hochhuth's *The Representative*
(1963) (in America, *The Deputy*), which focused upon the alleged
betrayal of German Jews by Pope Pius XII during the Second World
War, Eric Bentley attempted to explain the aesthetic reasons for the
impact of the stage portrayal of the Pope:

On stage, falsehood is not merely uttered, it seems to become truth. You see
Pius XII in three dimensions, *actually* doing those dreadful things which,
actually—but the second *actually* is weaker than the first—he did not do.[5]

To demonstrate even more forcefully the influence available to the
dramatist, it is necessary only to compare the Richard III of historical
record with the calculatedly deformed monster of Shakespeare's theatrical imagination and to recognise how much the popular conception of that monarch has been conditioned simply by the *theatrical*
incarnation. Shakespeare portrays Richard as deceitful, manipula-
tive, murderous and cruel, while at the same time endowing him with
the personal attractions of self-awareness, energy, wit and skill in
political manoeuvre. Nevertheless, in order to establish a perspective
from which his audience are to view and judge Richard, Shakespeare
makes him explicitly characterize himself as the comic devil of the
Morality Play. "Thus," declares Richard directly to the audience, "like
the formal Vice, Iniquity, I moralize two meanings in one word"
(*Richard III*, iii.i.). Shakespeare's characterisation of Richard has been
judged by traditional "New Critics" to represent, in the political context of the play, a piece of Tudor propaganda. By "New Historicist"
critics it has, more recently, been interpreted somewhat less specifically but rather more subversively, as embodying a criticism of the
duplicity attendant upon all political power. In the former interpretation of the play Richard is seen as the mental and physical embodiment of that new satanic Machiavellianism which Shakespeare and
his contemporaries saw as an insidious threat to their established
world order.

According to one's critical stance, the play can therefore be judged
as a frightening propagandist warning, cloaked in the colours of the
previous dynasty, of the threat posed to Shakespeare's contemporaries by the new politics. It may also be viewed as representing a
wider vision of the nature of political power in which the current
administration is not directly indicted. In "New Historicist" terms it
may also be used to support the view that, as in this play and in the
Histories Shakespeare chose to examine the political rather than
divine or hereditary aspects of the English monarchy, in practice he
was subversively questioning and even diminishing the status of the

monarchy itself.[6] Whatever the correct interpretation may be, it is indisputable that, in consequence of that authority bestowed by theatrical representation, Shakespeare's Richard III has subsequently transcended his Elizabethan literary and political context to become an integral and apparently irremovable part of the nation's mythology. As this example demonstrates—and, as dramatists and national rulers have always recognised, as a consequence of the human tendency to reduce complex experience to simple and easily comprehended patterns—myth, which is one example of this process, generally achieves more potency than historical fact. As a result, in almost every period of theatrical history, governments have sought to promote that mythic history which conformed to their own ideologies or have attempted to suppress those which do not.

Most historical dramatists view themselves first and foremost as dramatists and only fleetingly as historians. Few write only historical drama. Although those such as Peter Cheeseman of the Victoria Theatre, Stoke-on-Trent, who were responsible for the creation of the so-called "Documentary" plays which achieved popularity during the 1960s, often preferred to work from a profusion of primary source material rather than to rely upon academic histories, the majority of individual dramatists tend to rely almost exclusively upon such secondary historical sources. As E. H. Carr has pointed out, the latter, however, inevitably already embody the ideological assumptions of their author and period. Dramatic works will therefore often either exhibit the influence of their source material and/or reflect an affinity between the ideological viewpoints of their dramatists and those of their chosen historian(s). For example, Peter Shaffer's source for *The Royal Hunt of the Sun* (1964) would appear to have been largely W. H. Prescott's *The Conquest of Peru*, published in 1847. The book was by no means the most recent or comprehensive study of the subject available to Shaffer, but it was obviously one that accorded with his own perception of history. Its romantic, Victorian approach is reflected both in the play's atmosphere and in the individualised treatment of the central characters.

In contrast, David Hare, Trevor Griffiths, Howard Brenton and Ian McEwan have all acknowledged a debt—if not always in terms of source-material, then for its fresh perspective upon a familiar historical period—to Angus Calder's *The People's War* (1969).[7] Calder's book offered a history of the Second World War on Britain's "Home Front" as seen through the eyes of ordinary people. It was compiled partly from records of a research group known as "Mass Observation", which documented public opinion just prior to and throughout the wartime period. To the above dramatists, each of whom could be considered to a greater or lesser extent, like Calder, to be socialist in outlook, *The People's War* offered, in the words of David Hare, "a complete alternative history to the phoney and corrupting history I was taught at school".[8] In fact Calder's approach to history was but one example of a gradual shift towards social and Marxist history which had been taking place amongst British academic historians during the previous forty years. Although at least since the turn of the century there had appeared a growing body of social history, the emergence of Marxist history in Britain during the 1930s marked an important stage in the gradual democratisation of historical subject-matter and was to prompt a comprehensive consideration of the inter-active nature of historical processes, based upon the Marxist conten-tion that material production governs the formation of mankind's social relationships, ideas and beliefs.

Unfortunately for those dramatists and other creative writers hold-ing socialist views, early Marxist history generally espoused his-torical determinism. It therefore appeared to offer little scope either for the portrayal of the influence of individuals upon the historical process or for dramatic tension and character development. Later apologists of Marxism have, however, sought to modify the apparently deterministic implications of Marxist theory. In a book written to educate party workers, Ernest Mandel, for example, takes pains to emphasise that "if historical materialism is a deterministic doctrine, this is so in the dialectical and not mechanistic sense of the term. Marxism excludes fatalism". He further suggests that, "if humanity is the product of given social conditions, these material conditions are in turn the products of *human social practice*".[9] Such could also be seen to be implied in Marx's own famous *Theses on Feuerbach* XI: "The philosophers have only *interpreted* the world, in various ways; the point, however, is to *change* it." During the 1920s and 1930s Marxists such as Brecht were quick to seize upon the opportunity for human intervention offered by the Marx's Feuerbach statement in order to justify the agitational aims of their theatre which, in a world deprived of the possibility of revolutionary change, would of course be irrelevant.[10] In order to communicate and explore theatrically the relationship between material conditions and human social practice, Brecht also devised an "anti-metaphysical, materialis-tic, non-aristotelian" Epic form of drama. As it consisted of scenes dialectically complete in themselves which were united by a simple narrative thread or arranged in montage, the Epic avoided the neces-sity for the "dramatic" theatre's character development or plotting, devices which, Brecht believed, implicated the spectator in the situa-tion portrayed on the stage and thereby wore down his capacity for action. In the Epic drama characters were not to be universalized but were to be portrayed within a specific social context. They were to be

motivated by social rather than biological impulses and, most important of all, were to be portrayed not as being fixed in a pre-determined
pattern or role but as being "alterable and able to alter".[11]

Typically, bourgeois history may perhaps best be represented in
terms of discrete historical moments which are held forever in amber.
As suggested above, Marxist and Socialist history, on the other hand,
is primarily concerned with change. For both Socialist historians and
writers, history—even when it has involved set-backs for the working
class—is viewed as fundamentally a record of a long journey towards
an inevitable utopia. While it is difficult to consider David Hare as a
believer in utopia, in justifying his fondness for the history play in a
lecture delivered at King's College, Cambridge, in 1978 he was to
reveal, however, that faith in the beneficial nature of change was still
alive:

. . . if you write about now, just today and nothing else, then you seem to be
confronting only a stasis; but if you begin to describe the movement of history, if you write plays that cover passages of time, then you begin to find a
sense of movement, of social change, if you like; and the facile hopelessness
that comes from confronting the day and only the day, the room and only the
room, begins to disappear as and in its place the writer can offer a record of
movement and change.[12]

In Britain after the Second World War there was a marked
increase in the publication of Marxist history. This was also now less
rigidly dogmatic and deterministic than had been the case before the
war. During the 1970s, when political revolution appeared to many
on the Left to be incipient revolution, British dramatists were
increasingly to turn to such studies for inspiration and source
material. Marxist history provided evidence that could be used both
to illustrate those factors which have advanced or impeded the progress of socialism in Britain and to expose the part played in British
history by ordinary people. Trevor Griffiths is but one of a number of
dramatists who have acknowledged the influence of Marxist history,
in this case E. P. Thompson's comprehensive historical account of *The
Making of the English Working Class* (1963) and Raymond Williams'
studies of the evolution of British culture such as *The Long Revolution* (1961). A more direct influence was probably exercised upon
Peter Whelan's play *Captain Swing* (1978) by E. J. Hobsbawm and
George Rude's important study of the nineteenth-century "swing"
uprisings of agricultural workers, also entitled *Captain Swing* (1969).
Unlike some of their predecessors in the 1930s, in their re-interpretation of the past these Marxist historians were neither agitational
nor propagandist. Theirs was a quest for what Arthur Marwick has

described in *The Nature of History* (1970) as "historical revisionism".
To this, Marwick suggests, Thompson contributed by "bringing into
proper perspective the aspirations and conscious efforts of the working people, too often treated by other historians as an inert and faceless mass, passive to the central forces in history",[13] while Hobsbawm
and Rude rescued "the great and moving story of England's last
agrarian rising, that of 1830, from the oblivion to which an exclusive
interest in the development of the state, and an exclusive preoccupa-
tion with the winners in history, had consigned it".[14] Such historical
revisionism was similarly to play a part in the historical drama of the
1970s.

The emphasis placed by Marxist and Socialist historians upon the
part played in history not only by political leaders but also by ordinary people and their attempt to offer an account of the experiences
not only of the winners but also of the losers of the past, stood in
direct opposition to the individualism of bourgeois history.[15] The latter was clearly exemplified in the work of the nineteenth-century historian, Thomas Carlyle, and expressed in the famous dictum, "history
is the biography of great men". Although this viewpoint would not
have been voiced so forcefully by the liberal historians of the early
twentieth century, it nevertheless continued to underlie academic
history in Britain until well after the Second World War. Echoes of
Carlyle's assertion also continue to resound to this day in Britain's
popular conception of its history and its national mythology. As
David Hare implied in an earlier quotation, the history taught in
school to many of his fellow dramatists in the years following the
Second World War continued to be centred upon the influence of
great monarchs, politicians, parliamentarians and national heroes—a
history derived from Victorian Britain's confidence in itself and in its
liberal institutions. It was this type of history that was to be parodied
so grotesquely by Edward Bond in *Early Morning*. It was also to be
reflected by the monstrous children of Howard Brenton's *Gum and
Goo* (1969) whose words reflect their parents' simplistic view of history as a struggle between comic-book heroes:

PHIL: My Dad says, Hitler was a man terribly wronged.

GREG: My Dad says Hitler was the biggest bad man who ever lived. And
Winston Churchill got him: BANG.

   (*MICHELE'S moaning grows.*)

   Winston Churchill stood on the cliffs of Dover in his battle-dress and he
   made this speech 'bout filling up the hole with the English dead. Then
   Winston Churchill took out this great big gun and he SMASHED Adolf
   Hitler.[16]

Central to the employment of history in the majority of the historical drama of the New British Theatre after 1956 was the displacement of the individualistic approach to history referred to above which had been the basis for the historical drama that had preceeded it. While, from the 1960s, academic historians were providing the appropriate source material, the new theatre's social conscience was also to offer both the platform and the necessary motivation for dramatists such as Wesker, Arden, Bond, Brenton, Griffiths and Hare to alter the focus of historical drama from the *personal* and *individualistic* towards the *public* and *private*. During the 1960s this shift of focus was to result predominantly in what might be described as a "populist" historical drama. However, with the emergence of the political theatre movement during the 1970s, the deconstruction and reconstruction of the public's perception of history was to become a major feature of an attempt also to displace Capitalist values. As a character was to declare in Peter Flannery's play, *Our Friends in the North*, which was produced by the Royal Shakespeare Company in 1982, "There's a war being waged right now, right here this minute for control over people's perception of the last twenty years. History is being rewritten."[17] In fact by the 1970s the theatre's struggle for people's perception of the past did not merely relate to the previous twenty years but was concerned more fundamentally with the manner in which the nation conceived of history itself. By the mid-1970s the public/private approach to historical drama, sometimes overtly political, sometimes not, had become all pervasive throughout the British theatre from the Fringe to the institutions of the Royal Shakespeare Company and the National Theatre. How this evolution began is the subject of the next chapter.

2

Presenting the Past

In common with much else in the British theatre in the decade following the end of the Second World War, the historical drama performed in the then dominant commercial theatre was well into its old age. Plays such as Norman Ginsbury's *The First Gentleman* (1945), Joan Temple's *The Patched Cloak* (1947) and Terence Rattigan's *Adventure Story* (1949), which, in turn, dealt with the Prince Regent, Henry VII and Alexander the Great, reflected an individualistic view of history which would not have been out of place in the late nineteenth century. In these plays was also perpetuated a type of theatrical realism that had evolved during the 1920s and which reflected in its characterisation and action on the social and ethical values of the predominantly middle-class audiences of that period.

Historical drama had enjoyed particular popularity at the turn of the twentieth century when, in common with many contemporary non-historical plays, it offered the excuse for colourful scenes and costumes and romantic action. Its characterisation and broad acting-style were likewise in keeping with the theatrical conventions of the day, and its period settings allowed ample opportunity for the satisfaction of the contemporary taste for picturesque staging. Popular plays of this period were William Devereux's *Henry of Navarre* (1908) and, with only a loose connection to history, Baroness Orczy's *The Scarlet Pimpernel* (1903). This tradition of "decorative melodrama", as it was known at the time, was to reappear in the early 1920s in Madge and Lester Howard Gordon's *The Borderer* (1921), which dealt with the perennial romantic martyr-figure, Mary Queen of Scots. Such romantic melodramas were, however, soon to be replaced in the 1920s and 1930s by a new approach to historical drama which was to stimulate an increase in the popularity of the genre. As even a selective list of the many historical plays of the period makes clear, the dramatic focus was now firmly upon individual personalities. It would appear to have been John Drinkwater's much acclaimed *Abraham Lincoln* (1918) which provided the model for subsequent plays such as H. F. Rubinstein and Clifford Bax's *Shakespeare* (1921), Bax's own *Rose Without a Thorn* (1932), Reginald Berkley's *The Lady with the Lamp* (1929), Rudolph Besier's *The Barretts of Wimpole Street* (1930), George Daviot's (the pen-name of Elizabeth Mackintosh) *Richard of Bourdeaux* (1932), Alfred Sangster's *The Brontes* (1933), Norman Ginsbury's *Viceroy Sarah* (1934) and Laurence Houseman's *Victoria Regina* (1934). Communicated by the dramatic form of these plays was the current "positivist" view of history seen "as it was". As Katherine Worth has rightly noted in her *Revolutions in Modern English Drama*, the dramatists of the interwar years were committed "to the pretence that the play has no audience, is not a play at all but history as it happened, the real thing".[1]

The replacement of the sensational and spectacular elements associated with the previous romantic approach to history by the creative discipline required by the new biographical character-drama was viewed by some critics as a welcome development in dramatic writing. In a prefatory note to the published edition of Rubenstein and Bax's *Shakespeare* (1921), A. W. Pollard commented warmly of the play that "coming after Mr. Drinkwater's 'Abraham Lincoln' it raises a hope that the English drama may escape from the monotony of artificial plots into the rich variety of human life by becoming biographical".[2] In fact, drawing from the sparse biographical material available, Rubenstein and Bax offered, in chronological order, five incidents drawn from Shakespeare's life, beginning with his debut as a dramatist in 1592 and ending with the writing of his will in 1616. Although they inevitably found it necessary to create fictional situations, in their "filling out" of Shakespeare's life the dramatists were cautious not to exceed the bounds of plausibility. The play makes reference to the development and curiously abrupt cessation of Shakespeare's creative output, but its major concern is with the dramatist's various emotional crises—the suspected relationship with the Dark Lady of the Sonnets, his unsatisfactory marriage, and the premature death of his son. Any sense of historical period is contributed by means of reference to contemporary figures and places, by costume and set, and by dialogue phrased in an acceptable pastiche of

Elizabethan English. The result is therefore that Shakespeare is portrayed not in the context of a society at a given moment in history, but primarily in terms of his personal relationships.

Generally absent from the above plays was either any sense of social criticism or any attempt to employ the past to comment upon the present. In Reginald Berkeley's *The Lady with the Lamp* (1929) a move is made in this direction but is soon abandoned. Early in the play, a response to Florence Nightingale's mother's assertion that the Chartists are being "led astray by scoundrels and traitors", Lord Palmerston, the British Prime-Minister, refers to political revolution, a subject that in the light of recent events in Russia and Europe, and in the wake of the British General Strike of 1926, was loaded with potential contemporary significance:

PALMERSTON (sardonically): Curious how political revolutionaries are invariably heroes if they happen to be foreigners plotting to overthrow a foreign Government; and equally invariably scoundrels and traitors if they happen to be Englishmen trying to bring pressure on our own![3]

To this liberal sentiment Florence's mother replies confidently, "Because our Government is a good Government". This exchange is, however, soon depoliticised by a subsequent reference to Florence's own "revolutionary" views, not, however, about politics but about nursing. It is revealed that Florence has inherited her opposition to bureaucratic and uncaring institutions from her maternal grandfather, a member of parliament whose radical views earned him the nickname "King Killing Smith". Thus a potentially contentious subject is defused by reference to individual personality and to the liberality of a British parliamentary democracy that can tolerate such radicals as Florence's grandfather. As an individual in confrontation with hidebound and outdated institutions and motivated not by ideology but only by her own personal sense of justice, Florence Nightingale is typical of the heroes and heroines of the biographical history plays of the inter-war period.

The realistic illusionism of these biographical plays ensured that an audience's attention was constantly focused within the reality of the play and upon the personal trials, tribulations and achievements of its central characters. Whereas psychological studies were generally avoided, as such an approach would have somewhat demagnified the hero or heroine, reference to minor moral weakness might usefully be employed to evoke empathy while at the same time not diminishing a character's iconic status. The result was therefore a celebration of *individual* initiative as the motivator of historical

change and a reassertion of the status of the acknowledged heroes
and heroines of Britain's national mythology, here humanised and
slightly sentimentalised by their domestic settings and their inevitable amorous relationships. The life style represented in these plays
was often one of refinement and grace and, although it was not suggested that the figures of the past inhabited an idyllic golden age, at
least the world portrayed in the plays could be seen to have been
more in tune than was their own age with the middle-class tastes of
the audience.

Such a biographical approach to history, often decked out in fine
costumes, may still occasionally be seen on the stages of the West
End. Nowadays, however, it most regularly appears in the form of
those television plays or serials which portray either a complete biography or crucial moments drawn from the lives of modern mythic
figures such as John F. Kennedy or Winston Churchill or romantic/
historic ones such as Henry VIII or Elizabeth I. These dramatic
accounts, in common with their antecedents, continue to reflect the
individualistic values of a bourgeois culture and perpetuate the spirit
of Carlyle's aphorism that "history is the biography of great men".

During the early years of this century there was at least one dramatist who viewed with scepticism the cultural mythology conveyed
by romantic and biographical historical drama: George Bernard
Shaw. Although a large number of his plays, from *The Man of
Destiny* (1898) to *In Good King Charles's Golden Days* (1939), were
set in an actual or fictional past and centred upon great figures
drawn from the history of Western Europe, in its treatment of those
figures Shaw's historical drama was alone to anticipate that transition from positivism and individualism to scepticism and populism
which was gradually to become widespread in British historical
drama after 1956. Shaw was a fervent believer in the benefits of
change and, as a Fabian Socialist, took as his personal mission the
release of British society from the stagnation and petrification
enshrined in its institutions. Recognising Britain's enslavement to
the traditions of the past, Shaw employed an often iconoclastic but
also witty re-interpretation of history in order to shake audiences out
of their complacency. Characteristically Shaw's historical drama contained a debunking and de-romanticising of British and European
historical icons; a rationalistic preference for dialectical discussion
rather than stage action or image; sometimes mischevious simultaneous presentation of a variety of conflicting views concerning an
event or topic; and, often, the employment of anachronism as a means
of linking events of the past with concerns of the present—all of this
communicated in an ironic but, at times, almost flippant manner.

Although it is not unusual to discover in the historical drama of the 1960s and 1970s techniques similar to those used by Shaw, his peculiar brand of socialism—which in its theatrical expression emphasised the importance to the process of change of the intervention of exceptional individuals such as St. Joan or Caesar, and exhibited little concern for the masses—was quite alien to post-war socialists. Likewise, Shaw's fondness for employing verbal wit and paradox as a means of provoking an audience to question its socially circumscribed attitudes could easily be viewed as a trivialisation of serious concerns and as a potential means by which both Shaw and his audience could distance themselves from serious consideration of spiritual, material or political realities. Thus, although Shaw, the moral revolutionary and enemy of institutionalism, revealed how the past might be framed to criticise the present, only in part could his radical but essentially individualistic approach to historical drama offer anything of value to Britain's left-wing dramatists of the second half of the twentieth century.

In 1945 the decisive electoral victory achieved by the Labour Party seemed to mark the beginning of a new era in British politics. In the minds of many it presaged the coming of the New Jerusalem whose arrival would sweep away those rigid barriers of class and privilege which characterised British society. The people's war would be replaced by the people's peace, and, as Angus Calder suggests in *The People's War*, the bureaucratic structures established to administer the planned national economy needed to fight a total war on both the home and overseas fronts would be utilised in the post-war environment to create a more equitable socialist society. The new British theatre of 1956 was, however, born out of a sense of frustration that these changes had not truly won the hearts and minds of a British public which, by the mid-1950s, appeared to be more concerned with obtaining the first material fruits of the new consumerism and with girating to American-inspired Rock 'n' Roll than in establishing a collectivist socialist utopia.

In retrospect it may be seen that one of the most characteristic features of the so-called New British Theatre after 1956 was its amorphousness. Some changes were clearly apparent. In contrast to the dominant theatre which had preceded it, The New Theatre did indeed introduce new and often shocking subject matter and replaced the earlier rational explorations of ethical, moral and spiritual concerns with often emotionally charged studies of various aspects of sexuality, of violence and of alienation. It also now encompassed a broader social mix of characters. No longer did the majority of plays centre upon middle- and upper-class protagonists, and banished from the stage was the stereotypical relationship between the middle- or upper-class master or mistress served faithfully by the usually comical but worthy servant. What did not emerge, however, was a new *school* of British drama marked by a common aim.

Although often anti-institutional and anti-Establishment in approach, the writers of the post-1956 theatre also exhibited no common political stance. Looking back in the theatre periodical *Encore* in 1958 over the first two years of the New Theatre, Edwin Morgan referred to the praise assigned in the 1957 Yearbook of the *Big Soviet Encyclopedia* to John Arden and other young writers for their "sharp critique of contemporary bourgeois reality". This praise, he noted, was nevertheless qualified by the additional observation that their critique was "uncommitted, anarchic, and tinged with individualistic bolshiness".[4] This criticism may also be applied more specifically to the *historical* drama of the 1960s in which, although greater emphasis than hitherto is placed upon the experience of ordinary people, there is no evidence of any generally accepted political ideology. In the absence of any such ideology, the anarchic and individualistic elements referred to in the *Encyclopedia* were, for a time, to exist side by side.

In spite of those changes described above, during the 1960s the commercial West End theatre continued to present romantic and individualistic historical drama similar to that produced before the Second World War. Peter Schaffer's *The Royal Hunt of the Sun* (1964), for example, gained much of its popular success in consequence of the opportunities it offered for colourful staging and costumes, and for masks, chant and pageantry, rather than for any obvious contemporary relevance offered to a post-colonial society by its dramatisation of the conflict between pagan and Christian values and in its exploration of one man's quest for faith. The survival of history as spectacle was still evident in 1971 in Robert Bolt's introduction to the published text of *Vivat! Vivat Regina!*, which had been produced in 1970. Bolt admitted that for him the primary attraction of historical settings was not on account of their intrinsic interest nor for their exemplification of the workings of historical or social processes, but because

She who plays the Queen may enter from nowhere along a red carpet to a fanfare of trumpets and express her predicament in speech of such magnificance and accuracy as no real woman ever spoke, yet cause the audience no discomfort. She who plays the wife of a suburban grocer must come in from the bus-stop, hang up her raincoat, and express herself as eloquently as is plausible. Small wonder that so many realistic plays have centred on our failure to communicate. The fanfare and the carpet are theatrical devices, with an historical excuse.[5]

As ever, history was being used to provide theatrical spectacle and to intensify the consequence of the play's moral, ethical or spiritual concerns. Alongside historical spectacle also survived romantic historical biography. In 1970 Ronald Millar received popular and critical acclaim with his *Abelard and Heloise*, a love-story based upon the actual letters of the twelfth-century French priest, Peter Abelard. In 1964 Millar had also written the book and lyrics for a musical adaptation of another historical love-story based, significantly, upon Rudolph Besier's 1930s play, *The Barretts of Wimpole Street*, and featuring the relationship between the poet Robert Browning and Elizabeth Barrett. In 1970 Terence Rattigan was to add *A Bequest to the Nation* to his other plays which had already portrayed the private lives of famous historical figures—*Adventure Story*, about Alexander the Great, and *Ross* (1960), which dealt with a period in the life of Lawrence of Arabia. In *A Bequest to the Nation* Rattigan focused upon Nelson's affair with Lady Hamilton. Here was a play written in what might best be described as the "history lesson" tradition of historical drama. This consisted of deftly but simply drawn characters each of whom was employed to convey, with apparent realism, a number of facts and dates from the past. It was primarily contrived to ensure that an audience, while adding a little to its knowledge of history, would also experience an entertaining evening's theatre. Reviewing the play in *Plays and Players*, Hilary Spurling drew attention to its technical merit, illustrated particularly in Rattigan's "manner of sewing together and finishing it [a scene] off with an exit line which snaps it shut like a press-stud", a technique that she considered to "belong to a line of playwrighting long neglected but by no means to be sneezed at".[6] In common with the type of historical drama referred to above, its focus and style appeared, however, to belong to an age now past.

In 1956 Brecht's Berliner Ensemble made its first visit to Britain. Although the company left in its wake a legacy of confusion concerning Brecht's theatrical approach, its revelation that Brecht's epic drama, far from being dour propoganda for communism, consisted of a highly theatrical mix of humanity, humour, song and poetry, aesthetic discipline and ideological commitment was enthusiastically received by many connected with the British theatre. One result of this visit was described in 1965 by the editors of *The Encore Reader*. "For the past few years", they wrote, "British drama had taken a long, hard, disenchanted look at the contemporary scene, and now almost every playwright one cared to name was rumoured to be writing an historical play".[7]

Although it may now, in retrospect, appear inconsistent in the light of the view that its author was to express in relation to *Vivat! Vivat*

Regina!, one play that at the time of its first production appeared to have been influenced by Brecht's example was, in its stage version, Robert Bolt's *A Man for All Seasons* (broadcast 1954, produced London, 1960). However, in a contentious critique of Bolt's play which so outraged the dramatist that he felt compelled to respond in print, Kenneth Tynan, with the enthusiasm of the newly converted, took the dramatist to task for superficially employing Brechtian techniques in what was fundamentally an individualistic character drama. "Mr. Bolt is primarily absorbed in the state of More's conscience", claimed Tynan, "not in the state of More's England or More's Europe." In the absence of any wider reference point for the actions of his character he added that Bolt "must reduce everything to personal terms: the gigantic upheavals of the reformation dwindle into a temperamental squabble between a nice lawyer who dislikes divorce and a lusty monarch who wants an heir".[8] Tynan went on to contrast the play's abandonment of the historical significance of the Reformation in favour of the portrayal of a personal dispute with Brecht's own approach in a play also concerned with individual conscience, his historical drama, *Galileo* (1943). As Tynan was to correctly imply, while Brecht's character is by no means simply an ideological cypher but is portrayed both in physical and intellectual terms as an individual, the dramatist nevertheless makes his audience keenly aware of the historical implications, both for his contemporaries and for our own time, of Galileo's actions. Brecht's Galileo is no conventionally heroic figure. He is human, earthy and fallible, he steals the concept of the telescope from Holland, he is not prepared to become a martyr for his beliefs and prefers to act covertly to record his discoveries rather than to take a public stand against those who are bent on their suppression. By creating a character who does not command the unquestioning sympathy of the audience, Brecht forces its members to make individual judgements concerning Galileo's actions. Brecht realised that, privileged by its knowledge of subsequent history, the audience is also constantly aware during the performance of the truth of Galileo's claim that the earth rotates around the sun and is therefore able to focus not simply upon the play's narrative but also upon the reasons for the suppression of this truth, upon Galileo's response and upon the wider consideration of the relationship between science and the state. Thus the audience is prompted to relate to the action of the play simultaneously both in private and in public terms.

Tynan's criticism of Bolt's *A Man for All Seasons* was that it did not address itself to such considerations. In spite of an episodic narrative which superficially resembled Brecht's epic structure and the inclusion of an "endistancing" Everyman character, similar to those employed by Brecht to discourage the audience's direct emotional involvement in the play's action and to stimulate contemplation, the play was in fact an historical character-drama not dissimilar to the biographical history plays of the 1920s. "It matters little", observed Tynan, "whether More's beliefs were right or wrong; all that matters is that he held them, and refused to disclose them under questioning. For Mr. Bolt, in short, truth is subjective; for Brecht it is objective; and therein lies the basic difference between the two plays."[9] As his references to subjectivity and objectivity reveal, what Tynan was here observing was essentially the difference between Bolt's private and individualistic and Brecht's public and materialistic interpretations of history. In summarising his views concerning Bolt's play, Tynan was to identify what was to become the major point of departure for the historical drama of the 1960s and 1970s, although, as I shall illustrate later, only in part as a consequence of Brecht's influence. In the Epic, Brecht attempted to dramatise the interaction between the individual and his environment. "The most important transactions between people could no longer be shown simply by personifying the motive forces or subjecting the characters to invisible metaphysical powers", he wrote, seeking to differentiate between the "Aristotelian" and epic theatre:

To make these transactions intelligible the environment in which people lived had to be brought to bear in a big and "significant" way.

This environment had of course been shown in the existing drama, but only as seen from the central figure's point of view, and not as an independent element. It was defined by the hero's reactions to it. It was seen as a storm can be seen when one sees the ships on a sheet of water unfolding their sails, and the sails filling out. In the epic theatre it was to appear standing on its own.[10]

As he explained in "A Short Organum for the Theatre" (1948), history was for Brecht, as it had been for Shaw, primarily important as a record not of continuity but of change.

. . . we must drop our habit of taking the different social structures of past periods, then stripping them of everything that makes them different; so that they all look more or less like our own, which then acquires from this process a certain air of permanence pure and simple.[11]

By conveying a sense of impermanence and thereby communicating that change was possible, Brecht aimed to encourage his audience to recognise that there was an alternative to Capitalism and that steps could and should be taken to replace it with a more equitable system that would acknowledge and foster humanity's innate goodness. Characterisation in historical drama should also convey humanity's

potential for change in that, while a character should be seen in relation to "the particular historical field of human relations in which the
action takes place"[12] rather than exhibiting simply an extension of
the spectator's own behaviour, he should nevertheless be "not quite
identical with those identified with him".[13]

In revealing his preference for the public rather than the private
approach, Tynan was to become one of the first during the post-war
years to proselytise for a theatrical treatment of history which would
accommodate a concern not simply with a collection of facts and dates
but with the workings of historical processes, and not with the deeds
of individuals but with the experience and influence of the mass of
ordinary people.

Although with *Luther*, in 1961, John Osborne also appeared to be
emulating the Brechtian Epic approach to historical drama, like Bolt,
in the portrayal of his hero, he too was unable or unwilling to abandon individualism. Inevitably, this factor was again to militate
against a broadening of the play's historical perspective. Like *Galileo*
(and *A Man for All Seasons*), *Luther* belongs to a long tradition of
plays of individual conscience and, in spite of Osborne's intention
that the intense private interest of Act 1 should be replaced in Act 2
by a "physical effect" which would be "more intricate, general, less
personal; sweeping, concerned with men in time rather than particular man in the unconscious",[14] he does not convey that interplay
between the historical figure and his peculiar historical environment
which, in Brecht's plays, resulted in the portrayal of man not only as
an individual but also as a member of society. *Luther* centres instead
almost exclusively upon the problems of personal belief and private
conscience experienced by one particular man who suffers from a
painful bowel disorder. Luther is portrayed, like Jimmy Porter, as a
disaffected outsider in his own society. He is an individualist who, in
consequence of his theological doubts and his desire to attain unmediated communication with God, finds himself in opposition to the
institution of the Catholic Church. Significantly, Osborne's chosen
source for Luther's characterisation was Eric H. Erikson's psychological study, *Young Man Luther* (1959), and the play returns repeatedly, often employing Luther's own words, to the character's
evident anal fixation.

If the source material selected by a dramatist reflects his or her
own perception of character and event and exercises a major influence upon the dramatic realisation of both, then the difference
between Osborne's approach and that of earlier biographical historical dramatists lies merely in his application of modern psychology
to the creation of his hero and in the scatological nature of the

expression of Luther's personal angst. As Simon Trussler points out in his study of Osborne's work, Luther "is conceived much more fully as a private man hemmed-in by his own physicality than as a politico-religious animal".[15] This is a viewpoint supported by such emotive stage action as Luther's epileptic fit which concludes Scene 1, and by the powerful visual image of a man sprawled across the blade of a huge butcher's knife which opens Scene 2 and which effectively communicates the physicality of Luther's anguish. Luther's individualism is also emphasised by the fact that, in spite of his own humble background and his role as a religious revolutionary, he has no sympathy for political revolution and arrogantly disassociates himself from the Peasants' Revolt which was partly inspired by his own radical ideas. When the Knight upbraids him with the accusation that, had he involved himself in the peasants' rebellion, he "could even have brought freedom and order in at one and the same time", Luther retorts that "There's no such thing as an orderly revolution. Anyway Christians are called to suffer, not fight." It becomes evident that he is personally afraid of the chaos that accompanies revolution, seeing it as "the devil's organ". "They deserved their death", he says of the peasants, for, as he tells Christ, "they kicked against authority, they plundered and bargained and all in Your name!"

The play ends inconclusively with a scene of extreme personal domesticity which involves Luther and his child, and our last image is of a very private person who has put radical activity behind him. In his critique of the play, Kenneth Tynan was again to recognise, as he had in the case of Bolt's *A Man for All Seasons*, that, in spite of its pseudo-Brechtian structure *Luther* was radical neither in its theatrical approach nor in its ideological standpoint. He concluded somewhat bitterly that Osborne, whom five years earlier he had praised for his contribution to the revolution in British theatre, must have been somewhat embarrassed to have been dubbed an apostle of social revolution when in fact, like Luther, "he preached nothing but revolutionary individualism".[16]

While emulating some of Brecht's stage techniques, both Bolt and Osborne were ideologically incapable of adopting his non-individualistic interpretation of history. During the 1960s there were nevertheless a number of British dramatists who, in their dramatisation of history, were to present alternative interpretations to those offered by the Establishment and successfully alter its focus from personal to public. For them, the past was neither merely a source of "human interest" stories, of romance, spectacle or nostalgia, nor even a context for the expression of universal spiritual or moral concerns or the exploration of personal angst. For these dramatists whose political sympathies, while not identical, were broadly socialist, all history was now to become contemporary history. It was to be employed primarily as a means of discussing the present and as a vehicle for confronting public rather than personal issues. Outside the West End, in various regional theatres, at the Royal Court and at the Theatre Royal, Stratford East, in the work of Arnold Wesker, Joan Littlewood's Theatre Workshop and John Arden, the new approach was to be expressed in the form of Social Realism, the Epic, or Documentary theatre. Although this new approach to historical drama should not be considered as intrinsically "better" than that which it replaced, it was, nevertheless, to be more in tune with the thoughts, feelings and political and social aspirations of its age.

3

Private and Public

During the late 1950s and early 1960s Arnold Wesker, John Arden and Joan Littlewood each displayed in their work both a clear antipathy towards individualistic characterisation and a preference for examining human behaviour in relation to public events. Although this common viewpoint was undoubtedly the outcome of a shared conviction in socialism, its dramatic expression ranged between Arnold Wesker's socialist utopianism and John Arden's anarchism.

In the years after 1956 Croce's assertion that "all history is contemporary history" might almost have been the chosen slogan of those British dramatists who gradually began to displace that individualistic approach to historical drama still current in the 1950s and early 1960s. Not only was the past now to be interpreted in terms of contemporary concerns and perceptions, but also, increasingly, reference was to be made to those events in Britain's recent history which were considered to have exercised a direct influence upon the shaping of the present. In total these references were, however, by no means to offer a comprehensive picture of post-war British history. For the most part they were selected to illustrate stages in the post-war decline of that socialist ideal of a meritocratic society for which an overwhelming majority of ordinary people had voted in 1945. This widespread faith in the potential of a future Labour government was expressed by a young Eighth Army officer towards the end of the war:

They stand for a square deal for you and me, with food, a house and a job for all who will do it. They stand for everybody having an equal chance and for more even distribution of the wealth of the world—not cigars at the Ritz and starvation at the Rhondda, not duck at the Berkeley and the dole at Barrow.[1]

In contrast, looking back in 1966, Arnold Wesker described his own generation's perception of the actual social and political atmosphere in the wake of the Labour government of 1945: "The war had been a formative part of our lives followed by the hope of 1945, and the general decline from then on." By the 1950s, he maintained, they were "tired of pessimism and mediocrity, and all the energy that was spent on being anti-Soviet and anti-Communist". They were in search of "a vision".[2] In 1954 G. D. H. Cole, a member of the Labour Party and a professor of politics at Oxford, reviewing the state of contemporary British socialism in *World Socialism Restated* (London 1956), commented:

Democratic Socialism is suffering at present from altogether too many inhibitions. It dare not frighten possible marginal supporters; and it dare not flout that so-called "public opinion" which is really newspaper opinion put about by the reactionary press. It dare not offend the Americans. . . . A Socialism that dares not is bound to fail; the fighting spirit which created the Socialist movement is no less needed to carry it through to its goal. The use of parliamentary and constitutional methods need not destroy this spirit—though it is all too apt to do so, when constitutional socialism has become respectable and accepted as part of the national political set-up, and when trade unions no longer have to fight for the right to exist and have become part of the recognised machinery of the capitalist order.[3]

His own call was for "a society of equals, set free from the twin evils of riches and poverty, mastership and subject". The 1945 Labour government had failed to achieve anything close to this.

It is political disillusionment that emerges as the major motif in the historical drama after 1956. As Wesker suggests, the disillusionment of the 1950s was, for those on the Left, provoked primarily by the failure of the post-war Labour government to establish a truly egalitarian socialist state and was also aggravated in 1956, particularly for Communists such as Wesker himself, by Russia's violent suppression of popular revolt in Hungary. The latter was to provoke Wesker and many others to abandon the Communist Party.

In 1956 Britain's own armed aggression against Egypt to prevent the nationalisation of the Suez Canal was also to distress many (represented in David Hare's *Plenty* by the British Ambassador, Darwin) who had hitherto believed in the probity of Britain's foreign policies. This venture was condemned by the majority of the members of the United Nations, including the United States, and was the cause of violent disagreement within the British parliament itself. Adopting a clearly non-individualistic approach to history, in *The Abuse of Power* (London, 1978) James Margach concludes that on this occasion Prime Minister Anthony Eden's misfortune was that "he was obviously a victim of history caught between the old Imperial might of the Empire and its total eclipse as a world power".[4] Indeed the affair was quickly cited as clear evidence of Britain's declining role as an international power. As the U.S. Secretary of State, Dean Acheson, commented bluntly in 1962, much to the chagrin of the British, "Britain has lost an empire and not yet found a role". Beginning in 1947 with India, and followed in 1948 by withdrawal from Pakistan, Ceylon and Burma, Britain had begun gradually to divest itself of its Empire. Although many both on the Right and Left accepted the inevitability of self-government for Britain's colonies and particularly for India, for some, like John Osborne's Jimmy Porter and Alison's father in *Look Back in Anger* or Archie Rice in *The Entertainer*, the "old-fashioned grand design" of the Edwardian twilight of British imperialism was compared nostalgically with the new "Brave New-nothing-very-much-thank-you"[5] world of post-war Britain. For others, particularly on the Left, the Empire was seen as the embodiment of outdated social values such as "the stiff upper lip" and "playing the game" and of class, racial and sexual stereotyping. Its passing was in no way to be mourned. Generally it was in these latter terms that colonialism was to be portrayed in the historical drama of the following decades. Of all Britain's colonies Cyprus was to continue as a colonial nettle until, after considerable violence, it was given its independence in 1960. In 1959, as a result of the violence with which, a year earlier, British troops had rounded up Greek Cypriots after the wife of a British soldier had been shot in the back while out shopping in Famagusta, John Arden was to write his "unhistorical parable", *Serjeant Musgrave's Dance*.

By the mid-1950s, under a Conservative administration since 1951, Britain had reached a level of affluence which the working class had certainly never before experienced. In July 1957, only a few months after he became prime minister, Harold Macmillan made his famous observation that,

. . . most people have never had it so good. Go around the country, go to the industrial towns, go to the farms, and you will see a state of prosperity such as we have never had in my lifetime—nor indeed ever in the history of this country.[6]

He did, however, recognise that some had not shared in the general prosperity and promised to help them. By many such as Wesker this growing affluence was, however, seen as the cause of widespread political apathy, particularly amongst the working class. Although on the one hand the new affluence brought material benefits to those who before the war had lived in almost intolerable conditions—a development that Socialists could only welcome—on the other hand it also appeared to be producing an uncaring, self-centred attitude which was anathema to those who still believed in the collectivist values of pre-war and early post-war British socialism. This new outlook was soon to become popularly epitomised in the phrase, "I'm all right, Jack". Along with political disillusionment, this tension between individualism and collectivism was to be the topic most frequently explored in the historical drama after 1956.

WESKER'S SOCIAL REALISM

It was in consequence of the feeling that the Left had failed to change British society and that it had "debilitated itself by being so violently anti-Communist, that somehow a halt had to be called"[7] that Wesker began to write *Chicken Soup with Barley*. In this and in *I'm Talking About Jerusalem*, Wesker was to attempt to identify and provoke the socialist conscience by means of a retrospective survey of the recent history of British socialism. The Left's idealism, its social aspirations, its utopian attempts to create a Jerusalem in Britain's green and pleasant land and its failure to do so between the years 1936 and 1959, were all examined in terms of the lives of ordinary, unremarkable people. The plays were not simply explorations of the workings of economic forces, nor were they celebrations of the nobility of the working class. Instead they represented an emotional response to working-class apathy and contained a call for a similarly emotional corrective, as expressed in Sarah Kahn's admonition in *Chicken Soup with Barley*, "You've got to care or you'll die!"[8]

Wesker's chosen vehicle for his saga of the lives of ordinary people was not the Brechtian epic but social realism. He created not historical drama—the characters were all fictional—but history plays in which the lives of the characters are associated with and affected by actual historical events and forces and in which attention is paid to the nature, function and influence of the society that they inhabit. The basis for the realism of the characters is therefore private rather than personal. Wesker was concerned not with individual psychology but with individual lives shaped by the social forces playing upon them. *Chicken Soup with Barley* centres upon the Kahns, a family of East-End Jews. By relating the domestic experience of the family, as presented onstage, to public events that are taking place, offstage, in the streets of London's East End or elsewhere in Europe, Wesker revealed how, over twenty years, the nature of the socialist struggle has changed and how the working-class political activism of the 1920s and 1930s had been replaced in the years following the Second World War by political apathy.

During the first act of the play Sarah Kahn, the energetic communist matriarch of the family, takes part in the Jewish resistance to Moseley's Fascists on the streets of London's East End in 1936. Some of her comrades and members of her family are to continue the struggle against fascism in the Spanish Civil War and World War Two. The action of the play's second act takes place during the years 1946 and 1947 against a background of post-war optimism reflected, as Sarah's son, Ronnie remarks enthusiastically, in "Plans for town and country planning. New cities and schools and hospitals. Nationalization! National Health! Think of it, the whole country is going to be organized to cooperate instead of tearing at each other's throat".[9] During this act, however, Sarah is faced with her daughter, Ada's, disillusionment with the working class, her husband, Harry's, first stroke, and her political comrade, Cissie's, reports of the first signs of political apathy amongst the workers. In the final act, set in 1955, Sarah's fight is now not against the easily identifiable enemy represented by fascism but, ironically, against the anonymous agents of the new socialist society—the Welfare State bureaucrats. The play's climax results from Sarah's continued belief in the ideals of communism, a belief that compels her to cry out against the political apathy that has apparently been engendered by the materialism of the newly born "consumerist society".

Throughout the play Wesker avoids resorting to the personal crises—the affairs, suicides, illegitimate births, family secrets and unexpected accidents—which normally constitute the plot of the family saga. Instead each of the family's crises or disagreements, some of which are referred to above, is linked either symbolically or realistically with the socio-political events and concerns of the period. By this means, the lives and attitudes of the characters, while provoking audience empathy, are also successfully employed to convey the wider political and social changes that had affected British society over two decades. This is most clearly illustrated in Sarah's relationship with her malingering husband Harry who does not share her enthusiasm for politics, the public and private aspects of the play being unambiguously brought together in her words, "All my life I've fought. With your father and the rotten system that couldn't help him."[10] During the course of the action Harry is paralysed by two strokes. In Sarah's view Harry is totally self-centred and does not "care" about the fate of humanity. Because he does not care he gradually dies, his physical decline symbolically paralleling the similar twenty-year decline into uncaring apathy of the British working class. Harry's increasing debility is accompanied, as the play progresses, by the gradual abandonment of political activism by various members of the Kahn family, with the exception of Sarah, and by their political comrades. The public expression of politics is, in each case, replaced by the adoption of personal concerns. This is most apparent amongst those characters who, before the Second World War, were ardent Communists. After the war, for example, Monty Blatt, who in the 1930s was a Communist activist, having been shocked by the post-war evidence of Stalinist tyranny and made to feel politically impotent in face of the gigantic threat posed by the atomic bomb, abandons socialist politics in favour of bourgeois individualism: "There's nothing I can do anymore," he claims, "I'm too small."[11] He purchases a small shop in Manchester, where no one knows of his Communist past, and creates for himself a new and private world. "There's nothing more to life", he tells Sarah, "than a house, some friends and a family—take my word."[12] After the war, Ronnie, the "intellectual" son of the family, leaves home to become a cook in Paris only to return in 1956, disillusioned by the Russian suppression of the Hungarian uprising, and launches an attack upon his mother's continued belief in communism. In 1946 Sarah's daughter, Ada, and her husband, Dave, who had fought with the International Brigade in the Spanish Civil War, abandon London to set up a utopian, William Morris, handmade-furniture business in the Norfolk Fens. For them, too, Sarah's public socialism and extended family is replaced by the typically post-war atomic family separated from its roots and, in this case, intentionally withdrawn from the world in general. Ada and Dave have both lost faith in the "splendid and heroic working class"[13] and intend to replace Sarah's public socialism with an idyllic private family existence. "When Dave comes back", Ada tells her family, "we shall leave London and live in the country. That'll be our socialism." For her, the realisation of self is now more important than caring for others: "How can we care for a world outside ourselves", she asks, "when the world inside is in such disorder?"[14]

The story of the failure of Ada and Dave's idealistic and unrealistic enterprise is told in *I'm Talking About Jerusalem*, which, as its title suggests, is closer in form to a parable than to the social realism of *Chicken Soup with Barley*. The lives of its characters are nevertheless still seen to be affected by social forces from which they attempt to isolate themselves but which prove to be beyond their control. In order to earn a living until his intended furniture business is established, Dave works for a local farmer but besmirches his intended utopia by stealing a roll of lino from his employer. The ultimate failure of his dream is therefore both the result of his inability to break with the corrupt "habits of factory-life"[15] and a consequence of the competition posed by industrial techniques that enable the production of cheap but acceptable furniture. Like Monty, he too retreats into a world of personal concerns: "Well now the only things that seem to matter to me are the day-to-day problems of my wife, my kids and my work."[16]

Ada and Dave leave the Fens in 1959 as a new Conservative government is returned to power, and with it consumerism is firmly installed as part of the British way of life. At the close of the play, from a socialist perspective, Ronnie sums up what has taken place in Britain since the war. His words are close to those of Wesker quoted above and likewise illustrate the latter's political motivation for writing the play:

RONNIE: . . . We put a Labour Party in power. Glory! Hurrah! It wasn't such a useless war after all, was it, Mother? But what did the bleeders do, eh? They sang the Red Flag in Parliament and then started building atom bombs. Lunatics! Raving Lunatics! And a whole generation of us laid down our arms and retreated into ourselves, a whole generation. But you two. I don't understand what happened to you two. I used to watch you and boast about you. Well, thank God, I thought, it works! But look at us now, now it's all of us.[17]

The defeat of the utopianism of the "Two Jews in the Fen",[18] as Ronnie calls them, was not intended by Wesker as a parable of the defeat of socialism in mid-century Britain but rather as a parable about the impracticability and futility of attempting to hang on to political ideals by "dropping out" and avoiding social reality. As Sarah asks, "What's socialism without human beings tell me?"[19] *Chicken Soup with Barley* and, to a somewhat lesser extent, *I'm Talking About Jerusalem* successfully integrated both humanity, in their presentation of plausible and vital characters, and political concern, in their evocation of significant moments in the recent history of British socialism. Its social realism belonged, however, to an earlier tradition of socialist art which turned out to have little appeal to the young left-wing historical dramatists of the 1960s and 1970s.

THE DOCUMENTARY

Arguably the most widely influential example of an alternative, non-individualistic approach to historical drama to appear during the early 1960s was Joan Littlewood's *Oh What a Lovely War*, which was produced in 1963 by Theatre Workshop in Stratford East, London. Its influence was to be widely felt for more than a decade in many of Britain's newly established regional theatres and was even to extend into the work of the political fringe theatre of the 1970s. The documentary form of *Oh What a Lovely War* was by no means new to Joan Littlewood. In the years leading up to the Second World War she had been involved in the production of radio documentaries for the B.B.C., and in 1938 the left-wing theatre group "Theatre Union", which she co-directed with Ewan McColl, had staged a "Living Newspaper" documentary entitled *Last Edition*, which dealt with events relating to Hitler and Chamberlain's Munich Agreement of that year. The play was performed, with topical emendations, until the outbreak of the war when it was halted by the police, and Littlewood and McColl were bound over to keep the peace. Having emerged in the years following the Russian Revolution of 1917, in 1938 the Living Newspaper had just come of age. After the Revolution, Living Newspapers, consisting of readings and skits, had been devised to disseminate information and propaganda to a widespread and often illiterate population. The form had been further developed in Russia during the 1920s by the touring "Blue Blouse" theatre groups, so-named because of their uniform costumes which consisted of workers' blue skirts and trousers. Their performances were more sophisticated than those presented by the Living Newspaper groups and consisted of a montage of different items of skits whose variety of styles included monologues, mass declamation, comedy sketches and songs, acrobatics and dance. During the late 1930s the Living Newspaper was to re-emerge in New Deal America where, in a modified form, its techniques were again employed, in such plays as *Triple A Plowed Under* (1935) and *Power* (1937), to educate, agitate and reform. The plays were now intended to mobilise the power of the people in order to change present conditions by means of existing democratic structures. A major feature of the structure of these plays was a carefully contrived historical perspective. Typically each began with an historical resumé of the events that had led to an unsatisfactory or unjust public situation, such as the domination of the production of electricity by private monopolies whose sole aim was to increase profits even to the obvious detriment of ordinary people. This was followed by a closer examination of the deleterious effects of the present state of affairs. The play concluded with the presentation of a number of potential remedies and the recommendation of one of these remedies as a possible course of action. The historical approach of these plays was therefore both functional and materialistic and concerned with change rather than nostalgia. In the hands of the creators of the Living Newspapers, history became a tool for the analysis and understanding of the present by demystifying the means by which those in power—be they the faceless bureaucracy of a monopoly industry or the political representatives of a particular interest group—maintained their supremacy at the expense of the ordinary citizen. For the most part then, this was not a history *of* the people, so much as a history *for* the people.

But to return to Littlewood and McColl. Immediately after the Second World War the couple founded Theatre Workshop, one of whose earliest productions, in 1946, once again emulated the form of a Living Newspaper. The play, *Uranium 235*, was written by McColl and dealt with a subject that was to haunt the post-war world—the problem raised by the discovery of how to harness atomic energy. In the play the type of historical education that had been but an element of the American Living Newspaper now becomes a dominant feature of the action. Much of the play's first half is used to trace the progress of the scientific discovery of the atom from Democritus to Mendeleev, while the second half continues the story into the twentieth century with the discoveries made by, among others, the Curies and Bohr. The second half of the play also features a corp de ballet which is employed to represent such abstractions as Mass Energy and Sub-Atomic Particles, a feature not unlike the acrobatics that appeared in the earlier Blue Blouse performances. As in the American Living Newspapers, the resolution of the concerns put forward in the play is intended to take place not during the performance itself but outside the theatre in the real world of the audience. The play concludes with the actors asking the audience to decide, in the light of its newly gained historical insight, whether it wishes the country's scientists to develop atomic energy for peace or for war. "Which way are we going",[20] asks the play's final line, leaving the audience to provide the answer.

A notable outcome of Joan Littlewood's involvement in the creation of such documentary plays as *Last Edition* and *Uranium 235* appeared in their undoubted influence upon her 1963 production of *Oh What a Lovely War*. This musical documentary ostensibly illustrates the causes and events that led to the First World War and chronicles the history of the conflict on the Western Front as experienced by ordinary soldiers. Central to the play is the contrasting of the jingoism and sentimentality expressed in the commercial songs of the period, with the much grimmer but nonetheless humorous songs composed by the soldiers themselves, in which is revealed the real horror and futility of war. The play bears obvious stylistic similarities to the Living Newspaper and Blue Blouse revues. Its revue-like episodic structure, which combines song, dance and realistic scenes in a pastiche of the kind of pierrot show that was at its height during the Edwardian period just prior to the First World War, is reminiscent of the Blue Blouse revue, a similarity further emphasised by the use of the uniform pierrot costume to which are added hats, shawls and belts in order to convey social role and status. Also,

as in such American Living Newspapers as *Triple A Plowed Under*
and *Injunction Granted*, documentary evidence, in this case in the
form of library photographs of dead or disabled men and war-torn
landscapes, is projected onto a screen at the rear of the stage. In addition, casualty statistics are communicated on an illuminated newspanel situated above the stage. Littlewood's utilisation of this
documentary evidence is, however, somewhat more sophisticated
than that of the Living Newspaper and in fact probably owes more to
Piscator's Documentary and Epic theatre with which Littlewood was
familiar from the 1930s, than simply to the American example.
Whereas projection was used in the Living Newspaper primarily for
informational purposes, in *Oh What a Lovely War* it becomes part of a
montage in which documentary evidence of the reality of war either
underpins the action and songs performed by actors who illustrate
the human response to the situations portrayed, or, particularly in
the case of the newspanel, produces an ironic tension between what is
being said on stage and what was actually taking place on the battle-
field. In Act 2, a man's voice is heard singing the romantic song,
"There's a long, long trail a winding"; at the same time, standing
before a projected photograph of Tommies advancing across no-man's
land, an actor, portraying General Haig, describes the advance,
finishing his speech with the line, "I feel that every step I take is
guided by divine will". At this point above his head the newspanel
reports "February . . . Verdun . . . Total loss one and a half million
men."[21] Thus, in true epic fashion, the audience is provoked into view-
ing critically the situation enacted before it.

In *Oh What a Lovely War*, as in *Uranium 235*, history dominates
the action. The play was, however, intended neither, as some have
thought, to celebrate the courage and resilience exhibited by the British Tommy in the face of the horrors of the First World War nor to
condemn those who led them. It is important for an understanding of
its true aim to note that its chronology ends not with the celebration
of the armistice but at a point just before the intervention of the
American forces whose additional numbers were to alter the course of
the war. The implication of this was somewhat obscured in consequence of alterations made to the original script when the play was
transferred to the West End. As a result an audience may miss or be
able to evade the issues that the play was intended to raise by focusing merely upon its humour, song and spectacle. With the play's
transfer from Stratford East a concluding speech, delivered by the
Master of Ceremonies, which linked the events of the past with concerns of the present was, for example, removed and replaced by a
reprise of songs from the show. "The war game is being played all
over the world by all ages", announced the M.C. in the original ver-

sion, "There's a part for all the family. It's been going on for a long time and it's still going on. Goodnight." The inclusion of these words was obviously intended to underline the audience's responsibility in relation to contemporary conflicts but would appear to have been considered too sober a conclusion for a West End audience. This theme of public responsibility is nevertheless an integral part of the play and is referred to at various points throughout a narrative that illustrates the mistakes made by an earlier generation in order to suggest that it is the moral duty of each member of the audience to think for him or herself and not to follow those who would lead the nation, sheeplike, towards self-destruction. Two scenes in particular are important in representing this argument. The first contains Mrs Pankhurst's speech to the "misguided masses" whom she considers to be perpetuating the war. It illustrates that, as the war progressed, those at home were trapped in an impossible dilemma. If they were to speak out against the futility of the war they might hasten its end, but in doing so they would be forced to admit that their menfolk were dying in vain. On a personal level, the women in the scene are unable to undertake this act of betrayal and are therefore implicitly permitting the war to continue. Ironically, they are thereby probably also condemning their men to death. The play's final scene drives home even more strongly the responsibility of ordinary people for the outbreak and conduct of war. A troop of French soldiers refuses to return to the trenches, but when their officer threatens to shoot anyone who disobeys orders the soldiers go, clothed in their "fool's" pierrot costume, like sheep to the slaughter.

At a time when C.N.D. was particularly active and less than five months after the Cuban missile crisis of October 1962 had brought the world to the edge of nuclear war, Littlewood's approach to the dramatisation of this particular period of history was, I am sure, intended not to offer a nostalgic excursion into the past but instead to sound an urgent call to the present. The play's aim was undoubtedly to face the members of its audience with their responsibility to resist those politicans who would prepare the nation for the even more catastrophic and pointless war that would result from the use of nuclear weapons.

Although its specific message may have been somewhat obscured by its medium, *Oh What a Lovely War* was to become hugely influential in the years to follow. Acknowledging its influence upon his own work, John McGrath, for example, claimed that "in the 60s it was performed and loved in almost every repertory in the country. A new generation of actors played in it, sang its songs and heard how Joan's actors worked on it".[22] Indeed *Oh What a Lovely War* inspired and lent its form to the new documentary drama which emerged in most of Britain's regional theatres from the mid-1960s onwards and which, during the 1970s, was to be politicised by dramatists such as McGrath himself. It was in the Documentary play more than in any other form of modern British drama that there would consistently be created a history that, being primarily concerned with their actions and aspirations, was written *for* ordinary people.

A feature common to Britain's regional theatres during the early 1960s was their attempt to attract new audiences drawn from a wider social spectrum than had hitherto been traditional. With the example of *Oh What a Lovely War* before them their artistic directors were quick to recognise that history, and particularly *local* history, potentially might be a useful aid to the achievement of this aim. Thus, after 1963, Documentary Chronicle plays of varying quality, such as Allen Cullen's *The Stirrings in Sheffield on Saturday Night* written for the Sheffield Playhouse in 1966, and Alan Plater's *Close the Coalhouse Door* produced at the Newcastle Playhouse in 1968, were devised and/or produced by various regional theatres throughout the length and breadth of Britain. The former play was concerned principally with the activities of one William Broadhead, the leader of the Sheffield saw-grinders' union during the 1860s, who, in order to discipline union members, employed ruffians to drop cans of gunpowder down their chimneys. The latter play dealt with the history of the mining industry from the nineteenth century to the present day.

The centre and model for Documentary Chronicle plays was, however, soon recognised to be the Victoria Theatre-in-the-Round Company which established its home in 1962, under the direction of Peter Cheeseman, in a converted cinema/bingo-hall in a working-class district of Stoke-on-Trent. Here, during the next two decades, Peter Cheeseman was to devise a number of musical documentaries concerned with various topics of local interest, ranging from the pottery industry to the closing of a local steel-works. Each of these documentaries portrayed history seen from below and often dealt with the working conditions and exploitation of the lower classes and their attempts, particularly through Chartism and Unionism in the nineteenth century, to obtain control over their lives. In spite of this subject-matter, the plays themselves were generally apolitical. Although this no doubt owed something to stage censorship, the major reason for this stance was that the regional theatres were setting out to reach not *class*-based but rather *community*-based audiences, for exclusivity—political or otherwise—would surely have defeated the theatres' primary aim of filling seats.

Cheeseman's plays consolidated the various formal elements established by Joan Littlewood in *Oh What a Lovely War* and were to offer a model for other documentary plays of the 1960s. Authentic folk-ballads, humour, mime, dance and the all-purpose uniform costume were features common to the genre. In addition the employment of a ballad-singer narrator, for example in *The Knotty* (1966), was reminiscent of Littlewood's use of the Master of Ceremonies in *Oh What a Lovely War*. In each case the figure identifies himself as a teller of stories. On one level he is independent of the audience—he knows the story, they do not—on another he is undeniably sharing the present occasion. Furthermore his existence in the play evokes in full measure the oral tradition of story-telling which was both a source of entertainment and a means of perpetuating the values of a specific community by passing on its communal history from one generation to the next. Cheeseman himself set out quite consciously to adopt this communal role for this theatre. The historical documentaries were the clearest exemplification of this philosophy in action:

One of the things wrong with our society is that too few people have a sense of history. We have lost in our society the sort of natural structure whereby old men pass down knowledge to the young in the community and people are not taught history intelligently. In this sort of atmosphere it seems to me that our obligation is to show people the past of their community in a way which will give them a sense of that past, in the knowledge that they stand not alone in the present but are part of a historical perspective. This will give them a sense of self-consciousness and importance.[23]

The company's most successful documentary was *The Knotty*, a play about a recently closed local railway loop-line which, before its amalgamation in 1921 with the London Midland and Scottish Railway, was locally operated as The North Staffordshire Railway Company. The actors themselves took part in the preparation of the documentary. Their research included tape-recorded interviews with local people who themselves had some connection with the Knotty. The voice of the play was therefore not merely that of the writer or the actor, but also that of the ordinary people of the community. The actors were to offer their theatrical skills in the telling of the community's story and, in consequence of the fact that they were constantly changing roles as the play progressed, it was they rather than the individual stage characters who were established as the common denominators to which the audience related. The employment, not only for research purposes but also during the actual performance, of the tape-recorded voices of members of the community in this and other of Cheeseman's documentaries parallels the *informational* use of documentary photographs by Erwin Piscator in his Documentary theatre and by Joan Littlewood in *Oh What a Lovely War*. Absent however was the irony that the *epic* treatment of such material was intended to produce.

In the absence of any firm ideological stance it would be easy for the presentation and celebration of a communal past to slide into romantic nostalgia. Indeed, on occasions, the Victoria Theatre's documentaries do incline somewhat in that direction. What holds them back is a feature more characteristic of Cheeseman's work in particular than of the musical documentaries produced during the 1960s by other regional theatres. This peculiar feature was the recognition and illustration of the reality and significance for both the individual and the community of work itself. Specific work-skills such as the operation of a steel-smelting furnace or the shunting of goods-wagons were emphasised by the use of detailed occupational mime, enhanced, where appropriate, by the studied employment of light and sound. In each case the tools used for the mimed task were the authentic ones used by the trade, and the actors were coached by a local expert to wield them convincingly. These activities served to reflect the pride that working men have in their skills, an occupational factor often ignored by industrial economists and politicians. This focus upon the activity of work is reminiscent of the documentaries of working life made by the General Post Office film unit under John Grierson in the 1930s, which themselves endowed familiar occupations with significance and dignity. While they set their characters against an industrial background, documentaries such as *The Stirrings in Sheffield on Saturday Night* or *Close the Coalhouse Door* did not portray or explore the actuality of work itself.

With the exception of *The Staffordshire Rebels*, which was concerned largely with the wider historical issues of the English Civil War, each of the Victoria Theatre's documentaries centred upon the ability of ordinary people to cope with and to assert themselves in the face of events that were generated elsewhere or instigated by those more powerful than themselves. Ordinary people were portrayed as being adaptable to change but also capable of fighting for acknowledgement of the value of their occupational skills and of their human dignity. Whereas in plays such as *The Stirrings* history would appear to have been used primarily to attract an audience to whom it offered period colour and local interest, in the Victoria Theatre's documentaries the aim was genuinely to create a "people's history" whose function would be as much to contribute to the formation of a communal identity as to entertain their audiences and fill the theatre.

At the close of the 1960s Plater's *Close the Coalhouse Door* was, however, to move a little closer towards the substitution of class for community. In this it was to prefigure the approach that would be taken in the historical documentaries of the 1970s. Nevertheless, it still remained a regional documentary, but with national pretensions and political implications. The play dramatised—from the point of view of the miner and within the realistic framework of the Golden Wedding Anniversary party of a fictional geordie ex-miner, Thomas Milburn, and his wife Mary Anne—the history of mining from the nineteenth century to the present. As in American Living Newspapers, the past was employed to reveal the cause of a problem in the present—in this case the closure of coal mines—but, unlike them, the play offered no solution. Its ending is indeed ambivalent, leaving the conflict that it has highlighted between society's need for cheap energy and the welfare of the mining communities ultimately unresolved. The "revolutionary weapon" which Plater recognised had been created "without revolutionary intent"[24] by the miners' union had yet to wait until 1974 before it was to be employed *with* revolutionary intent against Edward Heath's government. For the time being, the historical documentary also remained "without revolutionary intent", a vehicle for the celebration of communal history.

I shall conclude this examination of the changes that became apparent in British drama during the 1960s by referring finally to John Arden, a dramatist who, during these years, established for himself a very characteristic approach to history, and who was to figure largely in the politicisation of historical drama during the next decade.

JOHN ARDEN AND THE EPIC

In 1961 Arden admitted that he too had shared the widespread enthusiasm generated by the Berliner Ensemble's visit to Britain in 1956. Like Bolt and Osborne, he also appears to have been influenced formalistically by Brecht's dramatic treatment of history, but unlike them he was to show himself able to adapt Brecht's epic form to suit his own dramatic needs, at the same time realising its potential for endistancing, historification, and the presentation of a number of conflicting viewpoints of the same event. Arden also shared with Brecht a fascination with folk-literature, folk-ballad and folk-drama, a fascination which, for both, led to a preference for parables, ballads and the portrayal of characters primarily in terms of their public roles, for example as kings, soldiers, servants, gypsies, or beggars, and only secondarily as private individuals. The evocation, in an historical context, of recurrent ballad characters and themes such as the passing love and abandonment of a young girl by a soldier, marital infidelity, or political betrayal, enabled Arden to endistance the behaviour of his characters so as to remove it from the private to the public realm and thereby more clearly communicate its socio-political implication for the present. "Social criticism" wrote Arden in "Telling a True Tale",

tends in the theatre to be dangerously ephemeral and therefore disappointing after the fall of the curtain. But if it is expressed within the framework of the traditional poetic truths it can be given weight and impact derived from something more than contemporary documentary facility.[25]

In the same article Arden identified his own concern with "the problem of translating the concrete life of today into terms of poetry that shall at the one time both illustrate that life and set it within the historical and legendary tradition of our culture".[26] In pursuing this aim Arden fortunately also shared with Brecht an ability to locate his characters within a clear socio-political, historical context which, although different from today, could be seen to embody factors that were relevant to the present. In Arden's early plays these concerns were not, however, as in Brecht's work, associated with Marxism but with Anarchism. In this, Arden was allying himself with what may be considered to have been the most influential British "left-wing" political stance of the 1960s and one that played a significant part in the formation of the peculiar character of the historical drama of the period. In his early plays Arden was concerned essentially not with *class* but with rather more abstract considerations such as the exercise of political power, the maintenance of individual freedom and the difficulty of balancing the two. Thus in his three historical dramas of the 1960s, *Ironhand* (1963), *Armstrong's Last Goodnight* (1964) and *Left-Handed Liberty* (1965), Arden examines the incongruity between the natural human desire for autonomy and freedom and the necessity for order and conformity produced by the structure of a "civilised" society. Central to Arden's drama of the 1960s was a conflict between two forces which in 1968 in the introduction to the text of *The Hero Rises Up* he was to designate as "Curvilinear" and "Rectilinear". Curvilinearity referred to the primitive, spontaneous and passionate in human behaviour. In social terms it was culturally subversive and was associated either with the lower orders of society or with anachronistic social systems. In contrast, rectilinearity was associated with order, restraint and even oppression. Socially it was represented by the bureaucratic and/or authoritarian manner in which so-called civilised societies of any political persuasion are normally organised and ruled.

Like Brecht, Arden conceived of his characters not simply as individuals but also as members of particular social groups, each with his or her own role. The plays are peopled by groups of gypsies, brigands, courtiers or soldiers which in their turn are revealed to be part of a yet larger and more complex controlling structure whose figurehead is normally a monarch. His historical drama is, then, like Brecht's, essentially public rather than private in conception. In those plays written before 1968, both the individual and society are shown to have disparate—but for each in its own terms quite valid—claims upon the other, and Arden's plea, implicit in the plays, is that individual and social demands should each be adjusted to produce what in *Ironhand* his hero Goetz von Berlichingen describes as freedom and good order. *Ironhand* was Arden's first truly historical play. It was produced at the Bristol Old Vic in 1963. The play's overall concerns were with the nature of government and the workings of political processes, subjects that Arden was also to explore during the 1960s in two other historical plays, *Armstrong's Last Goodnight* (1964) and *Left-Handed Liberty* (1965).

Ironhand was not, however, an original play. It was, as Arden himself justly described it, "a free paraphrase"[27] of Goethe's romantic historical drama *Goetz von Berlichingen mit der eisernen Hand* (1773). In practice Arden's play may be considered by a modern audience to be an improvement upon the original in that it restrains some of the romantic extravagance exhibited in Goethe's play and clarifies some of the historical references. The play also gave Arden the opportunity to enlarge his social and political canvas, and the epic scale of Goethe's play, which itself was an emulation of Shakespearian historical drama, allowed him to experience the mechanics of organising a large number and variety of characters and to experiment with the narrative rhythm needed to link the multitude of scenes characteristic of epic drama. It was, however, above all the public nature of *Goetz von Berlichingen* which appealed to Arden. "It was apparently impossible for a dramatist writing in English at the end of the eighteenth century", he wrote in the introduction to *Ironhand*,

... to understand the appeal of a play that treated of historical personages in vernacular prose, that varied that prose from the stately conversation of princes and emperors to the slang of soldiers and the regional dialects of peasants, and that included in its scope not only battles, chivalry, and romantic love but also such wide-ranging historical questions as the dispute between the partisans of the Roman and Common Laws, the Peasants' Revolt of 1525, and the ideas of the young Luther.[28]

This comment undoubtedly betrays a strong sense of fellow-feeling. As Goethe, in turning to Shakespeare as the model for his historical drama, had rejected "the dried up classical theatre, hung over one hundred years from Racine and Corneille",[29] so Arden was attempting in his own historical drama to break with the romantic individualism evident in that of his own time.

Ironhand is by no means simply a slavish translation of *Goetz von Berlichingen* but is used by Arden to explore favourite themes of his own. This is most clearly illustrated in a long speech, totally of Arden's invention, which is delivered by Goetz just before his death and which clearly expresses that unresolved dichotomy between anarchy and the necessity for social order which dominated Arden's work of the 1960s. I have edited the speech in order to illustrate the point more emphatically.

... Weislingen told me I did not know what freedom was. He said it was not possible for me to be free when I inhibited the freedom of other good men. . . . I stood by myself and took no heed of nobody. All that I said was freedom: all Weislingen said was some sort of order. To put the two together: all the world is broken up, and yet we must break it and break it and break it. . . . I deserve my true freedom and so do they all! And we deserve to be told what are the true questions and what are the answers, and we deserve to be able to tell them to our sons! And all that is impossible. . . . You will break yourselves up, you will turn upside-down, you will destroy yourselves with it—there is always one possibility, that one day you will find it. You are made not to rest until you have found it. Freedom. And no warfare. Freedom. And good order. Freedom.[30]

Goetz is a sixteenth-century German robber-knight who claims to owe allegiance to his Emperor. However, as another character, Weislingen, remarks cynically, the Emperor "lives at a convenient distance"[31] and therefore leaves Goetz at liberty to rob merchant convoys and feud with other knights. He is presented by Arden as an anachronism, a romantic conservative who is out of touch with his time. He is a "curvilinear" character who, in common with all of Arden's curvilinear heroes, lacks sophistication, is arrogant and on occasions is capable of barbarity but whose evident vitality, spontaneity and bravery have their attraction. In opposition to him are ranged in the play various numerically greater and politically more powerful rectilinear forces. These are resident in large part in the figure of the Bishop of Bamberg whom Weislingen identifies not only as a member of the hierarchy of the church but also as a territorial prince whose interests are peace, prosperity and free commerce throughout the country. In order to achieve these aims Bamberg sets out to alter the judicial system, levy taxes and suppress the robber-knights. In so doing, he inevitably comes into conflict with those such as Goetz who wish to maintain their independent feudal lifestyle.

In common with the majority of historical plays, *Ironhand* is therefore set at a time of significant historical change. The old orders of feudalism and religion are being supplanted by a new and more complex materialistic society which, in order to operate efficiently and successfully, needs to establish firm centralised control over its citizens and their activities. As the play progresses we gradually become aware of the inevitability of the eradication of the old anarchism by the new politics of the Bishop and of the newly instated boy-emperor. It is Weislingen's role in the play to apply the new politics. Ironically, however, he perishes as a result of his attempt to control, by means of imprisonment or death, the anarchy that has invaded his private life in the form of his wife's anarchic sexuality and infidelity. Nevertheless even without him the violent squabbles and treachery of the few robber-knights ultimately give way to the even greater violence and treachery of the more powerful and far-reaching new state. Goetz is captured and imprisoned by Weislingen's troopers. He dies in chains in Heilbron prison having ruefully looked back over his life in the words quoted above.

In his role as representative of the old anarchistic world, Goetz becomes embroiled in the Peasants' Revolt. As Osborne's play *Luther* also records, the peasants undoubtedly took encouragement for their actions from the teachings of Martin Luther. Luther's advocacy of unmediated communion between the individual and God appeared to them to justify a concomitant rejection of the feudal *secular* hierarchy. In order to make this connection clear, Arden alters Goethe's scene in which a monk meets Goetz in the forest and is immediately aware of his greatness, to one in which the monk is explicitly acknowledged to be Martin Luther himself. In Arden's play the Peasants' Revolt is, however, later revealed to have been a consequence of the peasants' belief that the replacement of their "common" or "curvilinear" people's law, which was based upon the traditions and customs of the region, by the alien "rectilinear" Roman law, constituted an infringement of their rights and freedoms. The religious dispute provoked by Luther is merely employed by the peasants to justify what turns out to be a festival of murder and rapine which Goetz, in spite of his apparently non-authoritarian status and his sincere attempt to find a solution, is unable to curb. Thus here as in the play as a whole, through a shifting of emphasis, Arden imbues *Ironhand* with his own concerns—the exploration of the implications of a curvilinear majority's opposition to a minority ruling group's imposition of its authority, ostensibly for the greater good of the state. Nevertheless, like Osborne, although somewhat more sympathetically, Arden avoids any commitment to mass revolution by illustrating in Goetz's failure to halt the excesses of the peasants' rebellion the potential violence and chaos that revolution may release.

As Arden admitted in an interview, although *Ironhand* had been
"too far from the original, yet not far enough to be a work in its own
right", nevertheless "as a workshop piece it has served its purpose".[32]
He was subsequently to apply the lessons learned in writing it in the
preparation of his next two historical plays, *Armstrong's Last Goodnight* and *Left-Handed Liberty*. The parallels between *Ironhand* and
Armstrong's Last Goodnight are many. Gilnockie, the Armstrong of
the title, is a sixteenth-century Scottish border equivalent of Goetz.
He too is anarchic in temperament and is revealed as an anachronism
in a society undergoing a process of change from feudally fragmented
to bureaucratically centralised rule. In addition Gilnockie behaves
like a naughty child who frighteningly also possesses the adult ability to kill. On the one hand, he is capable of being friendly and hospi-
table and is even at times ingenuous. On the other hand, he is prone
to treachery, is uncouth and has no sense of taste in his personal
adornment. The boy-emperor of the earlier play is here replaced by
the boy-king James of Scotland who, in order to ensure peace between
himself and Henry VII, dispatches the poet and diplomat Sir David
Lindsay, author of *Ane Pleasant Satyre of the Thrie Estates* (1539), to
persuade Gilnockie to terminate the border raids which are upsetting
the English. Historically Lindsay is known to have sympathised with
the people rather than with the nobles and with the reforming party
as opposed to the churchmen. Indeed, the three estates that are sati-
rised, often bawdily, in the above work are the clergy, the nobles and
the merchants. There is, however, no record of Lindsay having
actually taken part in Gilnockie's downfall, but the peculiar nature of
his historic role offered Arden a useful combination of curvilinear artistic and rectilinear political characteristics which could be used to
explore both the precise nature of the conflict between the King and
Gilnockie and the dilemma faced by the liberal who finds himself
embroiled in a dispute in which he appreciates the validity of the
claims made by both sides. In contrast to Gilnockie, Arden's Lindsay
is civilised and artistic, a humanist who considers himself to be intel-
lectually superior to the barbarous but not unlikeable Scot whom,
arrogantly, he believes he can manipulate by means of "policy, nocht
force".[33] In his role of Lyon King of Arms, Lindsay is nevertheless the
servant of the King and is directed to bring Gilnockie under his master's control, notwithstanding Gilnockie's "convenient", self-protective
allegiance to Lord Maxwell which parallels Goetz's similar allegiance
to the old Emperor. In *Armstrong's Last Goodnight*, unhampered by a
pre-existing text, Arden was allowed more opportunity than in *Ironhand* to shape his themes. In consequence the robber knight who
was romanticised in Goethe's play is, in *Armstrong's Last Goodnight*,
reduced in importance, while Lindsay's role becomes the more signifi-

cant. Lindsay's diplomacy, the reasons for its failure and the political expediency that supplants it and culminates in his treacherous contribution to the ambush and murder of Gilnockie by the King, are the central concerns of the play.

In spite of Lindsay's central role in the play which involves a struggle with his own conscience, Arden does not permit *Armstrong's Last Goodnight* to become the kind of character-drama represented by Bolt's *A Man for All Seasons*. The meeting between Lindsay and Gilnockie, although it has private features resulting from the differences in the two men's personalities, is not dealt with on a personal level but is placed in a context of wider political considerations. Their meeting is shown by Arden to be the outcome of political decisions that to a great extent dictate Lindsay's behaviour. In the opening scenes of the play Arden carefully establishes the various levels of bureaucracy involved in the progression towards the ultimate decision to send Lindsay on his mission to Gilnockie. The first scene illustrates a meeting of English and Scottish Commissioners during which there is discussion of border incidents. The second scene involves the Commissioner's Clerks, left behind on stage by their superiors at the conclusion of the main policy meeting. It is they who are shown to be responsible for activating the policy agreed upon by the Commissioners when they brief their emissary, Lindsay, for a mission to Scotland. It is then finally left to Lindsay to put the policy into practice. Throughout the play Arden effectively conveys a sense of the mechanisms of political diplomacy and by this means ensures that it does not simply become the kind of character-drama represented by Bolt's *A Man for All Seasons* but is instead a much more far-reaching illustration of political processes in action in which the play's central characters merely play a part.

Arden has referred in some detail to the manner in which, in the construction of *Armstrong's Last Goodnight*, he linked an historical event recorded in the form of a folk ballad of Johnny Armstrong with recent political events in Africa to produce a political parable:

Well, *Armstrong* began with a re-reading of the ballad, which I have known for years. . . . Then I read Connor Cruise O'Brien's book about Katanga and considered *that* as a dramatic subject. But I knew nothing about Africa— besides, there was a language problem. Congolese Negroes talk French some of the time and their own tongue at others. How was I to find an equivalent for that on the English stage? But once I had connected the book with the ballad, I was happily working in the old North again.[34]

In this manner, issues raised by a recent war in the African Congo were transferred to the world of the Scottish ballad, itself rich in met-

aphor, to become a political parable in which the "civilised" is measured against the "primitive". Although he was careful not to limit the
implication of his play by following too closely the specific details of
the negotiations undertaken in the Congo between O'Brien and
Tshombe during its civil war of 1961, by locating these diplomatic
manouevres within a distant historical context provided by the ballad, Arden was able to explore the very nature of that international
diplomacy which inevitably remains a significant feature of the politics of our own time. Furthermore, Arden's reference to the folk-ballad tradition with its archetypal figures and events ensured, as it had
for Brecht, that the characters of his play existed not simply as figures in a socio-political tract but as vital, sensual and sometimes violent human beings who inhabited a society now past but whose
experiences could be used to throw light upon the present.

Arden's next historical play, *Left-Handed Liberty*, was structurally
to prove much less successful than either *Ironhand* or *Armstrong's
Last Goodnight*. The play was commissioned in 1965 by the Corpora-
tion of the City of London to commemorate the 750th Anniversary of
the sealing of the Magna Carta. Arden was soon to recognise that the
historical material "did not seem naturally to lend itself to dramatic
form".[35] In addition, in spite of its apparent reference to a significant
moment of historical change in the relationship between the Monarch
and his subjects, it proved difficult either to assimilate those themes
of freedom and order, curvilinear versus rectilinear, which Arden had
been recently exploring or to employ the subject-matter to make any
significant reference to contemporary issues. In consequence, the resulting play was, in Arden's view, "a bit of a chaos".[36] In an attempt to
invest the play with some contemporary relevance, Arden chose not
to dramatise the events leading up to the sealing of the charter but
to focus instead upon the period following, during which a civil war
was resumed and King John was to meet his death in the tidal cur-
rents of the Wash. "If Magna Carta is worth commemorating at all,"
commented Arden in what sounded suspiciously like desperation, "it
presumably is still relevant to our politics."[37] Such relevance Arden
worked hard to convey.

Characteristically, Arden did not dramatise his historical material
simply as a conflict between King John and a number of representative barons. Instead, around this central core of events, he attempted
to draw a portrait of an age. This is initiated in the opening minutes
of the play in the Papal Legate Pandulph's discourse on medieval
cosmology. As the play proceeds the hierarchy implicit in this cosmology is extended to encompass, sometimes rather too fleetingly, the
various stations of society ranging from King to commoner. Significantly, considering the source of the commission, an important con-

stituent of this secular hierarchy is the Mayor of London whose involvement, according to Arden, reflected "the first time that the commercial middle-class took part in English politics".[38]

In common with the two earlier historical dramas, Arden's *Left-Handed Liberty* ostensibly deals with a society at a significant moment of change. The play reveals, however, that the view taught in school—that the sealing of the Charter marked both the curbing of royal power and a turning point in the progress towards English democracy—was a myth unsupported by historical evidence. In reality, Arden discovered, neither the King nor the Barons had any intention of sticking to the agreement, and the struggle for power between them in fact continued right up until King John's death. The Magna Carta could not therefore be represented as an historical turning point whose influence and lineage could be clearly perceived in Britain's modern democratic institutions. In consequence, in order to pad out his historical material, Arden filled the play with a rag-bag of various themes, which included Queen Eleanor's introduction of the concept of "courtly love" which was to infuse contemporary poetry; a consideration of the role of women, centred upon the character of Lady de Vesci; and reference to the part played in love and marriage by spontaneity and repression. The latter is represented in the form of a scene involving a dispute between a goldsmith and his wife during which King John gives a judgement, similar to that pronounced by Azdak in Brecht's *The Caucasian Chalk Circle*, by which everyone including the judge himself is the recipient of a prize.

All of these themes are yoked uneasily together, none being fully explored, and all are presented in the form of discussion rather than stage action. In fact, in the penultimate scene of the play Arden almost abandons his attempted dramatisation altogether. At this point, with the houselights up, King John addresses the audience directly. He begins: "There comes a time in any stage-play, when the stage itself, the persons upon it, the persons in front of it must justify their existence—and I think this is the time now."[39] It might also be counter-argued that it is up to the play as a whole to justify its characters' existence and function. For any audience to require such justification must surely reflect failure on the part of the dramatist. Following this introductory statement comes a rambling lecture during the course of which the character removes his sword, crown and mantle in order to make the audience aware that, as an actor, he has lent his body to the recreation of the historical figure he represents. Soon the lecture turns to Arden's currently favoured theme of the evasion of authority, here associated with the nature of the charter. According to Arden a central feature of the Magna Carta was the inclusion of certain "kinks" that would permit those who agreed to it or were affected by it some opportunity for freedom of movement. Of these "kinks", Arden maintains, King John was perfectly aware: "I said: make those clauses general—lax, if you like—" remarks King John, "because by their very laxity they go some way to admit the existence of dandelion, of disobedient women, and ribbons of cloth-of-gold".[40] The phrases to which King John refers, as might be expected from Arden, are concerned with basic freedoms—"And no man shall be arrested or imprisoned . . . except . . ." and "To no man will we sell or deny right and justice".[41] Eventually this essentially undramatic scene, in which Arden's own voice is so clearly detectable, culminates with a warning against the acceptance of the perpetuity of any system of rule, for

. . . every single stone, brick, or granule of aggregate that help to build the buttresses which hold up the walls of the Temple of Authority are in peril from these clauses! Every buttress must be made afraid of you—and you must never fear the buttress: because a buttress is a dead thing, inert, fabricated, the result of a delusion—whereas you are men and women—I have shewn you your pattern. . . .[42]

The play's remaining scene retrieves some theatricality by illustrating, by means of mime, stage lighting and projection accompanied by dialogue in verse and prose, the drowning of King John and the loss of his baggage-train in the Wash.

Unfortunately, only in the introduction to the published text does Arden unequivocally make the link between past and present. Here he elucidates the "message" which, if not entirely lost, is certainly somewhat obscured in the "chaos" of the play.

I suppose it is that an agreement on paper is worth nothing to anybody unless it has taken place in their minds as well: and that if we want liberty we have to make quite sure that
a)   We know what sort of liberty we are fighting for;
b)   Our methods of fighting are not such as to render that liberty invalid before we even attain it;
c)   We understand that we are in more danger of losing it once we have attained it than if we had never had it; which is an Irishism, but clear enough for all that.[43]

Left-Handed Liberty offers a salutary example of how, if historical drama is to be more than a dramatised history lesson and is to offer lessons for the present, a dramatist possessed of a clear moral, social or political viewpoint must select those moments of history which best accord with his or her views and aims and not attempt to work from the opposite direction!

In terms of their subject matter and their success in dramatising a whole society, *Ironhand, Armstrong's Last Goodnight* and *Left-Handed Liberty* are plays *about* politics but are nevertheless not *political* plays. In each of them Arden examines political processes, but in none does he propagandise for any specific political ideology or even imply any particular political solution. During the 1960s Arden brought his historical drama to the threshold of politics. It was the activity of the New Left after 1968 together with the relaxation of stage censorship in the same year which was to encourage Arden and other dramatists to move from the dramatisation of the generalised concepts of "society" and the "people", with their abstract associations of freedom and liberty, towards a more precise analysis of society in terms of "class".

PART II

4

Freedom and Good Order

Whereas from the late 1950s and into the 1960s British historical drama had been characterised by the disillusionment arising from socialist promises unfulfilled, the historical drama of the 1970s was primarily concerned with protest and political activism and was to reflect the specific political concerns of the contemporary Left. During the 1970s the majority of dramatists, even when the perspective of their work was evidently left-wing, were, however, unwilling to view history merely in political and economic terms. They continued to be concerned with individual experience and the human cost of historical change. To this end they were repeatedly to re-invoke the Anarchist views that had appeared so potent during the previous decade, and were to seek the means by which theatrically the inter-relationship of private and public experience could be effectively communicated.

It was not only socialists who exhibited a growing disillusionment with parliamentary politics during the 1960s. According to David McKie in *The Decade of Disillusion*, workers of all parties who at election times during the decade went round knocking on doors received repeatedly "the weary complaint that there was 'nothing to choose between them'; that they were 'both as bad as each other'; that it 'doesn't make a blind bit of difference who gets in'."[1] Alongside this general apathy there grew also amongst still-committed Socialists an ever-increasing despair with the policies of the successive Labour governments led by Harold Wilson. Even as early as 1961, however, Raymond Williams had written in *The Long Revolution*:

. . . Labour seems to have very little to offer. A different version of community, a pattern of new consciousness, it has not been able to give. Its com-
promise policies combine the two irrelevant elements of appeal to old and
fading habits and memories, and of cultural adjustment to the present social
confusion. Old Left and new Right in the Labour Party are unconscious allies
in delaying any relevant analysis and challenge.[2]

Many on the Left accused Wilson's government of not only abandoning socialism but, for example, on the evidence of its Industrial Relations Bill of 1969, of acting flagrantly against the interests of the
working class itself. As noted by David McKie,

Mounting unemployment; curbs on trade unions, and wage restraint—not
even stopping short of the threat of prison; support for the American adventure in Vietnam; limits on immigration, culminating in the panic moves . . .
to slam the door on the Kenya Asians; the maintenance of an independent
deterrent; prescription charges, charges for school milk, and dearer school
meals, cutbacks in the rate of building new homes—all these and other similar practices, natural, if thoroughly disgusting, when the Tories were in
power, but unthinkable from any other source, were now seen issuing forth in
the name of a Labour administration.[3]

Galvanised by this increasing distrust of party and parliamentary
politics, the protest movements—initiated in 1958 by the Campaign
for Nuclear Disarmament (C.N.D.) in response to Britain's testing of
its first H-bomb in the Pacific in May of the previous year—were
during the 1960s to find growing support, particularly amongst the
young. Both the protest movements and the young themselves were
soon to become influential political forces. C.N.D. was the first post-
war protest movement to attract large numbers of young people, particularly from the middle-class and/or those associated with the arts,
and was effectively to direct their youthful idealism into political
action. In fact, as Hugo Young points out in his discussion of "Politics
outside the System", C.N.D. was to offer in the long run merely "a
necessary outlet for moral indignation which had one swift and, as it
turned out, deceptive moment of political promise."[4] The one fleeting
moment of political promise referred to by Young was C.N.D.'s
responsibility for the adoption of unilateral disarmament by the
Labour Party in 1960. In the face of more militant political protest
during the 1970s, C.N.D. was to lose some of its attraction but, as
David Edgar illustrates in *Maydays*, it was nevertheless to be rein-
vigorated during the 1980s by the opposition to the basing of U.S.
Cruise missiles in Britain.

   Looking back in 1972, Hugo Young provided a useful summary of
the rapid development of protest movements during the 1960s:

Before Labour lost the 1970 election, the politics of protest, transformed into the protest "movement", appeared to be a good deal more durable than C.N.D. That one extraordinary incursion upon the consensus was now a puny and irrelevant memory. Protest encompassed not merely ragged idealists, backing worthy causes by constitutional means, but seemingly a whole generation with a comprehensive philosophy, a radical life-style and a contempt for the old methods of restrained persuasion. "Protest" was inclusive and badly defined. But it could safely be said to operate outside the system, and to aim variously at political, social and cultural revolution, with an impact which quite overshadowed conventional pressure-groups working, like C.N.D., to influence and thereby strengthen the system of parliamentary democracy. During the Labour years, the movement seemed capable of making an indelible mark on British politics.[5]

Disillusioned both with the Labour Party and with Soviet communism, young people in Britain during the 1960s began to look elsewhere for their socialist ideals. Firstly they turned to anarchism and then, when at the close of the decade this appeared to have been defeated by the forces of the establishment, they were to re-examine the words and deeds of earlier, *successful* revolutionaries such as Mao Ze Dong and Lenin, or the arguably less successful Trotsky, in order to discover a *method* of revolutionary change which would recognise equally the claims both of the individual and of the state.

The impetus for the move from the passive protests of C.N.D. towards a sometimes more aggressive phase of extra-parliamentary activity was provided during the early 1960s by U.S. military involvement in Vietnam. The protests against U.S. action were soon to become politicised, for gradually not only America itself but the whole western capitalist system was identified as the cause of the inhumane treatment of a small country by a world power. Thus by 1966 the anti-war protests had turned into a wider call for the revolutionary overthrow of a morally bankrupt political system. In this, students were to play a major part. Their protest was, however, also extended to encompass the "paternalism" and "institutional violence" of their own college authorities who were, of course, easily identifiable as the custodians of discredited values of a corrupt political system. This student activism was to take the form of a series of university sit-ins which began with the student occupation of the London School of Economics in March 1967 and reached their zenith in 1968.

Significantly, also in 1968 the Radical Student Alliance, a group formed within the National Union of Students and one that had played a leading part in the activism described above, changed its name to the Revolutionary Socialist Students Federation and thus clearly initiated a transposition into the wider world of revolutionary

extra-parliamentary politics. Its aims were declared unequivocally in
its manifesto:

R.S.S.F.'s aims cannot be achieved through parliamentary means and it
therefore constitutes itself as an extra-parliamentary opposition. . . . It commits itself on principle to all anti-imperialist, anti-capitalist and anti-fascist
struggles. . . . It commits itself to the revolutionary over-throw of capitalism
and imperialism and its replacement by workers' power. . . .[6]

In this the R.S.S.F. were aligning themselves with other student
groups throughout Europe and the United States and for a short
while in Europe it seemed that the international student movement
might forge itself, in alliance with the workers, into a wider political
movement which might even achieve its revolutionary aims. This,
however, was not to be. Even in France, where in 1968 the workers
and students were almost united, the movement was defeated on the
streets of Paris in May 1968 by the Gaullist government. In Britain
the students and workers were unable to overcome their mutual class
antagonism and in addition the various radical groups—such as
International Socialism, the Young Communist League, The International Marxist Group and the Young Liberals, who had allied
themselves loosely under the umbrella of the Vietnam Solidarity
Campaign in 1967—were by no means united in their aims. As David
Edgar illustrates in *Maydays*, this lack of unity amongst the various
groups bent upon revolution was to continue well into the 1970s and
was to contribute to the downfall of the Labour government in 1978.
During the 1960s this amalgam of various political views was nevertheless united to some extent by the presence of the Anarchists who,
on the one hand, were broadly socialist and therefore could appeal to
disaffected Communists and disgruntled Labour supporters, while on
the other hand, with their emphasis upon the rights of the individual
over those of the state, could also attract those middle-class intellectuals who felt themselves to be alienated from the establishment.

Before the 1960s the political status and influence of anarchism in
Britain had been relatively marginal. It had nevertheless been a feature of British political philosophy since the publication in 1783 of
William Godwin's *An Enquiry Concerning Political Justice*. In the
years after the Second World War it was kept alive in the works of
Sir Herbert Read and Alex Comfort, but in the 1950s, at about the
same time as the eruption of the new British theatre in Sloane
Square, anarchism was also to emerge vigorously onto the political
stage and, along with the new British drama, was to flourish during
the following decade. It was also paradoxically both to revitalize and
to diffuse the ideology of the Left.

"Anarchism is the politial elaboration of the psychological reaction against authority which appears in all human groups", wrote Nicolas Walter in a short Anarchist tract published by the Freedom Press at the height of the Anarchist revival in 1969. "Throughout history the practical tendency towards anarchy", continued Walter, "is seen among individuals and groups rebelling against those who rule them."[7] Such apparently innate rebelliousness is often associated with the process of growing up, and it may therefore be no coincidence that the Anarchist revival of the 1960s and early 1970s took place largely amongst the young, becoming indeed a major feature of the so-called "youth-culture" of the period. Writers of the plethora of Anarchist publications that appeared during those years sought, however, to establish that the movement was not simply a youthful fashion but was in fact a reflection of a deeper political consciousness. One of these writers, Colin Ward, in 1971 enthusiastically cited recent events as evidence of the international significance of the Anarchist revival:

. . . in Paris in 1968 anarchist flags flew over the Sorbonne, and in the same year they were seen in Brussels, Rome, Mexico City, New York and even Canterbury. All of a sudden people were talking about the need for a kind of politics in which ordinary men, women and children decide their own fate and make their own future, about the need for social and political decentralisation, about workers' control of industry, about pupil power in school, about community control of the social services. Anarchism, instead of being a romantic historical by-way, becomes an attitude to human organisation which is more relevant today than it ever seemed in the past.[8]

Many of these topics and, explicitly, the Anarchist approach to the organisation of people had already been explored in social terms by Arden during the 1960s but were now to be dealt with in a clearly political context in the historical drama of the 1970s.

In order to explain the apparent contradiction between freedom and organisation implied, for example, in the above quotation, Anarchists tendered the possibility of *spontaneous* order and organisation. They illustrated this concept by reference to such, in conventional terms, "unorganised" and leaderless post-war social phenomena as the occupation of abandoned army camps by families of squatters during the summer of 1946, the revival of "squatting" in the late 1960s, the pop-festivals of the same decade, and the uprisings in Hungary in 1956 and Czechoslovakia in 1968. Each of these events was considered in some measure to have achieved the Anarchist ideal of *communal individuality*.

The Anarchist movement of the 1960s was extremely conscious of its own historical evolution. A knowledge of this history also contributes to an understanding of aspects of the historical drama of the 1970s, where its concerns and conflicts are often directly examined in plays such as Trevor Griffiths' *Occupations* (1970) or Steve Gooch's *Women Pirates* (1978). Modern anarchism is usually considered to have begun in 1872 with the exclusion of Bakunin and his followers from the Congress of the Communist International at the Hague. In response Bakunin had angrily branded Marx as "an authoritarian and centralising communist". It was in fact this divergence of, on the one side, the libertarianism of the Anarchists and, on the other, the centralism and collectivism of the communists which a century later, in the light of the failure of the leaderless *communal organisation* of the student risings of 1968, was to be repeatedly examined in the historical drama of the period.

In "Anarchists in Britain Today" (1971), David Stafford argues that the creation of the so-called "New Left" in the late 1950s—a mixture of mainly Oxbridge graduates consisting of Communists who had resigned from the party over its support for the Russian action in Hungary and Conservatives who disapproved of the invasion of Egypt and inspired by Ralph Samuel and Stewart Hall—owed much to Anarchist theory. Its broad aim, expressed in such periodicals as *Universities and Left Review* and the *New Reasoner* which later merged to become the *New Left Review*, was to establish a new type of socialism, to "re-emphasise the *moral* concern and imagination of socialism", to reject the reduction of social issues to simple political formulae", and "to establish a new *ethically* based politics for the Left".[9]

Anarchist influence can undoubtedly be detected in the adoption by the New Left of the passive resistance and civil disobedience which characterised the C.N.D.'s demonstrations and Aldermaston marches in which a number of dramatists, including Arden and Wesker, took an active part during the late 1950s and early 1960s. Of the next generation of dramatists Howard Brenton is one who has acknowledged the influence of anarchism upon the form and content of his work and has portrayed the part played by it in the youth movements of the 1960s and upon the formation of the New Left. In a *Theatre Quarterly* interview of 1975, "Petrol Bombs through the Proscenium Arch", he referred to the 1960s "Situationists"—themselves an offshoot of the Anarchist movement—whose advocacy of cultural subversion would appear to have largely dictated the aesthetic subversion attempted by himself, David Hare and Snoo Wilson as dramatists of "Portable Theatre". Indeed David Hare has explicitly described the aim of Portable Theatre as being to take "anarchist plays around the country in order to shock people by putting plays on in places where they weren't expected."[10] "Situationism" first emerged

in 1957 and its followers were to play a major part in the events of
May 1968. Their particular belief was that the modern bureaucratic
system of industrial society, although apparently less physically cruel
than the labour exploitation of nineteenth-century competitive capitalism, had, in order to perpetuate itself, developed a "spectacular"
society supported by the creation of specious "needs". In this society
everything, including the individual, is treated as a commodity. In
the Situationist analysis "culture", in the form of the Arts or Education, is also employed by the "spectacular" society to manipulate the
individual into an acceptance of his or her role within the system. It
follows, therefore, that any revolutionary activity must not only
attack economic or social structures but must also subvert all man-
ifestations of establishment culture.

As noted above, the New Left found a catalyst for its activities during the late 1960s in the opposition to the Vietnam War and in the
May riots in Paris in 1968 and began to circulate its ideas widely in
the pages of *Black Dwarf* and *Red Mole*. It now advocated violent,
liberating, revolutionary action. This was, however, to be free of the
authoritarianism evident in the so-called socialist societies of, for
example, Eastern Europe. As Howard Brenton has described in his
1975 *Theatre Quarterly* interview, "Petrol Bombs through the Proscenium Arch", the New Left also set out to erect elements of a new
society within the framework of the old.

With this aim in mind, student Situationist groups in the French
universities of Nanterre, Strasbourg, Nantes and Bordeaux set out in
1967–68 "to organise chaos" on the campuses. They thereby con-
currently revealed a delight in *paradox* which, along with their
attack upon establishment culture and their wish not merely to *trans-
form* society but also to *change life itself*, illustrated their relationship not only to anarchism but also to Dada and Surrealism. As
Richard Gombin has suggested, inscriptions such as "Never Work"
which appeared on the walls of Paris in 1968 were themselves the
direct descendants of the Surrealist slogans of the 1920s.[11]

History was viewed by the Situationists as but another spectacular
official fiction which it was necessary to *disrupt* in order to provoke
that radically new perception of reality necessary for life to be fundamentally changed. This view was to be absorbed into the revolutionary programme of the New Left. The cultural disruption and
demystification needed to accomplish this radical realignment was
soon seen by dramatists such as Brenton to offer an ideal opportunity
for the theatre, with its potential for shocking immediacy, to play an
active role in the political struggle.

The attempt made in 1968 to reinvent the revolution rather than to
emulate the Russian model of 1917 was to revive again the funda-

mental conflict between Anarchists and Marxists which had been revealed in the dispute between Bakunin and Marx over whether a revolution should be conducted by a popular collective or by a party machine. In the wake of the failure of the revolutionary activity in 1968, which has since been taken as a convenient symbol for the defeat of the utopian socialism and anarchism of the 1960s, the topic of how to run a revolution was to receive widespread consideration in the historical drama of the following decade.

During the 1960s anarchist dramatists such as John Arden, and Edward Bond with *Early Morning*, employed historical settings, figures and events in analysing the mechanisms of authority, the means by which the individual is controlled and oppressed. In the following decade Howard Brenton and other post-Situationist dramatists such as Howard Barker followed the example of Bond's *Early Morning* by using the very structure of the play itself as a means of disrupting and subverting the audience's perception of authoritarian social structures. In addition, on a thematic level, Brenton was also repeatedly to refer to the apparent failure of Anarchism in the face of the *organised* forces of either capitalism or Marxism. Both *Fruit* (1970) and *Magnificence* (1973) reflect the influence of the Situationists in their reference—for example in the words of Jed in the latter play—to the society of spectacle, "the obscene parade".[12] In *Fruit*, Brenton also refers to the "Syndicalists", another Anarchist movement which was "very active in the London Docks just before the First World War" and which held the view that social organisation should be based upon the trade unions, who were the natural representatives of the working class. Significantly, they too looked to a revolution that did not reach fruition. "There may have been an English Revolution growing", commented Brenton, "which was stopped by 1914."[13]

In *Magnificence* and *Weapons of Happiness* Brenton was concerned with the very nature of revolution and with its potential realisation in England. Once again there is a connection with the events of 1968. This time it is implicit in the title of *Weapons of Happiness*, which is taken from a slogan painted on the wall of the "squat" that is the opening setting of the earlier play, *Magnificence*, the paradoxical nature of the statement linking it both with the Paris slogans of 1968 and the Surrealistic ones of the 1920s. The setting of the "squat" was itself also significant. "Squatting" was an activity that, both because of the relative spontaneity of its direct action and its attack upon bureaucratic red tape, was favoured by the Anarchists but not by factions of the New Left. It therefore provided for Brenton an important area of disagreement within the Left around which could be illustrated the potential effectiveness of the various forms of direct action in bringing about political change.

Neither Brenton's references to anarchism nor those found in the work of other dramatists of the 1960s and 1970s should, however, be taken as evidence of a firmly held political conviction. Instead they should, I think, be seen as symptomatic of a desire to evoke the possibility of a new form of socialism which would be neither bureaucratic nor tyrannical, which would be free of Marxist dogma and which would recognise individual autonomy.

This desire was evident in the dramatic treatment of historical events, particularly in relation to character and inter-personal relationships. Similar sentiments to those expressed by the Anarchist, Gustav Landauer, appear, for example, in a number of the plays and prefaces of Edward Bond. As Landauer suggested,

The state is not something which can be destroyed by a revolution, but is a condition, a certain relationship between human beings, a mode of human behaviour; we destroy it by contracting other relationships, by behaving differently.[14]

"Justice is allowing people to live in the way for which they evolved", wrote Edward Bond in his Preface to *Lear* (1971).[15] Bond also went further in the direction of Anarchism by warning that "if your plan for the future is too rigid you start to coerce people to fit into it. We do not need a plan for the future, we need a *method* of change".[16] As if in reply, another Anarchist writer has emphasised the need to "build up a theory of non-government, of non-management, from the kind of history and experience which has hardly been written about because nobody thought it all that important".[17] With the challenge of anarchism in the air, during the 1960s and 1970s a large number of politically aware British dramatists began to perceive the significance of such "history and experience" for an assessment of the moral and political state of contemporary heterosexual-white-male-capitalist-dominated society.

After 1968, the rise of the political theatre movement marked a distinct change in the use of history. There emerged a new generation of political dramatists who, joined by such old-timers as John Arden and Edward Bond, began to move away from that utopian socialism or anarchism which had been communicated in the historical drama of the 1960s, towards a more politically self-conscious and radically revolutionary socialism and Marxism. History was now carefully appropriated as part of the armoury of the left-wing political theatre, and the supplanting of personal by public history was also, for reasons described by Colin McArthur in his monograph, *Television and History*, now clearly identified as an ideological concern.

The emergence of the capitalist mode of production with its characteristic economic relations where individual men and women are "free" to sell their own labour power or buy that of others required a concurrent philosophical definition of men and women as separate and autonomous entitities, precisely as *individuals*. Just as in our society the notion of usury has become naturalised, regarded as a timeless "fact of life", so too has the notion of men and women as individuals. In fact, this notion had to be labouriously constructed as an ideology of the rising bourgeoisie to render coherent its throwing off of feudalism.[18]

Faced with this dominant and all-pervasive ideology communicated particularly in television's treatment of history, it therefore appeared imperative for the socialist dramatist not only to alter but also to aggressively demystify and deconstruct the apparent "naturalness" of such individualism. In so doing, the aim was to reveal that such a view of humanity was, as McArthur suggests, merely a philosophical construct and as such could be deconstructed and reconstituted in other forms. During the 1970s this radical treatment of history was intended to achieve a number of political aims. These were variously: to convince ordinary people that they could be agents of their own destiny; by means of iconoclasm to demythologise bourgeois history; to suggest the reasons why, during the post-war years, socialism had not won the hearts and minds of the British public; to present history in Marxist terms as one of class conflict; and to utilise dramatic form in order effectively to achieve these ends.

The question of what might be an appropriate dramatic form for the construction of a socialist historical drama was much discussed in prefaces and interviews by the dramatists themselves. Here developed a debate between those left-wing dramatists, such as John McGrath, who were employing a version of Agit-Prop theatre to illustrate the workings of economic and class forces, and those who considered such an approach outdated, oversimplified and incapable of dealing with the complex nature of the political and social forces at work in post-war Britain. As David Edgar notes in 1978 in his survey of "Ten Years of Political Theatre", central to Agit-Prop was a process of abstraction which involved the removal of personal and private experience in order to reveal "only the assumed objective essence of a situation".[19] This meant that, for example, a play's characterisation left the audience in "no danger of misinterpreting the actions of the capitalist in terms of his individual psychology: his class-motivation is all too clear".[20]

In David Hare's view such a simplistic, propagandist approach was an insult to the audience's intelligence. "Why", he asked in the same year, "do we so often have to endure the demeaning repetition of slogans which are seen not as transitional aids to understanding but as ultimate solutions to men's problems?" Such sloganising he considered ineffective as a means of adequately addressing the complexity of the current political situation. "Why the insulting insistence in so much political theatre", he asked rhetorically, "that a few gimcrack mottoes of the left will sort out the deep problems of reaction in modern England? Why the urge to caricature?"[21]

In this search for new forms of political drama both sides in the debate were to reject the unqualified emulation of Brechtian models. Edgar claimed that some new writers were already "conscious of the degeneration of Brecht's techniques to the condition of theatrical cliche",[22] while Hare contemptuously asserted that "Brecht uncoils the great sleeping length of his mind to give us the godlike feeling that the questions have been answered before the play has begun".[23] Even John McGrath, an active Marxist, while recognising the immense contribution made by both Brecht and Piscator to political theatre, decried their commitment to "working *within* the Berlin smart bourgeois theatre, albeit as 'oppositional' forces"[24] instead of attempting to create, as he himself wished to do, a popular, working-class political theatre.

In "Ten Years of Political Theatre" David Edgar rejected Agit-Prop as inadequate for dealing with the political situation of the 1970s. In its place he proposed a form of drama that would deal with those questions of conscience which precisely because agit-prop techniques portrayed "only the assumed objective essence of a situation" were beyond its scope. He considered elements of such a fresh approach to be already latent in the plays of some of his fellow-dramatists— namely, Edward Bond, Trevor Griffiths, David Hare, Howard Brenton and Caryl Churchill—and in the work of such theatre groups as Monstrous Regiment. A major feature of this approach was the use of shocking images, which were intended not as in Brecht's theatre to *endistance* the audience, but rather to *involve* it. In common with Brecht, however, in order to create an aesthetic dislocation that would betray the audience's expectations, these dramatists often abruptly altered familiar theatrical forms or endowed them with uncharacteristic subject matter. Such parodistic techniques were, of course, not new to the theatre, having been favoured most recently not only by Brecht but also by Ibsen and Shaw. In each case parody was employed as a means of disturbing or attacking a social group whose values the parodied form could be seen to reflect. Such was the parallel drawn by Ibsen in *A Doll's House* between bourgeois values and the clichés of the well-made play. With, as I have illustrated, some justification, Edgar attributed the direct inspiration for the revival of these techniques during the 1970s to the "spectacle disruptive situationist era of the later 1960s".[25] What may also have been derived from this era was the feature that Edgar considered to be central to the newly emerging political drama: the attempt to give weight to the expression of *both* public and private experience by eliciting from a dramatic situation "the dynamic between how people subjectively perceive that situation and the underlying reality".[26] How this might be achieved was further discussed by Edward Bond in "The Activist Papers" in 1980. He proffered a new form of drama based upon the epic which he described as the "epic-lyric":

The artist tries to show reason in experience and appearance—and the lyric is the daily appearance, the commonplace dress of reason. It's the footprint on the pathway. In the epic-lyric the individual and the particular are no longer isolated but are placed in a historical social human pattern. That's why there's a political way of cutting bread or wearing shoes.[27]

In consequence of the need to translate large public events into interpersonal interactions within the restrictions imposed by live performance, the historical dramatist must inevitably make a decision concerning the balance of the relationship between the lyric voice of the individual and the epic concerns inherent in historical change. Bond described in some detail how in the epic-lyric it would be possible to acknowledge and inter-relate both elements.

In this form events and incidents wouldn't only be aspects of historical movement. They'd show the pattern and nature of that movement. Instead of history being filtered through an individual, reduced to him (as in King Lear), the play's figures and incidents would embody and demonstrate the total historical movement. History wouldn't be shown as immanent in an individual, individuality would be transcended by the historical pattern which it represented. Incidents would be chosen to show how historical moments arise and how they lead to resolutions. Movements spread over long periods and involving masses of people might be reflected in stories, often simple stories. The characters wouldn't be moved by personal motives but by the forces of history. They'd be epic in analysis but not necessarily in size—after all a mouse can be the hero of an epic. The forces wouldn't be shown as abstractions. We need to show the historical abstraction but at the same time we need to show the individual characteristics—they're the means through which history works. That's really the reason we have art—we need to show the general in the particular in order to understand ourselves. So we'd show individual quirkiness. Indeed we'd show the power of historical forces by showing the individuality, ordinariness and human vulnerability and strength of the characters who live in it.[28]

I have quoted Bond at some length because here he sums up the wider aesthetic aims that, during the 1970s, motivated the attempt to create a public/private historical drama and were realised variously by dramatists according to personal taste, intended audience and individual ideology.

In the aftermath of the Left's political setbacks of May 1968 which were attributed by John McGrath and Trevor Griffiths to an absence of organisation and leadership, it was appropriately on the subject of leaders and public heroes that, in the following November, John Arden and his wife Margaretta D'Arcy staged *The Hero Rises Up*. In so doing, Arden was again to play a leading part in the evolution of public historical drama. The tongue-in-cheek "Necromatic Prologue" delivered by "an Academic Representative of the Authors" leaves the audience in no doubt about the play's significance in the topical debate concerning the nature of socialist revolutionary leadership:

To what extent the history of the human race is determined by the abstract and indeed scarcely tangible, though none the less mensurable, forces of economics, population-growth, routes of communication, geographical barriers, pastoral and/or industrial systems of production—and similar kindred phenomena—must at the present time be regarded as subject to controversy. No less controversial is the importance we should accord the individual human being in such a universal *schema*. . . .[29]

From the start, therefore, the Ardens draw our attention to the challenge posed to the bourgeois concept of the hero by the Marxist historian's materialistic analysis of historical processes. However, their academician then proceeds to point out that the modern Left, in spite of its philosophical objection to individualism, would also appear to be possessed of a need to create heroes of its own. "Even in the regrettable realms of radical–syndicalist–insurrectionary leftism there are the potent mythical figures of Che Guevara and Mao Tse Tung and —so on and so forth."[30]

The aim of the play, we are told, is to resurrect the figure of Nelson, a hero of *both* the ruling class and the people, in order to explore how we ourselves may create, or become heroes. From the prologue it would appear at first that by focusing upon Nelson's *personal* rather than his *public* life the Ardens are, like Terence Rattigan in *A Bequest to the Nation*, intending to proceed in the bourgeois tradition of historical drama. "I want you to meditate, as pungently as you can," the Academic Representative tells the audience, "upon the sexual congress of Lord Nelson and Lady Hamilton."[31] In fact the audience are not to be treated to a romantic (like Rattigan's) nor even to a lascivious biography of Nelson. Instead it is to witness a repetition of the iconoclastic treatment of a national hero which had been first seen in the post-1956 British theatre the year previously in Charles Wood's *Dingo* (1967). Here Wood had satirically presented a character who *could* be interpreted as representing Montgomery, the Second World War general. Whereas in *Dingo* Wood had, by means of iconoclasm, attempted to demystify the romanticised heroic "aftermyth" of the Second World War, in *The Hero Rises Up* the Ardens were concerned to question the implications behind the very concept of the bourgeois hero. The intention in employing iconclasm here and in the large number of plays in which it was soon to figure during the 1970s was not indeed to assault the personal status of the historical figures themselves, but to attack their iconic role within the nation's bourgeois mythology and their place within the capitalist superstructure of social, moral and ethical values.

The Hero Rises Up takes the form of a parody of the type of nineteenth-century nautical melodrama that celebrated heroically both Britain's contemporary military might and those national heroes who were responsible for its world supremacy. Like many such melodramas the play concludes in an appropriately patriotic manner with the apotheosis of the hero, Nelson. The songs and dramatic action of the parody are used to question the nature of Nelson's heroism and also to reveal *how* such a figure may be appropriated and employed as part of the establishment superstructure.

As both nineteenth-century and modern political cartoons reveal, political lampoon, of which theatrical iconoclasm is a variety, relies much upon the exaggeration of physical appearance and the reference to alleged mental or physical disability. Like Shakespeare's Richard III, the icon is often viciously demagnified in order to dethrone the often god-like figure enshrined in myth. Likewise in *The Hero Rises Up*, the "hero" who bursts through the paper screen that initially hides his *real* self from our view is revealed to be diminutive and grotesque in stature. He is skinny and has a "little cock-sparrow head",[32] an eye-patch and a missing arm. He nevertheless immediately commences to harangue the audience arrogantly. "If you don't know who I am you ought to be ashamed of yourselves, God damn your eyes"[33] are the first words we hear from his lips, an introduction hardly likely to inspire either admiration or empathy! In the initial production at the Round House in London, the part of Nelson was played by Henry Woolf. It was probably no coincidence that it was he who had earlier played the similarly iconoclastic role of the comedian who satirically imitates the war hero Montgomery in Charles Wood's *Dingo*. His portrayal of Nelson would appear to have provoked just the kind of critical response intended by the Ardens. "Arden's Nelson", wrote Robert Cushman in *Plays and Players* (ignoring Mar-

garetta D'Arcy's contribution), "exists only to be cut down to size." He
then went on to explain the intended significance of his words: "And
when I say cut down to size . . . I know Nelson was physically a small
man, but to cast Henry Woolf (you know Henry Woolf, he looks and
sounds like Dudley Moore) is to give the game away before playing
it." D. A. N. Jones in *The Listener* for his part noted that "Henry
Woolf plays Nelson as a murderous little clown"[35], and Benedict
Nightingale in *The New Statesman* described the actor's "strutting
marionette of a Nelson".[36] D. A. N. Jones had previously responded
similarly to *Dingo*. His views on that occasion may be used to illustrate his standpoint in criticising the Ardens' play and may also convey some impression of the nature of the usual critical response to
such iconoclasm. Having in general registered his admiration for *Dingo* as a play and his regret that it had been exiled to the Bristol
Arts Centre rather than being performed by the National Theatre, in
common with most liberal critics Jones requested that matters of
fact be treated not with indignation but with balance:

Exciting, serious, comic and healthy though it is, I found the play foul in both
senses—revolting and not fair. Because of sick motivation, like the very natural desire for glory and triumph shared by Churchill and Montgomery and
countless others, World War II is exposed as a racket. Big questions are
dodged: "What about the Jews? What about the Camps?" the only answer is
the Groucho-Marxist line: "We don't know about that yet."[37]

As the "Groucho-Marxist" reference makes clear, as usual the alternative historical viewpoint is automatically assumed to be "political",
whereas the accepted establishment interpretation is taken to be ideologically unmediated or "natural".

Such iconoclastic dramatisations of historical figures are usually
considered and generally intended to be offensive. Nevertheless the
indignant dramatist responsible for this iconoclasm would undoubtedly claim that those values personified within the nation's mythology by the selected historical figure were, to him or her, equally if not
more offensive. The aim of the offensiveness is not, however, to
provoke audience antipathy to the dramatist's viewpoint. To do so
would, of course, simply be counterproductive, and therefore the iconoclastic play is normally also spiced through with less insolent comedy. The overall intention is to *alienate* the audience in the Brechtian
sense, to assault its accepted view of history in order to reveal and
demystify those values that history implicitly contains.

It soon becomes apparent from the play that the John Arden who
co-wrote *The Hero Rises Up* was politically not that same Arden who
in *Anger and After* (1963) had been identified by John Russell Taylor,

and even projected elsewhere by Arden himself, as a liberal who, in relation to the conflicts presented in his plays, was unable to take sides. Perhaps partly as a result of the contribution of the more politically conscious Margaretta D'Arcy, it was now quite clear which side Arden was on. "And in case you miss the point", claimed Robert Cushman in his review in *Plays and Players*, "there are one or two choric figures around to drive it home. And nobody (which really makes this sub-standard Arden) makes any attempt to undercut *them*."[38] The explicitness of Arden's political stance, which was now at a point of transition between anarchism and revolutionary socialism, was for Cushman and a number of other critics to signal a decline in the quality of Arden's dramatic output.

Initially Arden's characterisation of Nelson appears similar both to that of such curvilinear characters as Gilnockie or Goetz, and, in that he is in the service of the rectilinear establishment, also to that of Lindsay. As its prologue explicitly states, the play is about a man who took up a rectilinear profession, who in himself was of an unusually passionate asymmetrical curvilinear temperament but was "done properly" by the English establishment and "wasted his extraordinary energy, courage and humanity upon having men killed (in the end himself killed): and then finally installed as a National Monument."[39]

One of Nelson's peculiar curvilinear qualities, made much of in the play and shared also by Gilnockie, is his sexuality. It is indeed not too fanciful to interpret the play's title not only in terms of the apotheosis with which the play culminates, but also as an expression of Nelson's sexual prowess with Emma Hamilton and others. Of the latter, Nelson's step-son Nesbit, who is one of the play's so-called "chorus" characters, does not approve. Early in the play, while his step-father is revealed upstage cavorting not with Emma Hamilton but with a girl brought on board ship for his pleasure, Nesbit remarks disdainfully to the audience that, "he was always a very venereal kind of fellow"[40]. Nevertheless, although Nesbit does not approve of this kind of behaviour, we are shown that, for its part, the English establishment is prepared to overlook Nelson's sexual relationship with Emma Hamilton outside the rectilinear *institution* of marriage in return for his skill in battle, while for their part the ordinary people applaud the relationship for its defiant curvilinearity. According to the Ardens, Nelson's popularity during his lifetime was therefore the result of his innate ability to please, at a particular moment in history, both the rectilinear and the curvilinear elements of society.

Although the Ardens' Nelson does battle for the rectilinear rulers of Britain, his tactics are typically anarchistic in that they take the form of a devolution of responsibility to a level of structured disorganisation. He reveals to his officers that his strategy for the battle of Trafalgar will consist of the unconventional division of his fleet into two columns which will penetrate into the midst of the French and Spanish line and create an "accumulated crescendo of haphazard destruction". "In effect then", concludes Nelson, "there is no battle-plan once the pell-mell has been set loose, and I intend to give no further orders during the engagement."[41]

It is Nelson's willingness, out of arrogance, to put his curvilinear skills at the service of the rectilinear establishment that is portrayed by the Ardens as his major character-flaw. They ridicule him by having him, during one scene, strut about the stage bedecked with medals and honours and wearing a hat surmounted by a wind-up plume which he has received from the "Grand Turk" as a reward for the victory of the Nile. Nelson's hubris allows him to mislead himself into believing that his status as a national hero actually means that he is able to exercise influence over his political masters. He also mistakenly assumes that, after his death, a grateful nation will honour and support Emma Hamilton simply for having been *his* mistress. From the Arden's point of view most damning, however, was the fact that, in order to maintain a monarchical power structure, Nelson also consciously betrayed the aspirations and lives of ordinary people. Throughout the play we are made aware of the revolutionary ferment sweeping Europe and Britain in the aftermath of the French revolution—rebellion in Italy, riots in Manchester, rick-burning in Dorset, workmen's combinations broken up in West Hampshire, presumed Jacobins under surveillance in Sheffield. Even the first meeting of Nelson and Emma takes place while our hero is illegally, on his own initiative, helping the King of Naples in his bloody suppression of the rebellion that has deposed him. To please the King he also goes as far as hanging from the yard-arm of one of his ships the leader of the rebellion who earlier had surrendered himself honourably into Nelson's hands. As Nelson openly admits, the King of Naples is "a pot-bellied timorous mountebank: but by Christ he *is* a king!"[42]

In a period when many, including the Ardens, were appalled by American support for an obviously corrupt regime in South Vietnam, Nelson's similar actions made him a useful means of drawing attention to the immorality of America's behaviour. Whatever the political justification, each was shown to be an enemy of the people. This lack of concern with humanity in general is further emphasised in Nelson's case by his claim that "I was the first naval commander who understood and put into practice the theory of the entire and total destruction of the enemy fleet, at whatever cost to my own".[43]

The play concludes with the assertion that Nelson was, however, duped by his rectilinear masters who, during his life-time, employed him to fight their battles but after his death attempted to remove any record of his curvilinearity and installed him, as a rectilinear hero beyond the reach of ordinary mortals, on the top of an appropriately phallic column in Trafalgar Square. As the words spoken at Nelson's funeral by the establishment's clergyman reveal, the hero, having wasted his energy in killing for the state, was indeed "done properly" by his political masters. Referring to Nelson's bequest of Emma Hamilton to a "grateful" nation, the clergyman considers it best to draw a discrete veil over an affair which cannot be condoned. It is, however, left to Nisbet to conclude that Nelson not only did not succeed in supporting Emma but also did nothing at all to help the *people* who had worshipped him as their hero. He suggests that, in one sense, for this they have themselves to blame, for, as a result of their need to create a hero, "we never tried/To do without him on our own".[44] By revealing how and why a hero is created as part of the establishment's superstructure, the play's aim has therefore been to warn the audience of too easily accepting icons that embody values that may, in practice, be employed to the disadvantage of the mass of ordinary people.

In the spring of 1968 the Ardens had collaborated with C.A.S.T., the first political theatre group to appear during the 1960s, on a production of *Harold Muggins Is a Martyr* at the Unity Theatre. Nevertheless, as the subsequent *The Hero Rises Up* revealed, as yet their target remained not a specific political ideology but such generalised representations of authority as the "establishment". The production of the latter play did, however, mark a move by the Ardens towards a more active personal resistance to Establishment values. In this case the Establishment was represented by the management of the Institute of Contemporary Arts, with whom the Ardens could be witnessed "brawling on the doorstep"[45] of the theatre in consequence of a dispute concerning the manner in which the play should be staged.

From this moment on the Ardens were to set themselves firmly against what they began to identify as the "capitalist" structure of a theatre that appeared prepared to accept only a particular kind of product that conformed to its own pre-defined aesthetic values. With their own wide experience of community drama behind them, they wanted to import into the mainstream and institutional theatre its often anarchic and spontaneous qualities. In place of a stylish production of their plays which would satisfy the aesthetic demands of the rectilinear theatre establishment, they favoured a lack of polish which, romantically, they considered conveyed that rough vitality which they associated with curvilinear art-forms. As with *The Hero Rises Up*, so, four years later, with the Royal Shakespeare Company's presentation of *The Island of the Mighty* (1972), they were again not

permitted to exercise any direct influence upon the form of the production itself. In this case they were to become so incensed with the
theatre management's assertion of its right to perform the play as it
saw fit, to *do things properly*, that Arden declared that he would
never again submit his work to the British institutional or mainstream theatre.

The Ardens' *The Hero Rises Up* has provided a useful means of
introducing some of the factors that must be considered and accommodated in creating a public historical drama. The play was to be
followed during the 1970s by an upsurge in the production of politically orientated historical drama. It is to the broader nature of this
politicisation that I shall turn in the next chapter. During the 1970s
those on the Left who had been involved during the previous decade
in passive protest and Anarchist revolt either began to espouse some
variety of Marxism or found themselves in conflict with those who
wished to follow a planned progression towards a revolution based
upon the Marxist–Leninist model, a situation dramatised most
clearly by Trevor Griffiths.

A Usable History

The rejection of Labour Party politics by the New Left, the post-1968 increase in left-wing extra-parliamentary activism, the abandonment of theatre censorship in that same year and the emergence of a politically conscious fringe theatre movement were to combine during the early 1970s to provide a climate in which left-wing political plays would be eagerly received. Some of the resulting plays were primarily propagandist, others were intended to activate the theatre as a forum for dialectical debate and yet others commented satirically upon the present state of England. For the most part the historical drama of the decade also took a radical stance and was characterised by an attempt on the part of some dramatists to create what Trevor Griffiths has described as a "usable history", that is, a left-wing history that would offer, in terms of perspective and/or subject matter, an alternative to the Establishment version of the past and, most importantly, would be directly applicable to the social and political concerns of contemporary Britain. Thus was created an historical drama that placed emphasis primarily upon social class but whose dramatists, as the decade progressed, were increasingly concerned to find ways of effectively communicating the private experience of public events. Its themes were to offer a clear reflection of the aspirations, activities, and worries of the Left during the 1970s, while the particular theatrical forms in which they were expressed revealed much about the dramatist's personal ideology. The most prevalent of these themes was that of political revolution.

In order to argue the need for political change and to provide a context for dialectical debate, as Christopher Bigsby has suggested, there was a tendency amongst left-wing historical dramatists to return to "a social context in which class antagonisms were closer to the surface, economic injustices more apparent, and in which, it is presumed, the working class had not yet internalised the values of the dominant group".[1] In essence this could refer to any historical period prior to the Second World War, but in fact the choices tended to be confined to those periods in which class antagonism had taken the form of civil insurrections such as the Peasants' Revolt, the English Civil War, the "Swing" agricultural uprising and the Chartist riots of the nineteenth century, the Russian revolution and the "Red Clyde" factory occupations of the 1920s. In her introduction to *Light Shining in Buckinghamshire* (1976) Caryl Churchill clearly illustrates the nature of that linking of past and present which she and other historical dramatists of the period sought to achieve. On one level her intention in writing the play was that of demystification—to expose "the simple 'Cavaliers and Roundheads' history taught at school". On another, it was to draw attention to the reasons for the failure of a social revolution that was now again being attempted some three hundred years later. "We are told", she writes, "of a step forward to today's democracy but not of a revolution that didn't happen; we are told of Charles and Cromwell but not of the thousands of men and women who tried to change their lives. Though nobody now expects Christ to make heaven on earth, their voices are surprisingly close to us".[2]

In *Occupations* in 1970, in the wake of the failure of the 1968 student uprisings, Trevor Griffiths turned for his subject matter to the widespread factory occupations that took place throughout Italy in September 1920, during which it appeared for a while that an industrial dispute might be turned into a full-blown political revolution. His intention was to employ the past to speak to the present and to focus attention upon what he considered to have been the reasons for the ineffectiveness of the revolutionary action of 1968 and the lessons that might be learned from it.

When you have a failure like May '68, there's often only one image of revolution left. . . . From the ashes of every failure or disaster there is the image of a Kabak or a Stalin saying we *will* succeed. Psychologically, the authoritarian and the libertarian live very close in my Left sensibility and in most Left sensibilities that I've encountered, and that is also an important dimension in *Occupations*.[3]

Occupations does not argue the need for revolution; that is taken for granted. This was a play directed at the militant Left and intended as a starting point for discussion concerning *how*, in the light of history, a revolution should be conducted. Griffiths' words, quoted above, express feelings common to the majority of left-wing British dramatists who, during the 1970s, were to make reference to revolutionary activity. While in the second half of the twentieth century any reference to revolution inevitably evoked the spectre of Stalinist totalitarianism, the failure of 1968 revealed to Griffiths and others on the Left a need for revolutionary organisation and resolute leadership.

It was the resulting dilemma of how the latter might be attained without sacrificing the claims and rights of the individual which was central to *Occupations*. The exploration of this topic is constructed dialectically in the play around the characters of Gramsci, a socialist intellectual, and Kabak, an executive member of the Communist Party of Bulgaria and a Representative of the Communist International in Moscow. Gramsci, who unlike Kabak was an actual historical figure, is concerned with transforming the industrial action into a genuine political revolution but, at the same time, is unwilling to view the masses as the expendable cannon-fodder of revolutionary action. Griffiths employs the character of Gramsci to represent the humanitarian view that even in a revolutionary conflict the leadership must pay attention to private values and must recognise the claim not only of the political cause but also of the individual. In his argument with Kabak, Gramsci moves from the private relationship to the public, maintaining that without the former the latter is meaningless. "How can a man bind himself to the masses, if he has never loved anyone himself, not even his mother or his father", he asks rhetorically, "how can a man love a collectivity, when he has not profoundly loved single human creatures." His own answer is that, "I began to see the masses as people and it was only then that I began to love them, in their particular, detailed local, individual character." Here Gramsci is summarising the dilemma faced by Britain's New Left. He concludes: "Treat masses as expendable, as fodder, *during* the revolution, you will always treat them thus. (*Pause*) I tell you this, Comrade Kabak, if you see masses that way, there can be no revolution worth the blood it spills."[4] In opposition to Gramsci's oration Kabak's words are characteristically blunt: "You cannot *love* an army, comrade. An army is a machine. This one makes revolutions. If it breaks down you get another one. Love has nothing to do with it."[5] Although the hoped-for revolution does not materialise, Gramsci is not necessarily proved wrong. He is, however, forced by the workers' subsequent decision to abandon their action, in return for the material bribes offered by the employers, to admit the need for strong leadership and disciplined organisation. Addressing a factory meeting after a referendum has ended the strikes, Gramsci now declares that "a revolutionary movement can only be led by a revolutionary vanguard, with no commitment to prior consultation, with no apparatus of representative assemblies". He concludes by delivering the "message" of the play and, in doing so, evoking the name of Lenin who in much of the left-wing historical drama of the period becomes an icon for disciplined revolutionary organisation. "Today we have the referendum," says Gramsci, "it must not be made the occasion for despair and dissolution. Rather we must see it as an urgent lesson from history; as a call for tighter, even more disciplined action."[6] As Kabak's views illustrate and as nothing in the play actually denies, the organisation and discipline that Gramsci now considers necessary may result in Stalinist authoritarianism. There is, therefore, no neat resolution of the play's dialectic. No right course is confirmed and the dilemma remains for the audience to resolve.

Although *Occupations* is predominantly realistic in approach, as suggested above its underlying structure is that of a dramatised debate between Kabak and Gramsci. This debate is given political context and is sometimes influenced by such external forces as the worker's referendum and Kabak's negotiations with the Italian industrialists. The major setting is a hotel room in Turin. This, Griffiths suggests, may, however, be represented simply by furniture, the most important piece of which is a large bed occupied almost constantly by Angelica, Kabak's dying, aristocratic mistress. Any realistic illusion established is interrupted between the scenes by the projection of slides onto the back wall of the set. These are obviously intended to set the action within a particular historical field and depict Russian revolutionary paintings, library photographs of the events described and, at the close of play, photographs of the Italian Fascists who took power soon after the abortive revolutionary events referred to in the play, Mussolini's subsequent alliance with Hitler and the signing of the pre-war non-aggression pact between Russia and Germany. At two points in the play Gramsci delivers speeches directly to the audience, the first time calling for revolutionary action and the second time, after the occupations have collapsed, for organisation and discipline. In these cases realism is nevertheless maintained by treating the theatre as a meeting-hall and the audience as the Italian workers. The combination of slide-projection and direct address, the latter albeit within the realistic convention, serves explicitly to link past and present and to convey effectively the impression that the debate portrayed is of a certain relevance to a 1970s, New Left audience.

As I have already mentioned in Chapter 1, Griffiths' depiction of Gramsci was sharply criticised by Tom Nairn, who maintained that the dramatist had irresponsibly distorted the historical reality of both character and event. In his defence Griffiths referred to the concepts of "historicity" and "typicality" put forward by the Marxist critic, Georg Lukacs. By Lukacs' definition a "typical" character was *both* an embodiment of historical forces *and* an individualized figure. Nevertheless, while such a character should be "typical" of an historical moment, it should not represent universalised class-types such as the Capitalist, the Worker, the Revolutionary—in other words *fixed* archetypes—for this would convey a very un-Marxist sense of immutability which would inhibit the communication of the possibility of political change. Griffiths's characterisation is broadly in line with Lucaks' concepts. Gramsci represents "mucking about with love and revolution".[7] He advocates the anarchistic view of revolutionary activity evident both in the Italian factory occupations of 1920 and in Paris in May 1968. As Nairn correctly pointed out, Gramsci's personality is, however, conveyed somewhat too sketchily. In response to Nairn's criticism Griffiths made some attempt to justify biographically his portrayal of Gramsci. In fact he had little interest in the man's personal or even private life but was only concerned with the typicality of the character in relation to the politico-historical issues examined in the play.

In the case of the other major character, the fictional Kabak, Nairn criticised Griffiths for making the character deeply ahistorical. Indeed, Kabak's typicality exhibits Russian political attitudes that extended over a period of time greater than that covered by the action of the play, and, compared to Gramsci and other characters, Kabak is burdened with the representation of all too many of the political factors that were at work within and between the communist and capitalist worlds of the period. Of these, central to Kabak's character is deception. Even his bourgeois clothes are intended to appear as though "the form were somehow at war with the content".[8] On one hand he is an advocate of world revolution, on another he negotiates with world capitalists in order to modernise and expand Russia's economy. The irony of his visit to Italy is that, had a political revolution been successful, his mission would have been rendered irrelevant for, with capitalism overthrown, its finance would no longer have been available. Kabak's characterisation is essentially public, but the private side of his character is revealed to some extent through the presence of Angelica, his mistress. This, however, only serves to illustrate that his love of individuals has very definite boundaries, and even this is overshadowed by Angelica's overtly symbolic role as the representative of a dying and no longer productive (she is dying of cancer of the womb) aristocracy. Griffiths' attempt to endow his dialectic with a human dimension by providing his characters with a private as well as a public persona while at the same time avoiding the deterministic implications of Naturalistic characterisation was to be repeated by many but not all political historical dramatists throughout the decade. For them neither the political nor the theatrical analysis of society could be adequately served simply by reference to the "masses". In the case of *Occupations* the attempt only just succeeds and, as I have suggested above, the play remains fundamentally a dramatised debate whose dialectic is only barely clothed in human flesh.

Four years later, having in the meantime explicitly examined the reasons for the failure of May 1968 and debated the requirements of revolutionary strategy in *The Party* (1973), Griffiths returned once again, in *Absolute Beginners* (1974), to the exploration of the necessity for and nature of revolutionary leadership. The year is now 1903, the year in which Lenin and the Bolsheviks took control of the shaping and organisation of the future revolution, and the settings of the play, written for television, are variously London, Brussels, Geneva and Tsarkoe Selo. As in *Occupations* Griffiths is not propagandising for the Left but is addressing those who, like himself, consider that revolution is a political necessity but who must decide how best to conduct it. Central to the play are anarchist/authoritarian, private/public antitheses similar to those represented through the characters of Gramsci and Kabak in *Occupations*. At one point in *Absolute Beginners* Lenin publicly refuses to discipline one of the party's agents, Bauman, who has caused the suicide of the wife of another member of the party. To Martov's assertion that "You can't separate private from public like that. . . . Party morality is more than just loyalty to the party . . . it's the highest level of ethical consciousness yet afforded the human species . . .", Lenin replies, "Metaphysics, Julius. Another time, perhaps, we may speculate. Just now we're trying to make the revolution *possible*."[9] In Lenin's private life personal emotion is also strictly rationed. When his wife, Krupskaya, asks whether she should continue singing to him, he replies, "No. No more music. It's too . . . moving. (*Pause*) It softens."[10] As the play develops and Lenin attempts to ensure acceptance of his view that for success a revolution needs to be directed by a centralised *party* organisation, rather than relying upon the enthusiasm of a disorganised social class, he is accused in turn by his colleagues of being a Robespierre, a Napoleon and a bloody Tsar. These accusations are significant when one considers that it was this very centralised, authoritarian organisation set up by Lenin which was to enable Stalin to establish himself as a dictator—an interpretation Griffiths prefigures by having Trotsky utter the sarcastic comment, "Comrades, we are priv-

ileged to be listening to the sound of party debate—new style".[11] If
Lenin may be equated with Kabak, Trotsky is also similar to Gramsci. In opposition to Lenin's hardness and ruthlessness stands
Trotsky's idealistic and humanistic vision of revolution as "the
boundless horizon of beauty, joy and happiness".[12] As in *Occupations*,
while evidently sympathising with Lenin's call for disciplined
organisation Griffiths leaves the audience with an historical warning
concerning what such centralised and disciplined organisation may
ultimately lead to. In Griffiths' view, while organisation is a necessity, the opinions of a Gramsci or a Trotsky concerning the treatment
of the individual must somehow also be accommodated.

The propagandising for revolution, or at least for political activism,
rather than merely the discussion of its principles, was to appear
elsewhere in different theatrical guise. With the abandonment of theatre censorship and the increasing activism of the political Left after
1968, the British historical documentary, which during the 1960s had
often teetered on the edge of nostalgia, now in the early 1970s began
to take a clearly political stance in relation to its dramatised
material, which on occasions recalled its Agit-Prop antecedents. Significantly, in the first issue of *Theatre Quarterly* in January 1971,
alongside an article describing the theatrical techniques employed in
producing documentary plays at the Victoria Theatre, Stoke-
on-Trent, there appeared, in contrast, "The Material and Models:
Notes Towards a Definition of Documentary Theatre" written by the
German documentary dramatist, Peter Weiss, in which the author's
view of Documentary Theatre was explicitly politically agitational
and propagandist. Weiss's major contention was that "Documentary
Theatre takes sides".[13] Its aim, he contended, was to expose the
mechanisms by which those in power ensure their continued
supremacy, and he listed a number of questions that should be asked
in order to accomplish this. One of these questions is particularly
pertinent to this study and illustrates how the documentary could be
transformed from a nostalgic chronicle into a political tool. "Why is
an historical figure, a period, or an epoch, eliminated from the history
books?", the creator of Documentary theatre is exhorted to enquire.
"Whose position is strengthened by this suppression of historical
facts? Who gains from the deliberate distortion of decisive and significant events?"[14] Weiss went on to advocate a Marxist "public" treatment of character in which "actions motivated by social and economic
factors are shown, not individual conflicts. Documentary Theatre is
concerned with what is typical as opposed to mere externals, and does
not deal with stage-characters and backgrounds. It is concerned with
groups, with areas of influence, with tendencies".[15] Whether or not

directly influenced by Weiss's article, it was nevertheless on a similar basis that the historical documentary was to be re-established within the Fringe political theatre of the 1970s.

To a remarkable number of politically committed writers on the Left, the historical documentary appeared to offer an ideal vehicle for political agit-prop which would be acceptable to the mass or ordinary people whose political consciousness they hoped to raise. The results were a number of "People's Histories"—Marxist histories constructed for and about ordinary people, portraying their historic political struggles for rights and liberties. One of the first of these politicised historical documentaries was Steve Gooch's *Will Wat, If Not, Wat Will?* presented in 1972 at The Half Moon, a small theatre that had recently opened in London's East End and was soon to establish for itself a reputation for producing socialist-minded plays. Gooch's play was an attempt to demystify history by telling the story of the peasant uprising of 1381 from the viewpoint of the peasants themselves. Nevertheless, the play was not merely a sociological study of peasant life in the fourteenth century, but was also an illustration of the ruling-class oppression that led to an uprising by the lower orders which was ultimately betrayed and violently suppressed and its leaders executed. The historical perspective is clearly Marxist, and from the opening scene the audience is introduced to a history concerned not with individual relationships, heroism or villainy but with the exploitation of a *class* and the identification of that particular *economic* structure which made such exploitation inevitable. Early in the play the peasants sing a song which, perhaps somewhat unsubtly, begins with the words, "Money, Money" and goes on to explain that,

The ploughman himself does dig and delve
In snow, frost and rain
Money to get with labour sweat
But much pain and small gain.[16]

History was carefully angled to reflect contemporary political and labour concerns. The play's first half deals with the various factors that Gooch considered to have provoked the uprising: Edward III's militarism which demanded increased taxation in the form of a new Poll Tax to finance the army; the increasing influence and political ambitions of the merchant class which believed itself to be the main creator of the nation's wealth; the Black Death and the imposition of the Statute of Labourers which on the book-jacket is described as exercising "the first legal restraints upon the workers' freedom of employment"; and, finally, the reduction and then freezing of peasants' wages. The two latter factors had, of course, particular relevance to the industrial situation in Britain during the early 1970s.

Owing to the absence of any detailed factual information concerning the lower classes in *The Anouimalle Chronicle*, which evidently provided Gooch with his major source material, in the first half of the play the dramatist was forced to create representative *fictional* peasant characters. In the second half, which deals primarily with the kind of *public* events that are contained in such historical chronicles, he was, however, able to take a more clearly documentary line.

The uprising itself is revealed in the play (written, it should be remembered, at a time when the relative merits and drawbacks of spontaneous revolution as opposed to party organisation were being hotly debated in left-wing circles) not to have been an organised revolution but rather a series of spontaneous, isolated eruptions which took place predominantly in various parts of south-east England and which gradually coalesced into the loose federation of forces that was to elect Wat Tyler as its leader and to march on London. Here, possibly for the first time in the historical drama of the 1970s, appeared a Marxist interpretation of the role and status of the leader in the revolutionary struggle. As suggested above, Wat Tyler was in no way the instigator of the revolt and is described in the play as its agent—"the voice of our body"—whose election to leadership was a matter of organisational necessity. "For more than one [leader] will divide us and send our arms and legs, our toes and fingers spinning in all directions",[17] says John Ball, another leader of the revolt and historically an early advocate of communistic principles. Furthermore, Gooch also exhibits awareness of the dangers attendant upon revolutionary leadership when he has Geoffrey Lister, the rebel leader of the peasants in Norwich, remark that "a leader of ordinary people must be their servant or power can run away with him".[18]

In a further attempt to emphasise the contemporary relevance of his treatment of the Peasants' Revolt, Gooch dramatises the part played in the defeat of the rebels by the middle classes of fourteenth-century English society. Early in the play the representatives of the Victuallers' Guild of London are portrayed attempting to win the favours of the young Richard II by means of bribery, while his father Edward III lies dying. With the outbreak of the revolt their support for either the King or the peasants divides according to their conception of what will best preserve their own position. As Walworth, a victualler and the Major of London, tells King Richard during the peasants' occupation of the city, "many of your loyal merchants and knights who saw this rebellion at first as a protest against inherited privilege and Church domination and remained neutral, now see it as purely destructive. They stand to lose everything they've worked for all their lives."[19] Into Walworth's mouth are placed words that also cannot help but identify him and his class as the true enemies of the people and therefore the real villains of the play: "It's not just freedom they want", Walworth tells the King, referring to the aspirations of the peasants, "they want to govern their own lives."[20] As the aristocracy have become a somewhat spent force, the middle classes are shown furthermore to have been testing their power and influence in relation to the King. Spurning their own lower-class backgrounds and, out of self-interest, employing their financial muscle upon the King, they seek to frustrate the legitimate aims of the peasants. At the close of the play it is Walworth, Bamber and Philpot of the Victuallers' Guild who betray and kill Wat Tyler during negotiations between the rebels (the "True Commons") and the King. For this exploit they are knighted. In the aftermath of the rebellion while, as a direct announcement informs the audience, other uprisings which had broken out from Peterborough to East Anglia were being violently suppressed by the King and their leaders executed, "middle-class leaders like Thomas Farringdon and Alderman Horn generally escaped with only blemished reputations".[21] Although he is undoubtedly on the side of the peasants, Gooch does not shirk reference to their sometimes excessive violence but, unlike Osborne in *Luther*, places it firmly within its proper historical context where all sides employed violence with equal relish. In spite of these excesses, Gooch's portrayal of the peasants' obvious moral justification in wanting to achieve the freedom simply to govern their own destinies cannot help but ensure that for a modern audience they become the unquestioned heroes of the play.

Having illustrated the economic causes of the revolt, analysed its nature, indicted its villains and revealed the outcome—all from the point of view of its losers, the peasant insurrectionists—Gooch concludes the play on an agitational note intended to arouse the audience's political sympathies and to underline the parallels between past and present. He quotes the words of Richard II who, by this stage in the play's narrative, has revoked his earlier undertakings to the rebels and is busily executing those "traitors" whom he is able to apprehend. His words are calculated to provoke audience antipathy:

For as long as we live, we shall do our utmost with all faculties at our disposal to suppress you, so that the rigour of your servitude will serve as an example to posterity. Both now and in the future people like yourselves will always have your misery before their eyes like a mirror, so that you will be cursed by them and they will fear to do as you have done.
—Richard II at Billericay, 28th of June, 1381[22]

John Mortimer's own reaction to the play in *The Observer* reflected both the effectiveness of Gooch's demystified people's history and the emotive impact of the play's agit-prop techniques. "By the end of the evening", wrote Mortimer, "I felt proud to have shared history with the peasants of Erith, Brentford and Romney Marsh: and ready to raise a bill-hook against all oppressors."[23] The sense of a shared history to which Mortimer refers was indeed carefully contrived by Gooch and his production team. They had learned from 1960s documentaries such as those of the Victoria Theatre, Stoke-on-Trent, that it was important to produce the sense of a shared experience by placing emphasis not upon empathy between the audience and individual characters but between the audience and the actors themselves. "The actors must contact the audience", advised Gooch, "though it's no good 'playing' this. They should be like people getting up at a family party and doing their turn."[24] Indeed, in order to create a relaxed and undaunting atmosphere the play was spiced with its fair share of music and comedy. This simulated party atmosphere was Gooch's solution to a problem apparent to all creators of documentary histories, that of finding a theatrical style that would both communicate the documentary material in an effective and unpatronising manner and promote that sense of group solidarity which, above all, the theatre could offer to the political propogandist.

As in earlier historical documentaries the actor, wearing a uniform peasant costume to which were added costume pieces which would indicate class and social roles, was therefore seen as the central element in the play. A noticeable difference from the documentaries of the 1960s, however, was that history was not to be shared in terms of region or occupation but in terms of *class*. The aim was not to invoke a community spirit but to agitate for action by revealing that the plight of these fourteenth-century peasants (who actually speak in the play in a modern idiom) had factors in common with the contemporary political situation. Wage freezes and parliamentary attempts to restrict the power of the trade unions were, almost six centuries later, still being employed to maintain that Capitalist economy which had been the end result of the merchantile expansion of the fourteenth century. The People's struggles of the past are therefore identified with those of the present and, as Dan Garret aptly notes in his unpublished thesis on Documentary Theatre, indeed "it is as though the Peasants' Revolt is being waged by the Workers' Revolutionary Party".[25]

While Gooch had been one of the first 1970s dramatists to return the historical documentary to its agit-prop roots, arguably the most theatrically successful historical agit-prop play of the decade was John McGrath's *The Cheviot, The Stag and The Black, Black Oil*. Although, like Gooch, McGrath adopted a Marxist approach to history, his documentary material, which itself included reference to the

present day, more clearly linked the "capitalist" iniquities of the past
with those of the present. McGarth's aim was to induce the audience,
in a Brechtian "Epic" manner, to "see anew", to re-evaluate the given,
Establishment version of events and to abandon not only its previously accepted interpretation of the past but also its perception of
the present. These aims are set out unambiguously in the notes to the
published text:

This play tries to show *why* the tragedies of the past happened: because the
forces of capitalism were stronger than the organisation of the people. It tries
to show that the future is *not* predetermined, that there are alternatives, and
it is the responsibility of everyone to fight and agitate for the alternative
which is going to benefit the people of the Highlands, rather than the multi-
national corporations, intent on profit.[26]

The play exhibits the political optimism of its time, the feeling that
British society could still be changed, that "socialism, and the
planned exploitation of natural resources for the benefit of all humanity"[27] was yet within reach and that the theatre could contribute
to that change by raising the consciousness and enlivening the
political awareness of the working class.

The Cheviot was first performed in 1973 by the Scottish 7:84 Theatre Company throughout the Highlands and Islands of Scotland and
subsequently reached a far wider audience when, in 1974, it appeared
in a slightly adapted form as a BBC television "Play for Today". The
play's theatrical success, which must have undoubtedly influenced
the decision to televise it, can in large part be attributed not simply
to politically receptive audiences nor to the prevalently left-wing
spirit of the early 1970s, but primarily to aesthetic factors associated
with the circumstances of its production. Most significant of these
was the availability of an indigenous form of *public* performance—the
Ceilidh.

As pointed out by David Edgar in "Ten Years of Political Theatre"
(1978), in order to reveal the political essence of a given situation the
agit-prop performed in Britain during the 1970s generally employed
parody of forms of entertainment with which its theatrically
"unsophisticated" audiences were thought to be familiar. Games
shows, advertisements, soap-operas and cartoons, all taken from television, were therefore adapted to subvert their intrinsic capitalist
values and associations.[28] The simple stereotypes of melodrama,
which was itself actually part of the working-class culture of the
nineteenth rather than of the late twentieth century, were also a
common source. Unfortunately, as McGrath himself suggested in his
book *A Good Night Out* (1981), for left-wing political theatre-workers

these forms of entertainment contained inherent problems. Over-simplication and the difficulty of presenting a sustained argument were the most conspicuous, but the bigotry, obscenity and stereotyping of much working-class humour were no less difficult to translate into a form that did not sound merely pretentious and which was able to convey the moral values of socialism. The initial success of *The Cheviot* also resulted to some extent from the fact that it was playing to audiences in the Highlands and Islands of Scotland, which were very untypical of the mass audience in Britain as a whole. Here in Scotland were audiences whose social structure—with its almost feudal identification with the "Laird" who owned much of the land on which the people lived, its pre-industrial rural environment and its own identifiable and often fiercely protected culture—was more representative of pre- rather than post-nineteenth-century British society. Most valuable of all for McGrath in finding an appropriate epic form for *The Cheviot* was the existence within the culture of the Highlands and Islands (also untypical of the rest of Britain) of a genuinely ethnic and vital form of entertainment, the Ceilidh, which crossed class barriers and which still played an important part in the lives of often geographically isolated Scottish communities. As the form itself provoked no bourgeois associations it was unnecessary either to satirize or to parody it. Its content could simply be altered to suit McGrath's purpose.

Ceilidhs normally take place in local village halls. Although they normally contain an element of performance, the distinction between performers and audience is blurred in that they are often one and the same—simply individuals offering their songs, jokes, stories or instrumental solos in the context of a village dance. According to McGrath, the form dates from the nineteenth century when it was a means "of reinforcing the Gaelic culture, which we were also trying to do, and of a political getting together".[29]

In performance, even as the audience enter the hall, *The Cheviot's* cast are directed to evoke the communal nature of the ceilidh, and during the performance they attempt to produce that sense of group solidarity which it is hoped will provide a positive example for the audience to follow even after the play has ended. The actors chat to the audience, one plays a fiddle and ultimately another announces that the evening's entertainment will begin with the communal singing "by special request" of the well-known Scottish ballad, "These Are My Mountains"—a song that is to gain ironic significance as the play's narrative develops. On the stage, which is merely a low, raised platform which hardly divides the actors from their audience, the company open a man-sized book to reveal a "pop-up" representation of

a Scottish mountain landscape, the light's go down and an actor
comes forward to deliver the formal introduction to the play.

M.C.: Later on we're going to have a few songs like that one—if you know
the words join in—and then we're going to have a dance, and in between
we'll be telling a story. It's a story that has a beginning, a middle, but,
as yet, no end—[30]

From here on the narrative proceeds chronologically. It is conveyed
by means of direct reportage from contemporary documents, dramatised events, cross-talk acts between caricatured historical figure or
characters representative of national or corporate interests, and
many songs, both traditional and specially composed for the production in Gaelic and English. As in previous documentaries, the public
nature of the narrative and its concern with groups and types is
emphasised by the donning of various costume pieces over a fairly
neutral uniform costume. The "story", told from a Marxist standpoint,
focuses upon three periods during which Scotland's natural resources
have been exploited, each time at the expense of the mass of the indigenous population—the clearance of crofters from the land in the
early nineteenth century in order to make way for the grazing of
Cheviot sheep; the use of the land by absentee landlords, from the
late nineteenth century onwards, for hunting and later for tourism;
and, finally, most recently, the exploitation of Scotland's oil and gas
resources, by various international oil companies aided, the play contends, by a succession of submissive British governments. The fact
that the story has "a beginning, a middle, but, as yet, no end", that
the first two elements deal with the exploitation and occasional resistance of the people and attempts to counteract the school-book loyal,
noble-savage Scotsman image, leaves the completion of the narrative
to the audience itself. This is emphasised by a speech delivered by an
actor, out of character, at the conclusion of the play: "We too must
organise, and fight—not with stones, but politically, with the help of
the working class in the towns, for a government that will control the
oil development for the benefit of everybody."[31]

The Cheviot's historical perspective is not, however, simply paro-
chially nationalistic. Its economic analysis also encompasses Scotland's place in England's wider colonialism. This colonialism, as in
other plays of the period, is also itself revealed to be an inevitable
part of the evolution and consolidation of capitalism. The colonisation of North America (whose countrymen, ironically, are shown to
have returned to exploit Scotland's oil reserves) is related directly to
the Highland Clearances of the late eighteenth and early nineteenth
century. The latter are revealed as yet another apsect of the

enclosure movement which, from a Marxist standpoint, is likewise indicted in other plays as an historical prerequisite for the evolution of Capitalism. We learn here that it was the *victims* of the clearances who, having being forced to leave Scotland, were in their turn to oppress the native populations of other "undeveloped" countries. Gradually, claims the play's narrative,

The highland exploitation chain-reacted around the world; in Australia the aborigines were hunted like animals; in Tasmania not one aborigine was left alive: all over Africa, black men were massacred and brought to heel. In America the plains were emptied of men and buffalo, and the seeds of the next century's imperialist power were firmly planted.[32]

In common with previous creators of Agit-Prop, in *The Cheviot* McGrath also employed caricature to reveal vividly the objective essence of capitalist economic exploitation. Nevertheless, unlike many of his predecessors, he was aware that such comic caricature could in fact lead an audience to underestimate the reality of the power and influence that it was intended to expose. Significantly, McGrath took steps to counteract this possibility at a moment in *The Cheviot* when the chronological sequence has reached the present day. After a comic song which reveals the present *owners* of Scotland to be, in addition to the old aristocratic families, the property dealers, the shipowners, construction men, distillers and merchant bankers who are the new ruling class, one of the actors addresses the audience in a more serious tone of voice. "One thing's for certain" he warns, "these men are not just figures of fun. They are determined, powerful and have the rest of the ruling class on their side. Their network is international."[33] He is, however, only placing added emphasis upon an aspect that has already been a fundamental feature of the treatment of the caricatured figures of the play. Such figures have not been portrayed, however, simply as the one-sided targets of class abuse; they have been placed in an ironic context which exposed the gap between what is said in public and what is done in private. McGrath's aim was to communicate at one and the same time that those in power in government, commerce and industry were by no means all-powerful, but that nevertheless they would not willingly surrender their power. To this end he employed the simple technique of role reversal.

An example of this appears towards the end of the play when the cowboy oil-man, Texas Jim, initiates an American hoedown. Accompanied by lively fiddle-playing, he shakes hands with the audience and begins a song which parodies the calls used in square-dancing. All is amicable until, masked at first by Texas Jim's cheerful smile, the words of the song become more and more aggressive: "Screw your landscape, screw your bays / I'll screw you in a hundred ways." As the song progresses further the accompanying square-dancers stand aghast as Jim becomes more and more frenzied: "You poor dumb fools I'm rooking you / You'll find out in a year or two."[34] Having viewed the character initially as a harmless fool, the audience is quickly alienated by his aggression and its hostility is aroused towards the American oil-industry which he represents. The spectator is also forced to realise that in reality there is much more to these figures than the mere laughter and scorn of a theatrical audience is capable of eradicating. It is the successful creation of repeated moments of such interaction which elevates the play above the unsophisticated and soon hackneyed preaching and sloganising of most Agit-Prop theatre. By means of irony the play *involves* the audience in the actual *process* of demythologisation rather than solely bombarding it with undisguised foregone conclusions.

By the close of the play, with the enemy—capitalist exploitation of Scotland's natural resources—clearly identified, an alternative political solution is called for. That solution, according to McGrath, is not to halt progress, be it in oil extraction or tourism, but instead to ensure that "the people must own the land. The people must control the land. They must control what goes on it, and what gets taken out of it."[35] In spite of surface appearances the play's demand is not for nationalism but for socialism. Indeed, McGrath is careful to avoid branding either the Scottish as victims or the English or American *nations* as exploiters. The Scottish people, the play contends, should not lament their history but should rouse themselves into taking action so that the exploitation that history and the play records will not simply be repeated once again to the detriment of the Scottish people.

In *The Game's a Bogey* (1974) and *Little Red Hen* (1975), which were targeted at an urban rather than a rural Scottish audience and were thereby deprived of a "living" form of popular culture, McGrath was somewhat less successfully to employ a mixture of realistic scenes, monologue, pop and folk song, and parodies of game shows and of music hall in order to address the Scottish working class, not only about resistance but also about political *organisation*. By focusing upon the fierce class confrontations of the 1920s and 1930s which have now been endowed by the Labour movement with something resembling mythic status, he attempted to employ the lessons of history to stimulate political activity amongst contemporary socialists. Indeed *Little Red Hen* is itself structured in the form of a lesson concerning the days of the "Red Clyde" some fifty years earlier, which for a while placed a truly socialist Scotland within grasp but which, like the Italian factory occupations of the same period, ultimately came to nothing. The lesson, delivered by the grandmother of a young Scottish National Party worker to her granddaughter as a warning against repeating the errors of the past, is followed by a critique of the party itself. In *The Game's a Bogey* McGrath focused upon the political career of the Socialist leader John McClean, who played a major part in the formation of the socialist "Red Clyde". In this case, the final speech of the play leaves the audience in no doubt concerning its intended lesson for today's working class:

The revolutionary fervour of the Clydeside was systematically suppressed and diverted into minor social reforms. This certainly gained a few concessions for the working class, but it totally failed to overthrow the ruling class. And in 1974, even these very few gains were in great danger of being taken away. The capitalist class were in such a state of chaos that they took to making all out attacks on the working class and its unions, even to the stage of calling a General Election to give itself more powers of repression. Well, thankfully they failed. But now, even with a Labour Government, no matter how many bills and social reforms they push through, they're still only asking for more concessions. "Capitalism, that is the right to rob the creators of wealth, must be killed, and it can be done in twelve solid months starting anytime, if but the workers are ready".[36]

As might be expected from one inclined to Marxism, McGrath has, throughout his career, paid particular attention to Socialist history and has attempted to employ it, as above, to stimulate political activity and consciousness. By 1978 he would appear, however, to have been alone amongst the committed dramatists represented at the Cambridge conference on political theatre in still believing that the working class could be politicised by agit-prop theatre. After 1979 such theatre, its audience depleted with the decline in left-wing political activism, was to appear more and more inapplicable to the political climate of 1980s Britain.

In the early 1970s the English 7:84 Theatre Company, besides producing plays written by McGrath himself, on two occasions also performed plays by two already well-seasoned creators of alternative historical drama, John Arden and Margaretta D'Arcy. In *The Bagman* in 1969 John Arden had allegorically reviewed his past career and his role as a dramatist. Here he paid particular attention to a gradually increasing awareness that his sympathies as a dramatist lay with the plight of ordinary people rather than with the concerns exhibited in much of the drama presented by the commercial and institutional theatres. In the preface to the text, written two years after the play itself, Arden also offered a description of his recent encounters in India and in England with the "Forces of Law and

Order" and of his somewhat awkward personal involvement with a
"group of revolutionists, one of whom, a lodger in my house, was
arrested for throwing a petrol-bomb at a policeman during an extraordinary demonstration in front of Ulster House, London."[37]

After 1969 this combination of factors led him increasingly to adopt
a socialist and even militant stance in his plays. Although Arden
referred to them, the events of May 1968 appear to have meant less to
himself and Margaretta D'Arcy than they did, for example, to
Howard Brenton and John McGrath. For the Ardens their personal
experience of the situation in Ireland together with their visits to
India and America appear to have been the major influences that
shaped their political outlook during the early 1970s. Indeed, in the
preface to *The Bagman* Arden already appeared to be well on the way
to the adoption of a revolutionary stance. There he quotes Mao Ze
Dong—"Whatever the enemy opposes, we must support: whatever the
enemy supports, we must oppose." Furthermore he is able to identify
unequivocally the enemy as the "fed man, the clothed man, the shel-
tered man, whose food, clothes, and house are obtained at the expense
of the hunger, nakedness, and the exposure of so many millions of
others".[38] In 1972 the Ardens worked with the English 7:84 Theatre
Company. They took on tour Arden's *The Ballygombeen Bequest*, a
play concerned with absentee-landlordism in Ireland which was soon
suppressed by court order, and which Albert Hunt has suggested was
the first of Arden's plays to take up "a clear Marxist position".[39]
Alongside this was performed a new version of *Serjeant Musgrave's
Dance*, rewritten in response to Northern Ireland's "Bloody Sunday"
and re-entitled *Serjeant Musgrave Dances On*. Although the relationship between the Ardens and 7:84 was apparently not always har-
monious, it would seem nonetheless that McGrath's work and
particularly his later play, *The Game's a Bogey*, with its evocation of
a public, socialist hero, may have influenced the two dramatists in
their similarly public dramatisation of the political life of the Irish
revolutionary, James Connolly, which appeared in the following year.

In 1977 in *To Present the Pretence* Arden claimed that, "twelve
years ago I looked on at people's struggles, and wrote about them for
the stage, sympathetically, but as an onlooker. Without consciously
intending it, I have become a participant".[40] In 1975, with their Irish
production of *The Non-Stop Connolly Show* it was very much as participants that Arden and D'Arcy once more turned to history, but this
time, like Griffiths and McGrath, specifically to socialist history. Ico-
noclastry now replaced iconoclasm and the play was neither "done
properly" nor even performed within the bounds of the theatre. The
Ardens' historical drama was not in this case to explore Anarchist
values but was now to illustrate socialist militancy.

Over the Easter Weekend of 1975, in the Liberty Hall in Dublin, home of Ireland's largest trade union, the TGWU, the Ardens presented a continuous 24-hour-long production based upon the life of the early twentieth-century Irish revolutionary leader, James Connolly. The play was appropriately entitled, *The Non-Stop Connolly Show*, and dramatised socialist history in clearly Marxist terms. In addition to its novel length, another factor that also made it unusual in the context of the political drama of the 1970s was the Ardens' attempt to formulate a true socialist hero. In so doing, in the light of their own lampooning of hero-worship in *The Hero Rises Up*, they also strove to avoid the very un-Marxist individualism of the Stalinist "cult of the personality". How they set out to achieve this feat provides an interesting perspective upon the inherent differences between private and public historical drama.

From the outset, the Ardens consciously avoided producing a "straight biography" of their hero. As far as possible they avoided details of Connolly's personal life and instead plumped for "a series of digressive stage-presentations of the events of his time which influenced his political views and consequent actions".[41] They thereby emphasised the external social and environmental influences that formed Connolly's public character, the character for which of course he is remembered, rather than exploring his individual psychology and personality. Indeed, throughout the play we are given virtually no clue as to whether Connolly was of a pleasant or an unpleasant disposition. In addition, although we learn that he had a wife and child, Connolly's domestic life is deliberately left indistinct. For the Ardens Connolly was, both as a man and as a theatrical character, one whose

. . . passions were chiefly moved not by what happened to him as an individual but by the success or failure of the working-class to organise, by the politico-economic connections between Great Britain and Ireland, by the problems of running a revolutionary party or producing a weekly newspaper with inadequate resources. He was not an adulterer, he did not fight duels, he did not get drunk, he did not run mad. The joys and sorrows of his private life, though no less poignant than anyone else's, were not the motivating force for the deeds of his public life.[42]

Throughout the play Connolly is portrayed as representing the aspirations of the people rather than as pursuing his own desires. He does not promote himself nor does he achieve personal wealth or even glory. Indeed, he is mostly portrayed as being *requested* by one socialist organisation or another to take part in their activities. Very unromantically he constantly meets with failure and, as a consequence, is repeatedly obliged to "go elsewhere" in order to work for the socialist cause.

In broad historical terms the play was intended to illustrate, through Connolly's political biography, the wider evolution of international socialism in Scotland, Ireland and the United States during the early years of this century and its temporary defeat in Ireland with the abortive Easter Rising of 1916. The Ardens teased from Connolly's biography a number of general thematic strands concerning the nature of revolutionary struggle in the twentieth century and thereby attempted to make him a "typical" example of a wider political phenomenon. The Ardens dramatically unified such "typical" elements as his proletarian origin, his involvement with international socialism, various trade unions and revolutionary parties, and his opposition to the capitalist/imperialist nature of the First World War by centring upon a dialectical rather than personal conflict which was "closely interwoven with each of the above aspect of his [Connolly's] life".[43] This conflict or schism was signally one which, during the 1970s, was much discussed by the Left and was provoked by the question of whether revolution or reform was the key to radical political change. The importance of this dialectical debate was in fact put forward by the dramatists as a justification for the play's extraordinary length. "In Connolly's case", they claimed, "this prolonged debate took so many shapes and faces that we felt it necessary to explore his experience at deliberately repetitive length—hence a cycle of plays rather than one clean-cut three-act summary".[44]

Connolly's public deeds are presented in a variety of theatrical styles ranging from agit-prop to realism, from mime to pageant. The play is divided into six parts, which open with Connolly's birth in Edinburgh in 1868, go on to deal chronologically with his work for various union and socialist organisations in Ireland, Scotland and America and culminate with his execution, tied to a chair because a leg-wound would not permit him to stand, by an English army firing squad as punishment for his part in the Easter Rising in Dublin in 1916. In performance the emphasis is consequently upon speed and rhythm with each scene intended to be viewed in a Brechtian manner as an independent entity each with its own "gestus" (*spirit, meaning*) and, in addition, as a bead on the unifying thread represented by the play's historical narrative. Having emphasised this in the introduction to the printed text, the Ardens point out that, as the actors should be "more concerned with understanding the political arguments and implications of the story than with 'creating character' in the normal theatrical sense",[45] even Connolly himself could be portrayed at various stages of his life by a number of different actors in turn. While the characterisation of Connolly and other *approved* working class and revolutionary characters is basically realistic, the approach taken to "recurrent social types (i.e. bourgois politicians, employers, military officers etc)"[46] utilises the masks and caricature of agit-prop theatre. Foremost of such caricatured characters is Grabitall, the Capitalist, who throughout the play repeatedly confronts the heroic (in the sense of brave and resolute) Connolly who nonetheless consistently pursues his true vocation as, initially, a people's hero and, subsequently, a people's martyr.

In common with other British left-wing historical drama of the 1970s *The Non-Stop Connolly Show* was inevitably intended to contain a political message for its time. In addition to examining the pros and cons surrounding the choice of revolution or reform, the Ardens emphasised the fact that their hero espoused not Irish Nationalism but International Socialism, a viewpoint that contained obvious relevance to the continuing struggle for a united Ireland. So that we are left in no doubt, this is underlined explicitly by Connolly's words to the Nationalist, Maud Gonne:

Understand the reality of soundly principled class struggle. Unite the British and Irish workers. Recognise the capitalist nature of exploitation. Unmask both monarchical and nationalist mysticism. Identify the enemy, identify the enemy upon the lines of correct analysis. Strengthen the position of the Irish Socialist Republican Party. . . .[47]

It was the Ardens' intention, therefore, not only to illustrate socialist history but also to employ the Connolly biography to argue for the subsuming of Irish sectarianism into a wider socialist movement which would treat the struggle for Irish unity as a fight for colonial independence not only from an *imperialist* but also from a *capitalist* foreign state. The play ends with an appropriately agitational exhortation by Connolly as, along with others responsible for the uprising, he is about to be executed by the English. "We were the first", claims Connolly, "we shall not be the last. This is not history. It has not passed".[48] His soul, like that of an earlier insurrectionist, goes marching on. The play's narrative is, then, of an unwaveringly good and wise hero whose life (born into lowly circumstances and dying for his beliefs at the hands of an occupying power) would appear to be intended to make him, in common with other martyr-figures, something of a secular Christ-figure. On the page his character appears too good to be true and therefore rather lack-lustre. Indeed Connolly's characterisation, particularly in terms of its sexuality, is in total contrast to the far from saint-like heroes, such as Gilnockie or Nelson, who appeared in Arden's earlier plays. Nevertheless, the play, which to those unfamiliar with the relevant historical background may on occasions appear to be a pedantic and rather too complicated history lesson, was undoubtedly intended by the Ardens to be transformed in performance by its music, comedy and pageantry into an epic narrative which would inspire in the audience a communal and festive spirit similar to that provoked by folk theatre or pantomime. To many critics, however, *The Non-Stop Connolly Show* appeared in performance to be even more confused and confusing, shapeless and ill-prepared than had the earlier promenade performance of *The Hero Rises Up*. "The Ardens', reported Paddy Marsh in an article in *Theatre Quarterly*, "had hoped that a 'non-professional' staging of the show would make it more readily accessible to the audience: in practice, the lack of rehearsal, the make-shift arrangement, and lack of organisation combined with the unindividualised verbal delivery to make the plays particularly difficult to understand." For Marsh, most damning of all was, however, the Ardens' authoritarian approach to the production which he considered "ill became self-confessed socialists".[49]

Throughout his career as a dramatist, in consequence initially of his preference for parabolic and ballad forms and, subsequently, his concern with Marxism, Arden has consistently shown himself to be most at home in the past. Since *The Non-Stop Connolly Show*, he has returned repeatedly to real or imagined history in plays written for the stage and radio and in his two novels, *Silence Among Weapons* (1982) and *Books of Bale* (1988). Although his historical drama cannot be said to have inspired considerable emulation, since 1968 it has nevertheless been marked by an attempt, which it must be admitted has achieved only modest popular success, to create a dramatic history *of* and *for* the people which would explain and explore in theatrical styles borrowed from "curvilinear" popular forms, important social and political issues of our time.

Popular resistance and revolution, usually dramatised in a public, documentary or semi-documentary manner, were to remain popular themes for historical drama throughout the 1970s. Unfortunately, as illustrated by the plays discussed above, British history could provide no record of a *successful* popular uprising. Caryl Churchill's *Light Shining in Buckinghamshire* (1976) described, for example, how the belief of many that the English Civil War would be followed by Christ's second coming to establish heaven on earth was disappointed and how the desire of ordinary people for greater liberty was thwarted by Cromwell. "What was established instead", claimed Churchill," was an authoritarian parliament, the massacre of the Irish, the development of capitalism."[50]

The nineteenth century provided dramatists with further material concerning the struggle of ordinary people for their rights and liberties. The emergence of Chartism, and the concurrent "Plug" riots which broke out in the Northern textile towns of England during 1842, were portrayed in 1978 in the Red Ladder Theatre's *Taking our Time*. The play records, however, that although Chartism survived, the "Plug" riots themselves failed to halt the expansion of the new, mechanised mills and did little to alter the pattern of boom and slump, apparently endemic to capitalist societies, whose lowest ebb was inevitably accompanied, like today, by a resuscitation of the ailing economy "at the expense of working people's living standards".[51] In *Captain Swing* (1979) Peter Whelan used the "Swing" uprisings of agricultural workers which broke out throughout England in 1830 to examine the justifiability of *violent* revolution.[52] The farm-workers' resistance takes the form not of violence against the person, but of arson, machine-wrecking and the sending of threatening letters "signed" by Captain Swing. Throughout the play, which is generally realistic in form, the ever-present threat of violence attendant upon the uprising is represented in a stylised manner by the menacing figures of the "Corn Men". These apparitions, which evoke the folk tradition, appear intermittently on the stage threateningly swinging their flails and, towards the close of the play, don judges' robes in order to impose the savage punishments of flogging, transportation, imprisonment and execution upon the rebels, thereby illustrating how, while the farmworkers successfully avoided violence, the state had no such qualms when suppressing their uprising.

In the plays referred to above, common land is enclosed, driving those who eke a meagre living from the common pastures into the towns, onto the roads or into crime. Machinery is introduced on farms or in factories, forcing down wages and depriving workers of their jobs. In each case, however, resistance on the part of ordinary people is shown to have been futile. What unites these plays is therefore the creation of a type of "peoples" history, lucidly described by John McGrath, concerned with

. . . the actual history of the working class, its formation, centuries of suffering and pride, the victories as the peopled moved towards a greater degree of emancipation, the distortions of purpose as they approached complete power, the lessons of the political struggle, the divisions within the people today and the mystification that prevails as the ruling class pretends it no longer rules. All this history has been suppressed, and needs to be shown to the people: it is a rich history, full of vivid episodes, odes, songs, strong characters and plenty of action.[53]

The only portrayal of a successful popular revolution appeared from what, at the time, may have been considered a somewhat unlikely source, the pen of David Hare. Hare's previous work had evoked an England of frustrated hopes and cynicism, but in 1975, in *Fanshen*,

he was to write a play that would use its source material optimistically to illustrate socialism in action. Although actually
written by Hare, the play originated in the workshop sessions that
were the characteristic working method of its commissioner, the Joint
Stock Theatre Company. This working method and the company's
penchant for the broadly socialist treatment of history undoubtedly
reflected the influence of one of its two directors, Bill Gaskell.
Gaskell had directed *The Caucasian Chalk Circle* in 1962 which,
although reminiscent of the earlier Berliner Ensemble production,
was nevertheless acknowledged to have been the "first fully successful attempt to translate Brechtian theory into practice in this country".[54] How far Gaskell actually influenced the form of *Fanshen* is
difficult to determine. Certainly the rehearsal and workshop approaches applied to its production were similar to those employed
by Gaskell in the earlier Brechtian production and must, in some
measure, have affected the play's ultimate shape. It is, however,
indisputable that formalistically *Fanshen* is noticeably different from
Hare's earlier plays, which normally focused upon a small and tightly
knit group of strong central characters. In contrast, *Fanshen* is concerned with a larger group of far less individualised characters and
exhibits a dialectical clarity worthy of Brecht. From his experience of
working on *The Caucasian Chalk Circle* Gaskill claimed to have
learned "that one must use a Socratic method in rehearsal—getting
the actor to think for himself, getting him to understand his responsibility to his part, to the play, and ultimately to society".[55] From
Hare's own description of the rehearsal approach adopted for *Fanshen*
there would appear to have been some similarities: ". . . slowly the
rehearsal methods took their shape from the political techniques
which had been developed in the revolution. It became important to
the directors that the production be genuinely democratic."[56] Indeed,
the techniques of self-criticism and public appraisal described in the
play were employed as part of the rehearsal process. In addition to
simulating the dialectic that is central to the structure and meaning
of the play, this approach seems to have proved an effective method of
meaningfully involving the actors in a play that was concerned not
with individual character-psychology but with the step-by-step *process* by which a *group* of people was attempting to realise social and
political change. ("Fanshen" means "to turn the body" or "turn over".)
The audience, which knows neither more nor less than the play's
peasant characters concerning the best means of achieving that
change, shares with them, as the play's action unfolds, a process of
learning.

The setting of *Fanshen* is the Chinese village of Long Bow during
the years between 1945 and 1949 when China was being sys-

tematically transformed into a Communist state. The action is based upon the experiences, recorded in his book similarly entitled *Fanshen*, of an American tractor technician, William Hinton. Hare claimed that his intention in adapting the book had been to write "a classical play about revolution, setting out the problems which will always arise when people try to change the relationship between leadership and the led. A European audience is asked to examine a process of change very different from anything which they might anticipate".[57] Significantly, the play's characters speak, and swear, not in a form of Anglo-Chinese dialect but in short and direct English phrases. The impression is thereby conveyed to the audience that it is not simply watching a documentary representation of events that took place at another time and in another country, but is present at the construction of a dialectical model which, while it is applicable to Britain today, is distanced by its time and location from current political partisanship.

One of the play's major strengths was that its display of dialectical discussion was neither located amongst a group of European intellectuals, theorising and jockeying for positions of power at the turn of the century in a small room in some European capital, nor set in the context of some political congress where influential figures from socialist history could expound their views directly to the theatre audience. Instead it simply demonstrated the application of political dialectic by ordinary people in the process of changing their lives. Referring for its evidence to Hinton's historical record of events, Hare illustrated, in a manner whose clarity of expression made it understandable by even the most apolitical member of the audience, how a new society *could* be constructed brick by brick. A major feature of this dialectical process is emphasised by the use, in an early scene, of a banner that, like those employed by Brecht, describes the subject matter of the ensuing scene. It bears the words, "Asking Basic Questions".[58] This process of asking questions in fact continues in various forms throughout the play and reaches its climax in the closing moments when, after one attempt to re-organise society has failed and new plans have been put forward for discussion, emerging from a cacophony of voices can be heard the repeated question, "What do you think about this".[59] The audience is therefore left with the impression that the questioning must go on and that failures must be recognised and, where necessary, new approaches adopted, for as one character remarks towards the end of the play, ". . . socialism itself is transitional".[60] This sense of transition is, of course, an historical concept unfamiliar to British audiences who are steeped culturally in an often stultifying sense of tradition. It is, furthermore, generally viewed by the political Right as a sign of indecisiveness and therefore

weakness. Considering that British audiences were so unused to
dialectical debate, the play was surprisingly successful during the
1970s in engaging its audiences in its dialectical processes and in
provoking them to consider, for example, the most fundamental question raised by practical socialism, "Who depends upon whom for a
living?"[61] In comparison to Hare's previous work and to the tone of
most of the radical historical drama of the 1970s the play concludes
on an unusually optimistic note. Out of a flood of red banners, the
"massive groundswell" of music and questioning voices, which make
up the climax of the penultimate scene of the play, emerges a lone
peasant who, in verse, announces with the resolute new voice of the
people a break with the past and confidence in the future:

There is no Jade Emperor in heaven
There is no Dragon King on earth
I am the Jade Emperor
I am the Dragon King
Make way for me you hills and mountains
I'm coming.[62]

In *Fanshen* Hare was concerned with the moral core of socialism and
how this might be practically applied. It was a play intended not to
agitate for action but to provoke debate, and in this it was certainly
successful.

   In their radical portrayal of history in the plays discussed above,
the dramatists were to emphasise the public rather than the private
lives of their characters. By this means they obviously intended to
discourage the kind of individualistic interpretation that would run
counter to the political message embodied in the play as a whole. As I
have suggested earlier, however, some dramatists such as Hare himself, David Edgar and Edward Bond began to look for ways to illustrate the process of history while at the same time revealing the effect
of that process on the individual. Their aim was, in Bond's words, to
"show the power of historical forces by showing the individuality,
ordinariness and human vulnerability and strength of the characters
who live it"[63] and to demonstrate, in Edgar's words, "the dynamic
between how people subjectively perceive that situation and the
underlying reality".[64]

Chronicles and Disillusionment

Although in *Fanshen* David Hare had offered a positive picture of revolution, this was by no means characteristic of his work during 1970s. In other plays he measured a contemporary England dominated by greed and corruption against how things might have been had the socialist ideals of 1945 been realised. His view of contemporary England was also shared by other young dramatists such as Howard Brenton and David Edgar who, after the defeat in 1968 of what seemed to be progressive forces, also looked back with disillusionment, like Arnold Wesker ten years earlier, over Britain's post-war history. Unlike Wesker's, their vision of British society was, however, now often satirical and was generally devoid of that humanism which had permeated the earlier dramatist's *Chicken Soup with Barley* and *I'm Talking About Jerusalem*. Although Hare, Brenton and Edgar were to a greater or lesser extent socialist in political outlook, they were by no means uncritical of post-war British socialism as represented by the current Labour Party. Neither were they encouraged by the political factionalism of the New Left, nor complacent, in spite of all the revolutionary sound and fury of the 1970s, about Britain's potential for political revolution. In contrast to McGrath, Gooch and the later Arden, amongst this group only Edgar was inclined towards Marxist agit-prop and even he began to leave this behind as the decade progressed in favour of more complex dramatic structures.

Hare, Brenton and subsequently Edgar, in common with Wesker, wrote what Hare has described as "history plays". Like *Chicken Soup with Barley* and *I'm Talking About Jerusalem*, the action of these plays centred upon a number of fictional characters whose lives were dramatised in the context of and in relation to a number of specific historical events. However, whereas Wesker had employed social realism, Hare, Brenton and Edgar were to incline towards a variant of the epic and were often to disrupt the surface reality of their plays in ways that appear to owe much to the technique of disruption employed by the Situationists during the 1960s. Hare has justified this portrayal of the inter-relationship between character and event in terms that were obviously influenced by Marxism and which may also be applied to the work of Brenton and Edgar. "It seems to me so clear about human beings that history and society have a radical effect on how they think and how they behave", Hare claimed in a recent television interview, "that not to represent that in a play is, I would go as far as saying, it's untrue".[1] In the case of Hare and Edgar, and sometimes of Brenton, the aim was indeed to convey, in a realistic manner, the private experience of the public events of recent British history.

David Hare and Howard Brenton first worked together in Portable Theatre, which was founded by Hare and Tony Bicat in 1968 "to take anarchist plays around the country in order to shock people by putting plays on in places where they weren't expected".[2] They have since intermittently renewed their association by jointly writing plays, firstly for the regional theatre (*Brassneck* for Richard Eyre at the Nottingham Playhouse) and subsequently for the National (*Pravda*). While apparently sharing a common view of society, Hare and Brenton differ markedly in their choice of dramatic focus. Hare is extremely sensitive to the internal workings of the small interest-groups of either business or politics and is good at creating female characters, particularly those whose emotional life is somewhat bleak. Probably in consequence of his more firmly established Marxist stance, Brenton, in contrast, is much more fascinated with the process of history itself and with its relationship, through mythology, to the cultural values of the present. While Hare's history plays such as *Plenty* have tended to dramatise the private somewhat at the expense of the public, Brenton's have emphasised such Situationist elements as shock, satire, iconoclasm and demythification more than the exploration of private experience. In *Brassneck* (1973) the two aspects are, however, united in a saga of post-war moral, commercial and political corruption.

Brassneck follows the fortunes of the fictional Bagley family between the years 1945 and 1973. Like Wesker in *Chicken Soup with Barley* and *I'm Talking About Jerusalem*, Hare and Brenton utilised what David Edgar has referred to as "that hoary old standby", the family saga.[3] Unlike Wesker, however, they undermined the form by making the Bagley family utterly loathsome. In addition, *Brassneck's* narrative departs from the family sagas so popular in the Victorian period in that it does not contain the traditional bourgeois parable in which rugged individualism and hard work bring their just reward. Instead it reveals that, as the Bagleys' wealth and power increases, so also does their involvement in corruption. To underline the topical relevance of their satire on business practices, Hare and Brenton chose to embroil the Bagley family in a venture similar to that of the "Poulson Affair" of the 1970s which involved the bribery of council officers and the over-pricing of such local authority projects as the construction of housing and hospitals. Referring to Angus Calder's book, *The People's War*, David Hare made clear that his and Brenton's aim in writing *Brassneck* was to write *"The People's Peace*, as seen, in our case, through the lives of the petty bourgeoisie, builders, solicitors, brewers, politicans, the masonic gang who carve up provincial England."[4] However, in creating this combination of public events and private history the dramatists consciously eschewed that individual psychology which would perhaps have allowed an audience to empathise with members of the Bagley family and thereby lessen the impact of the play's indictment. The family relationships are not presented in human, emotional terms but simply as extensions of the characters' attitudes towards the accumulation of capital. Indeed the unifying feature of the Bagley family lies not in love or mutual respect but in a shared acquisitiveness. The underlying grotesqueness, the monopathic characterisation and the evident indignation amounting often to sheer disgust is in fact reminiscent of that exhibited in Ben Jonson's city comedies and clearly reveals Hare and Brenton as fervent moralists.

The action of the play is set in the fictional Midlands town of Stanton. In an epic manner, scenes depicting discrete stages in the rise and temporary decline of the Bagley fortunes are interspersed with slide sequences which characterise either the historical period in which the subsequent section of the play is set—1945, 1945–50, 1953 and the 1960s—or the social milieu within which its action is to be located. The latter consists largely of tightly knit groups, such as the Freemasons or the golf-club, which must be penetrated and manipulated by the Bagleys if they are to obtain wealth and power. The various scenes are, as is usual in the epic, complete in themselves. Thus by setting public events such as Coronation Day 1953 against private ones such as the Bagley wedding, a satirical point is established, but no attempt is made to reveal or explain aspects of character or events that fall between these scenes which portray various stages in the development of the Bagley saga. As a result, the Bagley family is not made the centre of an individualistic portrayal of family life set against the background of public events, but is used to provide a private strand alongside a public presentation of history and to personify Hare and Brenton's vision of post-war Britain's moral decay.

Brassneck, whose title is a Midlands word meaning "cheek" or "nerve" and has criminal connotations, opens appropriately with a vivid example of entrepreneurship. In its first scene, set in 1945, the 77-year-old Alfred Bagley, en route from London to Stanton, buys from its driver a van filled with ex-Air-Force parachute silk. In the following scene Bagley is introduced to Stanton's Capitalist old guard headed by James Avon, an estate agent, each of whom, in the wake of the Labour victory of 1945, lives in fear of Nationalisation. Discussing this prospect, Bassett, a local brewer, warns his colleagues that "my father taught me there is a class war which you neglect at your peril."[5] The play, however, goes on to illustrate that in post-war Britain such a class-war was to prove far less important than the steady growth of that capitalist, consumerist society which has been a major feature of recent British social and economic history. Alfred Bagley sets out to shape his own new world and, having established himself in the town, feels confident enough in 1953 to expound his life's philosophy on the occasion of his niece's wedding. He claims defiantly that the principles by which he has lived were the outcome of his horrific experiences in the trenches of the First World War. There he learned "the full extent to which mankind can go", even as far as cannibalism, with the result that "in my long life nothing's touched me. No-one's touched me! E-state agents, architects, newly-weds, cannibals, none of you".[6] It also becomes apparent during this speech that in fact he killed his wife during the Second World War by pushing her down the steps of an air-raid shelter. Although, ironically, having delivered this speech he dies of a heart-attack, Alfred Bagley's values are perpetuated in the remainder of the play by his nephew Roderick.

The world inhabited by Alfred Bagley and his successors is, like the Victorian world created by Edward Bond in *Early Morning*, an amoral, capitalist one of dog eat dog. Hare and Brenton's moral castigation is not, however, directed only at the capitalist business-world. Characters such as Harry Edmunds, the Labour politician who sells himself out to Roderick Bagley; Tom Browne, the independent Communist who is disillusioned with the Kremlin and, while remaining a "big wheel" in Transport House, becomes Roderick's public relations man; and Raymond Finch, the Tory ex-cabinet minister who is prepared to exercise his influence to aid the Bagleys, are employed to suggest that wealth and power may exercise a hypnotic power which can transcend political principles and to illustrate the extent of the moral corruption available to the Bagleys. Edmunds is also used to suggest that the Bagley saga represents in microcosm England's betrayal of the political ideals that emerged from the Second World War. In the world according to the Bagleys, true fellowships has no place and barbarism is a means of accumulating profit. For this state of affairs, Edmunds admits, the Left is as much to blame as the Right.

We 'ad a chance in 1945. Finest government this country ever 'ad. But not good enough. Not quite good enough by half. By the end, in rags. What am I now? I know. Don't answer that, 'Arry Edmunds. 'Ow can we ever forgive ourselves? I can't forgive myself. Labour party, the party we all love. . . .[7]

Towards the end of the saga, having been embroiled in scandals concerning the illegal securing of local authority building contracts, the Bagleys become bankrupt. Their bankruptcy is not, however, offered by Brenton and Hare as the just punishment for their crimes. Instead it is employed to suggest the extent and resilience of capitalist corruption. Roderick is sacrificed as the scapegoat for the company's malpractice while, purely out of self-interest, Labour and Conservative councils alike assist the Bagley organisation by covering up their own part in the scandals. Tom Browne nevertheless points out that the continued and inevitable pressure for business to produce ever higher profits will, in the future, result both in tighter regulation and in greater limitation of individual freedom. He prophetically describes what in fact is now beginning to take place in the City:

The time is coming when business will be run like high security prisons. No action that is not accounted, no gesture that is not cross indexed, no indiscretion that is not costed and filed away . . . we can't afford less if we're to go on. Making profits. (*He smiles*) Great Britain Ltd.[8]

In spite of their setbacks, at the play's close the Bagleys, under the new leadership of Roderick's son Sidney, are poised to rise again with a new and even more lucrative commodity. Sidney himself clearly conveys the dramatists' view of modern consumer capitalism—he wears a city suit but carries a flick-knife and would be quite at home in a Ben Jonson comedy such as *The Alchemist*. The new business venture which he introduces to his family, assembled in his plush strip club, will centre upon "a product of our times, the perfect product, totally artificial, man-made, creating its own market, one hundred percent consumer identification, generating its own demand . . .".[9] The product is heroin, a commodity which in this context becomes a symbol of the fundamental immorality of Capitalist acquisitiveness and exploitation. The play also leaves the audience

with the view that capitalism is too deep-seated to be easily dismissed. Indeed its final line offers an ironic challenge to those on the
Left who, during the 1970s, were attempting to convince themselves
that capitalism was in decline. "As head of a great English family",
says Sidney, "I give you all a toast. The last days of Capitalism."[10] For
the Bagleys in 1973 capitalism was clearly not in its last days, but
instead was preparing itself to enter a new phase in its evolution. In
his controversial adaptation of *Measure for Measure*, produced in the
previous year, Brenton's Angelo had remarked, "I offer this view of
history. It is a paradox. The old order, unchecked, will bring forth a
new and far harsher form of itself".[11] Having referred to the history of
post-war British capitalism, in *Brassneck* this is the ultimate vision
conveyed by Brenton and Hare.

From the beginning of his career as a dramatist Brenton himself
has exhibited a particular concern with history. In his earliest published play, *A Sky Blue Life*, which was performed at the Little Theatre, St. Martin's Lane, in 1966, then by Brighton Combination in
1968 and, in a revised version, at the Open Space Theatre in November 1971, Brenton employed history to examine the possible role of
the writer in a post-revolutionary Communist society. In doing so he
was obviously speculating about his own potential role as a politically
committed left-wing writer. As in a number of Brenton's subsequent
plays written in collaboration with fringe theatre groups, *A Sky Blue
Life* takes the form of a collage of frequently altered situations, story-
telling, songs and mime built around a central historical figure who,
in this case, is Maxim Gorky. Its ensemble approach demands that
actors repeatedly change roles. Audience interest is therefore maintained by means of various theatrical devices rather than through
empathy with the central character, who often acts more as an
observer than as a participant in the play's action and who, even at
the close of the play, has not resolved his dilemma concerning his role
as a writer in post-revolutionary Russia.

In its 1971 published version, *A Sky Blue Life* consists of a series of
scenes which flow one into another and which dramatise stories written by Gorky and feature his meetings first with Tolstoy and then
with Lenin. In the play, Brenton was for the first time to
demythologise a "great man", an occupation that he was subsequently
to enter upon with great enthusiasm. The "great man" is not, however, Gorky but the "master novelist, Aristocrat, Freer of serfs, Mys-
tic and saint", "THE DADDY OF 'EM ALL"[12], Leo Tolstoy. Gorky
visits Tolstoy in his country retreat and asks him, "when will the
Russian people shake off their chains, and rise from the earth into
the light?" Tolstoy simply ignores the question and instead discusses
horticulture. He is no longer interested in ideas and his critical

response to one of Gorky's short stories is merely formalistic—"The stove was in the wrong place".[13] Ultimately he even denies being Tolstoy but then explains that he is now *un*writing his books and simply wants to abandon the corpse of the old Russia and to retire to "Live in a field. Be a peasant. Dig some tatoes".[14]

If Gorky learns nothing from Tolstoy that will help him to define his role as a writer, later in the play Lenin, in contrast, is quite unambiguous in stating what Gorky should and should not do. Lenin calls for a revolutionary play which fulfils one important criterion— "Can it be used. Now".[15] Plays that contain "lovely death scenes", in his opinion, "wet the knickers of the bourgeois theatre-goers, and DO nothing".[16] In the new Soviet state, on the other hand, utilitarianism should be paramount. As were many British dramatists to do after him, Brenton portrays Lenin as the "hard man" of the Russian revolution who, in this case, considers that reading works of literature simply wastes time which could be better employed in revolutionary activism. "You know what I read now? Daily", he asks Gorky, "Lists. Lists. Those to be shot, those to be fed. Corpses and potatoes, (*joking*) the true literature of revolution."[17] As he leaves, Lenin sets Gorky the task of writing some pamphlets. When Gorky enquires about their subject matter Lenin replies, "Me. Goodnight, Alexi".[18] Gorky's role in the revolution is therefore to be concerned not with the celebration of the proletariat but with the promotion of revolutionary individualism.

While these two scenes deal with the political dilemma facing Gorky, the dramatisation of his stories is employed to portray the country and the people in whose name the revolution has taken place. This is established in the words with which Gorky opens the play. "Factories and ditches. Fields. The great plain, going for miles. A landscape of millions. It was a hard life of bitter struggle. But sky-blue."[19]

In the first story, "Ice", the intellectual, Gorky, a peasant and a factory worker, who in total represent the various social strata of post-revolutionary Russian society, struggle together across the frozen Volga. In "Depths", set amongst the lowest in society, Gorky is told of a belief in a true and just land, which turned out to be a utopian fantasy. Significantly this dramatisation is halted by Lenin. The play's penultimate story reveals to Gorky the ignoble nature of the proletariat whom he is seeking to serve. It is set among illiterate and superstitious peasants in a plague-ridden village. The peasants try to persuade Gorky to read a funeral service; he resists but convinces them that he had done so, and in spite of his warning that they will spread the plague, they selfishly flee from their village. In the play's final scene Gorky at last discovers a role for himself by helping a mother give birth. This is, however, a humanitarian rather than political act and does not resolve either Gorky's or the audience's dilemma concerning the artist's contribution to the process of revolution. The play's themes are unfortunately not clearly expressed, partly because the enacted stories, which originally communicated themes of their own, are slightly at odds with the central theme of the present play and partly because of the confusing mixture of factual biography and literary fiction. In later plays Brenton was clearly to delimit each of these elements and thereby to make the clear interaction between them a more effective means of communicating his themes.

In the years following the initial production of *A Sky Blue Life*, although he was briefly to portray both Lenin and Stalin and refer on one occasion to Eastern Europe, Brenton was from now on to focus predominantly upon the demythologisation of *English* history. In *Christie in Love* he was to turn more specifically to English criminal history. The play was written in 1969 for David Hare's Portable Theatre under the influence of Situationism. Brenton challenged the popular myth surrounding the mass-murderer Christie by portraying his murders of women as bizarre but rather sad acts of love. Against this he contrasted the prurient fascination exhibited by the public and Christie's portrayal as a monster by the popular press which took perverse delight in the detailed description of his crimes.

The play is to be performed in a filthy enclosure bounded by chicken wire and strewn with popular newspapers, a set obviously intended both to evoke the garden in which some of Christie's victims were buried and to confront the audience with the evidence of its own fascination with the "dirty stories" reported by press. Christie, however, is portrayed naturalistically. He is above all a "normal" sort of man. The policemen who arrest and question him, and who would usually embody public morality and respectability, are portrayed by Brenton as grotesque and vulgar caricatures reminiscent of vulgar music-hall entertainers. Through their obscene limericks and sexually obsessive questioning of Christie, Brenton convey's the public's morally ambivalent attitude towards both sexuality and criminals.

In *Wesley* and *Scott of the Antarctic* Brenton was again to examine popular mythology, this time that associated with the iconic figures of John Wesley and Scott of the Antarctic. In *Wesley*, performed in a Bradford church in 1970, the founder of Methodism gives an account of "the dark night of his soul. His struggle with sin within. His struggle to know God. His journey to salvation".[20] In *Scott of the Antarctic*, performed on an ice-rink in the same city in 1971, Brenton was to attack the cult of heroism and particularly its association with Victorian imperialism. In combination the above plays may be seen as the prototypes for Brenton's later more extensive treatment of history. The characteristic sensationalistic manner, drawn from Situationism and exhibited in *Christie in Love* and *Scott of the Antarctic*, with which he assaulted the cultural myths and icons of establishment history, was to reappear in later plays, most notably *The Romans in Britain* (1980). The deconstruction of the cult of heroism and the concern with the particular myths of the Second World War, which was to become a characteristic feature of his later plays, were also explored in the early years of his career in *Hitler Dances* (1972).

In *Hitler Dances*, through the medium of a series of children's games, Brenton confronts various individual attitudes to the myths of the Second World War. Most importantly these include reference to the romantic depiction of the wartime exploits of the SOE heroine Violet Szabo in the 1958 British war-film, *Carve Her Name with Pride*. The heroic, romantic myths conveyed by the film are systematically de-romanticised by counterpointing them with speeches which recount the violent reality of warfare and suggest that Violet's fervent desire to kill Germans, which made her an easy recruit to the SOE, was motivated not by patriotism but by revenge for the death of her husband, who was killed during the African campaign. It is also revealed that the film's portrayal of Violet's torture by the Gestapo which, with the foreknowledge beloved by historical dramatists, her interrogator Feiffer tells her will be subsequently portrayed as "something sexy",[21] in fact did not happen. Owing to "administrative confusion",[22] her papers were lost and, after her initial verbal interrogation, Violet received no further attention from the Gestapo. She was later transferred to a concentration camp and executed. Brenton's attack in *Hitler Dances* was, then, upon that glorified mythology of war perpetuated by the entertainment industry which, as the performance of the play by "children" is intended to illustrate, is absorbed by successive generations of the young.

A theatrical device that Brenton had already employed in *Christie in Love* was to reappear in *Hitler Dances*, again in *The Churchill Play* and, in a slightly different form, in *Weapons of Happiness* and *The Romans in Britain*. It was a device, similar to that employed by Arden and D'Arcy in *The Hero Rises Up*, which was to communicate clearly the fundamental aim and nature of Brenton's theatrical reference to history. In each of the above plays a figure from the past— Christie, a German soldier, Winston Churchill, Joseph Frank and Julius Caesar—is placed in the present. In the case of Christie, the German soldier, and Churchill, the historical figure is actually *resurrected* from his grave in a parody of a Hammer Horror movie, and indeed in each of these plays the theatricality of the moment is emphasised as a means of alienating the audience from its mythic preconceptions. The technique brings the past into collision with the present in a manner that displays the very mechanics of historical drama and reveals with dramatic economy that history is the artifact of those who create it, that it is ideologically affiliated, that it normally reflects and is part of the present and that, by means of the mythology contained within it, it may exercise a profound influence upon the future. Brenton's resurrecting of Christie, Churchill and Caesar is in various ways iconoclastic. In each case he reviews the contemporary cultural status of the icon and thereby reveals and questions the myths that each embodies. Churchill, Frank and Caesar are, in addition, used to communicate similarities or dissimilarities between past and present and to illustrate and deconstruct those myths of the past which perpetuate socially devisive and destructive attitudes and behaviour.

The majority of the features described above were brought together in 1974 in *The Churchill Play*. Like *Brassneck*, the play was directed by Richard Eyre at the Nottingham Playhouse. Indeed, it was Eyre who had suggested to Brenton that he should write a play to mark the centenary of Churchill's birth. In doing so, Brenton united a number of contemporary political issues to create a heightened version of the present. Themes concerning the contemporary situation in Northern Ireland taken from an earlier play commissioned by B.B.C. radio in 1972, but rejected as part of its policy not to broadcast material referring to Northern Ireland which its management considered to be in any sense controversial, were combined with oblique reference to the then prevalent industrial unrest, which was to culminate in the Miner's Strike of 1974, and the threat of anti-trade union legislation, to make the play highly topical. Four years later, in 1978, in an even more volatile political climate in which politics had polarised and the threat of a right-wing backlash against the union activism was looming large, Brenton was to offer a politically somewhat tougher revised version of the play for production by the Royal Shakespeare Company at The Other Place in Stratford.

Formalistically, *The Churchill Play's* most notable features are its meta-theatrical approach, its disorientation shock techniques such as the resurrection of an historical figure, its iconoclasm and its demythification, all of which, as I have suggested above, had been experimented with by Brenton in earlier plays. In addition, for the first time Brenton was successfully to combine these features with the epic historical approach that he and Hare had employed in *Brassneck* and which, aided by documentary-style slide-projection, had set the public events of recent British social and political history against the lives of the new capitalists of post-war Britain.

Whereas in *Hitler Dances* Brenton had directly de-romanticised the image of warfare simply by deconstructing the establishment mythology of the Second World War, in *The Churchill Play* the iconic figure of Winston Churchill, while being used likewise to demythify aspects of the Second World War, is here also employed to illustrate capitalist values which perpetuate the oppression of the working class. The play is set in 1984 in Camp Churchill, an internment camp for so-called trade-union "activists" which was intended by Brenton to resemble the Long Kesh internment camp in Northern Ireland. The association of Brenton's chosen date of 1984 with George Orwell's novel which refers to that same year clearly signals the play's allegorical intent and, in the light of the novel's themes, inevitably evokes considerations of totalitarianism and the institutionalised division of social classes.

The realistic action concerns the creation and presentation by the camp's internees of a play that focuses predominantly upon Winston Churchill's role in the Second World War. This play-within-a-play is ultimately performed before an all-party parliamentary committee whose brief is to examine and report on camp conditions. Brenton's demythologisation of the Churchill legend begins with the theatrical coup with which the play opens. What at first appears to be a dimly-lit reconstruction of Churchill's lying-in-state in Westminster Palace, complete with stained-glass window, candles, catafalque and honour-guard of servicemen, is initially dislocated by the emergence of Churchill from his coffin in a pastiche of Hammer Horror Dracula films. The whole scene itself then disintegrates visually before the audience's eyes as neon lights shatter the gloom, revealing that the "real" setting of the play is an aircraft hanger in which "the stained-glass window is seen to be a flimsy paper construction" and the honour guard to be internees of a prison-camp, themselves guarded by soldiers with sten-guns. A tension is therefore immediately established between the past represented by the funeral, the present represented by the audience and the future represented by the prison guards and their prisoners of 1984. It is a dramatic tension which Brenton is to exploit throughout the play. In addition the play-within-a-play is used to demystify the workings of such "public" political strategies as capitalism's manipulation of the working class, while the prison staff and visiting parliamentary representatives are employed to give voice to those "private" concerns, prejudices and failings which motivate and maintain such strategies.

The demystification begins even before the lights reveal the sham nature of the setting. The "marine" guarding the catafalque accuses Churchill of "buggering" working people (an image subsequently increasingly favoured by Brenton) and explains that he will never be forgotten or forgiven in Wales for, as Home Secretary in 1910, sending soldiers against striking miners with the result that three of the strikers were shot dead. "But 'e won a war" responds another guard, this time a soldier, only to be contradicted by the marine: "People won the War", he retorts, "He just got pissed with Stalin. . . ."[23] In this manner early in the play Brenton establishes the discrepancy between the reality of Churchill's behaviour as perceived by ordinary people and the myth created by and about him during the war. It is at this point that Churchill breaks out of his coffin in order to defend himself. He claims that it was the *ingratitude* of the people which deprived him, the great wartime leader, of office in 1945. He identifies himself with the view that history is the biography of great men, a view which, we are to discover, is also shared by the Establishment, represented here by the camp commandant, Colonel Ball. Dismayed by the internees' characterisation of Churchill, and ironically, given the context, Ball reminds Thompson, the camp's doctor and organiser of the play-within-a-play, that "Winston Churchill saved this country from one thousand years of barbarism".[24]

Brenton's representation of Churchill's leadership appears to owe much to the book that had partly inspired him and Hare to write *Brassneck*, Angus Calder's *The People's War*. Calder's left-wing reading of the wartime relationship between Churchill and the British people is not one of a charismatic leader whose will was enacted by a submissive and grateful population, but rather as an interaction between leader and people. Churchill's wartime near-dictatorship (which is reflected in the play in the association of his name with a camp in which opponents of the capitalist system are interned and sometimes "dumped" or killed) was, in Calder's view, *accepted* by the population because it appeared to be the most effective way of conducting the war. "Churchill", he wrote, "appeared in May 1940 as the new man, thrown up by the very situation which he called on all classes to defy. He was part of that situation, he did not transcend it, he expressed defiance, he did not create it, and as those particular circumstances receded, so his magic dwindled."[25] He was granted power and support by the people for as long as the peopled deemed it necessary, and with the cessation of hostilities the people unsentimentally removed him from power. "He was essentially a war leader", claimed Calder, "and his rejection by the electorate in 1945 was the result of this long-standing image of him, not of any sudden excess of ingratitude."[26] Calder also provided the evidence for Brenton's illustration of Churchill's personality. This private aspect is used by Brenton to reveal that Churchill's view of the world was based upon a romantic historical fantasy which was pernicious for the working class in that it allocated them a place in an unchanging and unchangeable hierarchy. In creating his meta-theatrical imagery Brenton followed Calder in presenting Churchill as, perhaps even at times unconsciously, himself playing a heroic part in an imagined heroic drama. In the internee's version of *The Churchill Play* he describes a visit in June 1945 to the "Red Clyde", a visit which is described by Calder. Here Brenton's Churchill describes the moving personal experience provoked by his reception, which he interprets as one of a deserving leader honoured by a grateful nation. His romantic view of working-class Scotland is, however, countered by an internee, Mike:

MIKE: Old Man, we don't live in the same world.

CHURCHILL: It's not all ermine robes to wipe your bottom on where I come from.

MIKE: Nor is it all cloth caps and waving flags where I come from.

CHURCHILL: We're both of the Island Race. Out of the Celtic mist, the Saxon fen. And bitter dark green Normandy.

MIKE: I do not understand a word of that.[27]

Churchill's reference to the "Island Race" is, of course, an echo of his own romanticised approach to history in his *A History of the English-Speaking Peoples*. While here Brenton effectively demythologises Churchill as a man of the people and reveals his iconography to be essentially a threat to the working class, the dramatist is less successful in his attempts to use, for a similar purpose, Churchill's famous war-time visit to view bomb-damage in working-class Peckham. Central to Brenton's strategy here was the alteration of the phrase called out to Churchill during his tour by "Uncle Ernie", a victim of the bombing, which is reported in Churchill's memoirs as: "We can take it Guv. Give it 'em back." In Brenton's play within a play this is "corrected" in the words of another internee, Furry, to: "We can take it Guv. Give it 'em back . . . But we just might give it back to you one day."[28] As the "corrected" line is much longer than the original, the impression conveyed, however, is not merely that Churchill has misheard the comment, perhaps as a result of his inability to understand the aspirations of the working class (a reading of Churchill's character for which Calder provides some justification), but rather that Churchill has consciously altered the phrase to suit his own self-image. The power of the Churchillian myth cannot, however, be dismissed so simply. As some critics were to point out, the accusation of malicious intent rests more easily upon the doubly fictitious character of Uncle Ernie, played by Furry, and their creator Howard Brenton than upon Churchill himself.

Through the mouths of the actors performing the play within a play Brenton articulates the view that the Churchillian myth is an illustration of how Britain persists in clinging to those class divisions conveyed by the image of a paternalistic upper-class leader followed gratefully by a subservient working class. By referring to Churchill's private world Brenton again creates images that possess public implications. Churchill is, for example, shown to have been haunted by images of disintegration and disease. On the personal level he is concerned that he may have inherited syphylis from his father and suffers from bouts of depression which he calls "black dog". On the public level the resurrected Churchill describes himself regretfully as "a dying bit of Old England", to which one of the other actors in the play-within-a-play retorts, "Churchill, you left us nothing. . . . Bit a gas from our fathers about some darkest hour years ago. Gas only, not a single true human thought. Not a single true, human remain".[29] The play implies that it is such class-based attitudes represented by Churchill which have ultimately led to the establishment of the camp that bears his name, and Brenton uses the slide show of "post-war English history in reverse",[30] which is part of the internees' play, to signal to his contemporary audience the progress already made towards this situation in the years since the war. A slide showing the first Wilson government, which in the opinion of the New Left had abandoned socialism, reveals the actual political outcome of the hardships of the Second World War and the promised socialist future of 1945. Other slides depicting the Suez Crisis and Eoka "terrorism" in Cyprus represent Britain's post-war loss of empire and international influence. These slides are badly projected and the pictures distorted as, according to Brenton, was history itself.

The Churchill Play thus refers back to the moral and ethical decline of post-war Britain which had already been portrayed by Brenton and Hare in *Brassneck*. Within its central image of the internment camp this process is, however, also linked specifically with the betrayal and suppression of the rights and aspirations of the working-class. Uncle Ernie's assertion that "People won the war" is answered cynically by Mike with the retort, "And for what?".[31] A similar view that the working class was not the class that benefited most in the years after 1945 is neatly expressed in Calder's introduction to *The People's War*, in words that clearly summarise what was to be one of *The Churchill Play's* main concerns:

Thanks to their [the people's] energy, the forces of wealth, bureaucracy and privilege survived with little inconvenience, recovered from their shock, and began to proceed with their old business of manoeuvre, concession and studied betrayal. Indeed, this war, which had set off a ferment of participatory democracy was strengthening meanwhile the forces of tyranny, pressing Britain towards 1984. The new capitalism of paternalistic corporations meshed with the state bureaucracy was emerging clearly along with the managerial ideology which would support it.[32]

As he and Hare had already done in *Brassneck*, in *The Churchill Play* Brenton was also to suggest that the socialist ideals of 1945 had not only been diffused during the post-war years under the influence of capitalism but had also been betrayed by the Left itself. In this play the Labour M.P., Morn's, betrayal of these values is portrayed as being even more insidious than, in *Brassneck*, was the Labour M.P., Edmunds', or the Communist, Tom Browne's, connivance with the forces of capitalism. Morn has knowingly collaborated in a "vast conspiracy of obedience"[33] which has deprived the working class of their rights and freedoms. He now attempts, by turning to alcohol, to avoid the consequences of his party's collaboration with the Right which are the oppression of the working class and the establishment of internment camps such as the one that he is now visiting. Only when caught up in the prisoners' escape attempt does he admit to himself that action to consolidate and to ensure the continuance of socialism should have been taken earlier.

MORN (*rambling to himself*): We should have done it. Years ago. Factory floor, street level. Taken means of production, given power into people's hands. '45. '64. '78. We had the democratic space. But somehow there were always good reasons. Day to day, little crises. For not. Not.[34]

As the reference to 1978 suggests, this speech was added in the revised version of the play in order to cite the most recent of those failures which had haunted the Left during the post-war years.

Brenton was not, however, simply looking for scapegoats. Earlier in the play some responsibility for the present situation has also been attributed to those liberal middle-class intellectuals who largely constituted Brenton's audience. This group is represented in the play by Doctor Thompson, who attempts to turn a bad situation, which he is powerless to alter, into something more humane by at least allowing the prisoners to express their dissent under the guise of necessary recreation by means of the play-within-a-play. The prisoners, however, turn this politically ineffective artistic expression into an act of real rebellion by using it as a cover for their attempt to escape from the camp. As the camp commandant, Colonel Ball, correctly observes, from a right-wing point of view there is a spark of resistance in Thompson but, as becomes apparent in the latter's exchanges with the guard-sergeant, faced by the single-minded power of an army

which has been politicised in trade union disputes and on the streets
of Northern Ireland and whose non-commissioned officers and men
are capable of killing both their superiors and prisoners, Thompson
alone has little chance of altering the situation. Regarded by the
army as a misfit, Thompson appears no less so to the prisoners. His
spontaneous offer to join their escape in order to offer medical assist-
ance is disregarded on the grounds that it is much too late for him to
begin to rebel against a system that he has implicitly permitted to
become established. Thomson's wife, Caroline, is used by Brenton to
illustrate those private concerns which have allowed Britain to slide
thus into a right-wing dictatorship. Throughout the play she expresses a desire to run away from the reality around her. "It's not bad,
what I want, is it?" she asks her husband, "it's no disgrace? A house,
with a garden, in the south of England. Decent. Mild. Safe. Away
from this . . . rural slum."[35] It is in Jimmy's violent outburst at the
close of the play that Brenton answers her question. "You put me in
'ere",[36] Jimmy replies angrily to Caroline's question of why he wants
to destroy her way of life. By joining the "conspiracy of obedience"
she, like Morn, has passively contributed to what is taking place in
Britain. In the last minutes of the play the prisoner Joby emphasises
that the erosion of human rights which has culminated in Camp
Churchill has taken place as a result of public apathy. Democracy has
just been allowed to slip away without anyone really noticing, until it
was too late. "The bad temper. People's minds closing. Getting colder.
The country sliding down. Guns, Barbed wire."[37] Brenton's aim was,
therefore, to warn members at all levels of society to be aware of and
to resist any depletion of human rights before the time for action had
passed.

The 1974 version of the play ended with Glenda's words, "I don't
want the future to be . . .".[38] If we assume that the completed line was
intended to be "I don't want the future to be like this", then the play
stands as a warning against that vast conspiracy of silence to which
it is so easy to succumb. In the revised 1978 version, however, Brenton added new final words to what had now become a more violent
second act. The play now ended with Joby's cry, "The Third World
War",[39] words that in the manner of agit-prop now communicate
defiance and class warfare and which, at a time when the Left and
Right were in clear confrontation, were obviously intended to shake
audiences out of their political apathy.

In *The Churchill Play* Brenton discovered an effective way of
addressing contemporary political concerns by counterpointing the
public and private aspects of British post-war history. By demystifying the Churchillian myth he also offered a series of epic perspectives
which would relate the past (the history of the people's war) with the

present (the actual performance of Brenton's play) and the future (the Churchill Internment Camp in 1984). This permitted him to exploit the tension created by the interplay of fact and fiction, expressed in terms of public and private experience, to awaken the audience to processes at work in British society *at the present time*. By conjoining past and future Brenton was not therefore intent on prophesy but was attempting, by locating the audience in the midst of a long-term historical process, to reveal a pattern of events that he considered were leading inexorably to a more authoritarian and divided society but which if dealt with now could still be halted.

In 1976 in *Weapons of Happiness* Brenton was again to introduce a figure from the past into a modern fictional context. The modern context was, in this case, the intentionally somewhat trivial one of the abortive "revolutionary" occupation of a crisp factory by some of its employees. The progress of this occupation, which smacks of the romantic anarchism of the 1960s rather than any organised redistribution of power and wealth to the workers, is treated in an aggressively realistic manner which brings out the disparate private aims of each of those involved. The play opens with the lone figure of Joseph Frank who, we later learn, was a dedicated Communist who nevertheless was tortured and later hanged in the Prague treason trials of 1952. In a short speech he refers to the "ignorant English" who are asleep while "in the nightmare of the dark all the dogs of Europe bark".[40] Frank has been conjured up by Brenton from the "nightmare" reality of European Stalinist communism to provide a contrast to the revolutionary fantasy that he considered was being played out in contemporary Britain by the "ignorant English". The intrusion of international socialist history, old and decaying as it may be seen to be in the figure of Joseph Frank, was used by Brenton to test the value of current British left-wing political activism. In an epic manner the scenes of the play move backwards and forwards between Frank's interrogation in 1950s Czechoslovakia and the developing factory occupation in present-day England. The private attitudes to revolution of the various participants in the factory occupation are thereby revealed to be naively utopian in comparison to the harsh reality of Stalinism experienced by Frank. For him Stalinist dictatorship is not a historical political aberration but a painful personal memory which he now wishes to put behind him. "Funny how they do badges a all the others but not Stalin",[41] observes one of the would-be English "revolutionaries", thereby unwittingly acknowledging how the modern Left is avoiding the truth of history. It is Janice alone among these "revolutionaries" who has any sense of politics and appropriately it is she who comes closest to Frank on a private level by making love to him in the London Planetarium while, pointedly, the *Red* Planet rises above them. Nevertheless, even she wants to live only in the present. Although claiming to be a Marxist, she rejects Marxism's fundamental tenet. "There in't no history" she tells Frank, "never happened. And if it did, make it go away. (*She claps her hands*) Now is what I want. Now . . . That's what I love. The Now. My now. Lovely sexy here and now. Perhaps we just been made. A second ago. The world came into existence . . . Pop! . . ."[42]

When the workers' occupation collapses and its participants ignominiously escape from the factory through a drain, Frank tries finally to communicate to them the reality and seriousness of revolution. "You do not have a chance for revolt often. And, often, it is ridiculous. Fleeting. Difficult to think through. But it is rare. And not to be thrown away. It is the most precious thing on earth."[43] As the group flees to Wales in order to set up an "alternative" community, Frank advises them not to stay in the countryside, echoing the classical Marxist view that, "nothing revolutionary comes from agriculture, not in Western Europe. Make for another city".[44] They ignore his advice, only to discover, when they come across an empty Welsh farmhouse, that the previous occupant, a real farmer, has been unable to make a living out of the place and has abandoned it. Their alternative lifestyle also appears doomed to fail.

In the penultimate scene of the play, after the factory has been abandoned, the ineffectiveness of romantic, individual revolutionary gestures is illustrated metaphorically by Brenton in a manner that would inevitably remind an audience of scenes shown on television during the Russian takeover of Prague in 1968. A Russian tank with Stalin standing beside it appears suddenly behind Frank who is now alone on the stage. Frank runs towards the tank, throws his coat over the barrel of its gun and sinks exhausted to his knees. Stalin looks at him, laughs and calls him "an incurable romantic".[45] A blackout transforms the scene into the present and Frank is discovered dead in the factory yard. Although the play reaches no definite conclusion, its implication seems to be that emotionally motivated, spontaneous, unorganised revolutionary action, as was demonstrated in 1968 in both Eastern and Western Europe, must inevitably prove ineffectual. At this stage in his career Brenton was therefore joining with McGrath and Griffiths in believing that, for a revolution to be successful in Britain or elsewhere in Western Europe, Anarchistic spontaneity must be replaced by something resembling Leninist organisation. The figure of Lenin had in fact made a brief appearance to deliver various aphorisms in Brenton's previous play, *Magnificence*. Notable amongst these was the assertion that "Left-wing communism is an infantile disorder. Politics is an art and a science that does not drop from the skies".[46] In *Weapons of Happiness*, through the historical figure of Joseph Frank, Brenton appears also to be suggesting that revolution should, at the very least, be taken seriously.

Weapons of Happiness was the first new play to be commissioned and performed by the National Theatre in its new home on the South Bank of the Thames. Brenton defended himself against potential accusations that, as a politically committed dramatist, he was selling himself out to the theatrical establishment. He claimed in an interview published in *Theatre Quarterly* in 1975[47] that the bigger theatre better suited the kind of "public" drama which he preferred to write and was a test of his worth as a playwright. Some nine years later, in 1984 just prior to the opening of *Pravda*, David Hare was similarly to describe the attraction of working, in this case again with Brenton, for one of the two large institutional companies, The National Theatre or the Royal Shakespeare Company. Speaking of the National Theatre he explained, "I came here to experience on a really large scale", and continued,

I write social plays and you have to have a sweep of actors, a company of Shakespearian size, so that not only is every class represented but groups can argue within each class. You are talking about 15 to 20 players. And there are only three or four theatres in the country where you can use that number.[48]

Such were the demands made by *Pravda*. In 1978 the National Theatre had produced its first play by David Hare, *Plenty*. This was a production that demanded *only* fourteen actors but whose epic sweep over almost twenty years of post-war English (rather than truly British) history was to fully exploit the staging facilities offered by the Lyttleton Theatre. In this play the private experience, in this case of despair, took precedence over the public historical events of post-war England. Hare appears to have been very clear concerning his goal in writing this "history play". Although he was dealing with a character similar to that of Freddy in Terence Rattigan's *The Deep Blue Sea* "who has had a good war and can then find no role in the peace", Hare's intention was not to produce a similarly enclosed study of an individual affected by war experience, but instead, "to set one character's life against the days of English plenty".[49] Nevertheless, although focusing upon one particular central character, in common with many other young dramatists of his generation he too was to disclaim any concern with the "wearying personal fetish or even chronic personality disorder"[50] of individual psychology, and to express a desire to create characters whose lives had been demonstrably affected by those same social changes experienced by the audience itself.

Hare wrote *Plenty* while directing his first film for television, *Licking Hitler* (1978), and, perhaps inevitably, the two plays contain themes in common. *Licking Hitler* was set during the Second World War in an English country house which had been requisitioned for use as a military radio transmission centre. Part of the centre's function is to transmit "black propaganda" to Germany with the aim of lowering morale and promoting dissent. The action of the play concerns the gradual moral corruption of Anna Seaton, an upper-class girl assigned to the centre, by her participation in the preparation of the propaganda unit's broadcasts. The scripts for these broadcasts are prepared by an ex-journalist, Archie Maclean, who hails from that "Red Clyde" which appears to have become, for the left-wing historical dramatists of the 1970s, both a symbol of working-class resistance and an assertion of the possibility of a socialist revolution. The film concludes in a semi-documentary manner with a stills sequence accompanied by a voice-over summary of the post-war career of each of the characters. Anna, we learn, has drifted through a career in advertising, a marital breakdown and a relationship with an unmarried mother—a background and post-war existence paralleled by Susan Traherne in *Plenty*. In the latter play Hare moves forward chronologically to focus now upon the post-war experiences of Susan Traherne, who also, like Anna, is an upper-class girl whose life had been altered radically by the experience of war. In this, *Plenty* acts almost as a sequel to *Licking Hitler*. Indeed the words of Anna's closing voice-over establish the moral environment which in *Plenty* leads Susan Traherne ultimately to despair:

Over the years I have been watching the steady impoverishment of the people's ideals, their loss of faith, the lying, the daily inveterate lying, the thirty-year-old deep corrosive national habit of lying. . . .[51]

Chronologically *Plenty* begins where the action of *Licking Hitler* has left off. The influence of the past is, however, carried throughout the play by Susan Traherne, whose character has been shaped by her wartime experiences, like Anna's of a covert nature, as an S.O.E. courier in occupied France during the war. From this standpoint she reacts to the public events that made up what Hare has described as the "great, groaning, yawling festival of change"[52] of Britain's post-war years. Susan's experiences have left her hypersensitive, particularly to that process of moral and ethical decline described by Anna Seaton, which drives her ultimately to despair and to the verge of madness. We learn little about Susan's family background (other than from her assertion that her father was "a shit") or about the day-to-day intimacies of her marriage to the diplomat, Brock. In fact in the dramatis personae of the play she is referred to as Susan Traherne, not Susan Brock, although for much of the play she is married. This is only one of a number of similarities, such as the pistols, the shooting at a "friend", her desire for solitude and the sharp changes of mood, which link Susan's character with that of Ibsen's similarly socially alienated Hedda Gabler. However, while Ibsen's use of Hedda's maiden name was intended both to convey her alienation from those around her and to call attention to the hereditary factors that have formed her personality, Susan's likewise emphasises her isolation from close human relationships but merely hints at a middle-class background. Thus in Hare's characterisation there is a shift from the highly individualistic manner in which Ibsen portrays Hedda towards a concern with the *interactive* nature of the individual and her social context.

Although Hare attempted to avoid individualistic characterisation, the danger inherent in his portrayal of Susan in *Plenty* is that the extremes of her personality, which may easily be read psychologically, may dominate the audience's attention at the expense of the wider historical background. If this were to happen, Hare's intended use of the interrelationship of private and public experience to reveal the private spiritual anguish disguised by the gradual growth in Britain's public post-war material prosperity would be severely hampered. Hare was to realise that, on occasions, this had indeed occurred. In 1983, in his introduction to Faber's collection of *The History Plays*, he was to contrast the British and American productions of the play to make this very point.

In England the opposition to *Plenty* formed around the feeling that from the start Susan Traherne contains the seeds of her own destruction, and that the texture of the society in which she happens to live is merely irrelevant, for she is bent on objecting to it, whatever its qualities. This is certainly not what I intended, . . . I intend to show the struggle of a heroine against a deceitful and emotionally stultified class, yet some sections of the English audience miss this, for they see what Susan is up against as life itself.[53]

In Susan's opinion the war has for her been a positive experience by giving her the opportunity to experience intense personal relationships. For Darwin, the British post-war diplomat stationed in Brussels to whom she reports the death of her lover during an illicit holiday in 1947, it appears initially to have produced the utopian opportunity to build a new Europe. It is these two private and public strands that throughout the play Hare weaves around the character of Susan Traherne, thereby linking England's moral and ethical decline, as represented in the post-war activities of the British Foreign Office whose ethics are replaced by a kind of mannerism in which "behaviour is all",[54] with Susan's own mental deterioration.

This ethical decline and mental deterioration, ironically, is accompanied by Susan's, Brock's and the nation's attainment of greater and greater material wealth—the "plenty" of the play's title.

The play's opening scene, set in Susan and her husband Brock's expensive house in Knightsbridge in 1962, immediately establishes the "state of England". The house has obviously been recently "stripped bare" of its opulent trappings, some of which can in fact be seen protruding from the packing cases scattered around the stage. We are immediately made aware both of material possessions and of the bleakness which they are normally used to hide. This bleakness is emphasised by the play's opening line of dialogue: Alice, Susan's friend, having entered from the street and shaken off the rain, complains, "I don't know why anybody lives in this country. No wonder everyone has colds all the time. Even what they call passion, it still comes at you down a blocked nose".[55] This lack of passion is further conveyed by Susan's reference to the "turkey neck and turkey gristle"[56] appearance of Brock's penis as she distastefully examines his naked body which, throughout the scene, lies inert on a single mattress at the front of the stage.

Having tantalisingly established this situation, Hare then in subsequent scenes traces Susan's life from her wartime experiences in France in 1943 to the events of that day in 1962 which preceeded the situation with which the play commenced. Each of these scenes is associated either with some major event from post-war British history such as the Festival of Britain or the Suez crisis, or with a period of economic change, and each is employed by Hare to signal a stage both in Britain's increasing materialism and in its moral or ethical decline. It is almost at the end of the play, with the return to the first scene's setting of Knightsbridge at Easter 1962, that a climax is reached with Susan's despairing rejection of Britain's post-war "plenty". Having thrown her material possessions out of the window and given her and Brock's house to Alice for use as a home for unmarried mothers, she is accused by Brock of being personally "selfish, brutish, unkind. Jealous of other people's happiness as well, determined to destroy other ways of happiness they find".[57] At this point, although the chronology of the play has come full circle and has effectively been used to parallel Susan's private mental deterioration with the wider public moral and ethical decline of post-war Britain, Brock's words suggest the kind of personal, psychological explanation of her behaviour which Hare recognised had sometimes been grasped at by British audiences.

The play's penultimate scene which follows the one discussed above is set some six months later, in June 1962, in a dark and dingy hotel room in Blackpool. Susan has left Brock and is seeking a reunion with Lazar, the wartime agent with whom she had shared a brief but intense relationship during the war. In this scene the private concerns of the play are resolved with Susan's realisation that for her "there's only one kind of dignity, that's in living alone"[58] and with the revelation that Lazar, in an alternative response to Susan's resistance to the post-war situation, has compromised his life and idealism—"I gave in. Always. All along the line. Suburb. Wife. Hell. I work in a corporate bureaucracy as well. . . ."[59] If the visual seediness of this scene is intended to convey emotively that despair into which Susan and many others in Britain had fallen, then the contrast provided by the bright lighting and colour of the *coup de théâtre* of the play's final scene which now forms itself piece by piece before the audience's eyes is used by Hare to emphasise the sad irony of what might have been for Britain had post-war hopes been realised. "There will be days and days and days like this"[60] is Susan's and the play's ironic final line which unites her own and her country's tragedy and thereby neatly resolves both the private and public elements of the play's structure. I use the word "resolve" but, although there may be a structural resolution, the absence of any clearly defined ideological stance within the play means that the audience is still left unsure as to whether it has been watching a portrait of a woman in crisis whose destructive personality has a tendency to alienate both the audience and her fellow characters, or whether Hare intends the play not as an Ibsenite study of character but simply as a parable of England's post-war moral and ethical decline. On the basis of a statement made by Hare during his 1978 Cambridge lecture that "to me it would be sad if a whole generation's lives were shaped by the fact that a belief in change had fallen temporarily out of fashion",[61] it would appear that he believed that by depicting a human spirit yearning for the highest personal, social and moral values and inhibited from reaching them only by the amorality and spiritual destitution of post-war British capitalism, his chronicle would contribute positively in counteracting that stasis and defeatism which he saw around him. Bearing these factors in mind, the play can be described neither as political agit-prop nor simply as a pathological case-study of a deranged woman. Perhaps, then, the most appropriate description of *Plenty* is that it is a moral fable.

By 1980, when Brenton was once more to counterpoint past and present in his historical allegory *The Romans in Britain*, speculation about revolution was no longer appropriate. In the words of Catherine Itzin, "the Conservative axe had begun to hack the heart out of such socialist structures as had been built within Britain's mixed economy after the war",[62] and the Left now found itself forced increasingly to take up a defensive rather than an offensive posture.

Brenton in some measure reflected this change by abandoning the subject of potential socialist revolution which had been central to his work during the 1970s and turning instead in *The Romans* to the situation in Northern Ireland and, characteristically, to the historical myths that contributed to the perpetuation of its problems. In doing so he nevertheless continued to draw upon Situationist tactics which would administer a cultural shock to the audience. As theatrical history now records, the cultural shock in fact proved to be enormous. Ostensibly at least, this was neither a consequence of Brenton's irreverent treatment of national myth nor his reference to the politically sensitive topic of England's role in Northern Ireland, but resulted from the inclusion in one scene of the simulated homosexual rape of a Celt by a Roman soldier. As Brenton undoubtedly realised, it was the venue for this act—not a tiny fringe theatre but the Olivier stage of the National Theatre—which did more than anything to provoke the subsequent hysterical response from Mrs Whitehouse and the political Right. The National Theatre, in consequence of that status denoted by its name, is of course second only to national television in the potential impact of its product. In fact much of the discussion surrounding the play and the court action brought by Mrs Whitehouse against its director, Michael Bogdanov, was scarcely if at all concerned with the work itself but rather with the principle of censorship.

Brenton's treatment of history in *The Romans in Britain* has a number of features in common with that exhibited in his earlier works. Foremost of these lies in the interweaving of past and present, the aim here being to suggest that England's treatment of Ireland is yet another example of that process of colonisation from which, the play suggests ironically, the English nation was itself created. Associated with this is the demystification of that form of myth-making employed by one race to characterise another and thereby to justify its colonial ambitions. Set, in an epic manner, against such momentous historical events as the Roman army's reconnaissance of southern Britain in 54 BC, prior to its invasion of Britain in the following year, and the Saxon invasion of England in AD 515 are the perceptions of various ordinary people whose lives were either destroyed or radically altered by those historic events. Within the play these significant historical moments are structurally inter-related by means of the repetition of various themes and motifs, by the paralleling of individual experience and, overtly, by an individual English army major's humanistic attempt to construct a connection between past and present. In a preview interview with Philip Oakes published in *The Sunday Times*, Brenton was unequivocal both in his acknowledgement of the play's points of reference and in his admission of the political necessity for treating the topic of Northern Ireland in meta-phorical terms. The topic of Northern Ireland was, it must be remem-bered, a subject that, with the notable exception of the "outsiders" John Arden and Margaret D'Arcy, had been largely avoided by mod-ern British political dramatists. "What my play says is that all Empire is bad", asserted Brenton,

The Republican cause is just. The border is a crime. But bald statements are no good. To convince an audience of the truth of my arguments I find myself writing about Britain in 54 BC and a British officer going off his head in an Irish cornfield today.[63]

The initial link between past and present takes place at the end of Part 1 of the play, which has hitherto been concerned with the effects on the indigenous Celts of the Roman incursion and has introduced the historic figure of Julius Caesar. A slave girl brought from Ireland by the "British" Celts stands on the north bank of the River Thames in 54 BC holding a stone, having just killed the criminal Conlag. By means of the type of Situationist *coup de théâtre* which, as I have illustrated, was particularly favoured by both Brenton and Hare, she is transformed into an Irish child about to hurl a stone at the soldiers who emerge from upstage, dressed not as they were earlier in the Roman garments of Caesar's invasion force, but now wearing 1970s British Army uniforms and equipment. The girl is shot by the sol-diers and the transformation into the present is completed by the sound of an army helicopter whirring overhead and by the entrance of an army jeep containing Julius Caesar, who is now also trans-formed into a British army officer on patrol in Northern Ireland. The scene concludes with Caesar's justification of the shooting of the girl by his troops in language which has been used throughout the ages to vindicate militarism and imperialism, "that everyday life will begin again. That civilisation may not sink, its great battle lost".[64] The ubiquitous myth of imperialism is that of racial superiority. As here, it inevitably associates imperialist ambition with civilisation and jus-tice and characterises those who are oppressed as ignorant and bar-baric. Throughout the play, by repeatedly revealing the motives behind such myth-making, Brenton sought to provoke the audience to consider that, in fact, it might be English myths concerning Northern Ireland which were, in part, responsible for inhibiting any resolution of its problems.

The Romans is full of myth-making. Characters frequently recollect stories from the past or create myths about the present. This myth-making arises mainly out of a need to come to terms with things that are unfamiliar and therefore frightening. As Oakes points out in his preview, throughout the play Brenton successfully "describes legends and myths, rationalising their purpose without denying their magic".[65] Daui, the Irish criminal who is on the run at the beginning of the play, for example, describes the Romans to the Celts who capture him in this manner: "The sun shines out of their navels. Two navels. And big, very big men. In metal. When they walk they clank."[66] Unfortunately for him his attempt to use myth to assert his own superiority over the "farmer boy" Brac and to frighten those who threaten him fails, and he is up-ended and his throat is cut by Brac's brother, Marban. Later, the matriarch of their tribe pours scorn upon the stories concerning the Romans which describe them as having "Eagles instead of heads to scare the boys. Cocks of brass to scare the girls".[67] When the three Celtic brothers, Marban (who is subsequently raped), Brac and Viridio, first set eyes upon three Roman soldiers they realise that the latter are in fact human, that they have got neither eagles' heads nor brass balls that clang when they walk. Brenton sets these myths against the real secret of the Romans' military superiority and imperial success. This has been correctly assessed earlier in the play by a Celtic envoy who, unlike the majority of his countrymen, has himself actually seen the Roman invaders. Contrasting the Roman army with the feuding Celtic tribes he points out that they are united and therefore strong. The overall implication is therefore that only by not believing in myth, by facing up to reality and by uniting their forces will the Celts stand any chance of defeating the Romans.

While in *The Romans* Brenton exhibits once again his enjoyment of *demythification*, he also accompanies this with his equally characteristic technique of *demagnification*. At the end of part one, for example, he reveals the less glorious aspects of Roman imperialism. With the entrance of Julius Caesar we learn that, in spite of its military efficiency and superiority, the Roman army's invasion of Britain has, in its commander's opinion, "deteriorated into a squalid little raid".[68] We also learn that, in common with all attempts at colonisation, this one was motivated by nothing grander than material gain, in this case in the form of fresh-water pearls. This ignoble expedition will, however, be appropriately elevated in Caesar's official biography which, it appears, the civilian historian, Asinus, has been brought along to compile. Asinus is under no illusion concerning his role. He realises that he and his fellow historians are paid by Caesar simply to establish omens which can be seen to have marked him out for future greatness, while in practice "he does nothing. He only reacts. And he finds himself the master of continents".[69] Here again the heroic leader is viewed in Marxist terms not as one who initiates change or whose destiny it is to rule but, in spite of Caesar's attempts to suggest otherwise, merely as a public functionary elevated to greatness by the needs of the moment.

The Roman army is portrayed not as the efficient fighting machine of legend but as a force plagued by inept leadership, prone to barbarity and devoid of honour, dignity or internal loyalty. It is commanded by such upper-class twits as the Legate who has only obtained his commission in consequence of Caesar's seduction of his sister. His patron is, however, now tired of him and issues orders that he be discreetly killed. Caesar himself is portrayed as being more interested in self-aggrandisement than in the expedition upon which he has embarked. He is suffering from an aching tooth which, under the gaze of some of his troops, he ostentatiously extracts with his knife. These troops, when left to themselves, commit acts of casual violence, and in the notorious attempted homosexual rape scene Brenton intensifies the horror of their unprovoked assault upon the Celt, Marban, by accompanying it by the soldier's comic but obscene repartee. In this and in other confrontations between soldiers and the indigenous population in both the ancient British and modern Irish settings, the soldiers consistently dehumanise the natives by referring to them as wogs, niggers or bog-shitting micks. Killing such creatures becomes therefore no more remarkable than squashing an ant. This, Brenton implies, is the real obscenity of imperialism, one which is still perpetuated today by racialist and often obscene jokes such as, "Why are Catholic tarts the best?" . . . "Because they've got rhythm",[70] which, in the second part of the play, the British undercover officer, Chichester, employs to identify himself with the British army patrol that detains him in Northern Ireland. Throughout the play Brenton further conveys his contempt for the armies of occupation in a somewhat adolescent manner by means of the widespread employment of anal and excremental references. On our first encounter with the legendary Roman army we witness one of them attempting to bugger a Celtic youth (like the present English army the Roman soldier also fails to dominate the Celt), while Caesar himself is accompanied both by a latrine detail and by characters named Asinus and Primus Pilus. Of course all of this is intended to contribute to the play's predominant, angry assertion that British imperialism is "buggering" Ireland. It is, however, arguably too superficial a statement to be transformed into the most conspicuous image in the play.

The second part of the play opens in 1980 in a field in Northern Ireland where, as I have mentioned above, an undercover agent with the very English name of Chichester is waiting to meet and to assassinate an I.R.A. leader. The historical scenes in this part of the play are set during the Saxon invasion of Britain in AD 515 and concern variously the plight of an old Roman matron and of a number of Celtic refugees, all of whom are fleeing before the Saxon advance. The suggestion of alien intrusion embodied in the play's title and illustrated in its first part is paralleled in the second by a reference to the alien presence of English troops in contemporary Northern Ireland as akin to that of spacemen on the moon. Past and present are similarly linked by the parallel between the Irish whiskey and Iron Curtain gun carried by Chichester and the iron and wine carried by the Irish criminals who open the play, or by the modern English soldier's assertion that he is in Ireland to dig toilets, which refers back to the similar occupation undertaken, equally unwillingly, by the troops of the Roman empire. Most striking, however, are Chichester's own utterances which explicitly link the modern Irish with the ancient Celts and are used by Brenton to suggest that it is crucial that the English should understand and acknowledge that the difference between themselves and the Irish is not merely regional but fundamentally racial. In respect of this Chichester points out that, besides imposing *territorial* imperialism upon Ireland, the English have also been guilty of cultural imperialism, exemplified by their appropriation of the *Celtic* hero, Arthur, for their own mythology. Today, Chichester claims ironically, Arthur would be to the English simply one more Irishman, now fighting them as in earlier times he had fought the Saxons.

It is predominantly by means of such patterned repetition that Brenton conveys the constants of imperialism. When he introduces an Anglo-Saxon warrior in Act 2 Scene 4, the man speaks a language unintelligible both to the Celtic characters onstage and to the audience, thus making the point that his descendants, the English, were themselves just another alien race bent on colonisation. Conspicuously it is only the Celts who appear in each of the historical periods covered by the play. It is they alone, the play implicitly states, who in spite of repeated colonial incursion, have maintained their identity to this day.

In the penultimate scene Brenton uses Chichester's meeting with the I.R.A. man, O'Rourke, to draw together the common experiences represented in the play's various historical periods. Chichester confesses his true status and the purpose of his meeting with O'Rourke and speaks in condemnation of British imperialism in Northern Ireland. He also recognises that, historically, he is simply another link in a continuous chain of oppression and exploitation. He admits that ". . . in my hand there's a Roman spear. A Saxon axe. A British Army machine gun. The weapons of Rome, invaders, Empire".[71] In each period these weapons have been used against the native Celts. Out of a desire to free himself from the chain, Chichester unfortunately succumbs to liberal romanticism by talking of throwing down his weapons and resurrecting from the peat and water those who perished in earlier imperial wars. Up until this point the woman accompanying O'Rourke has remained silent but, provoked by Chichester's words, she now responds angrily, accusing him of not facing reality and of creating yet another myth concerning Ireland.

> WOMAN: What right does he have to stand in a field in Ireland and talk of the horrors of war? What nation ever learnt from the sufferings it inflicted on others? What did the Roman Empire give to the people it enslaved? Concrete. What did the British Empire give to its colonies? Tribal wars. I don't want to hear of this British soldier's humanity. And how he comes to be howling in the middle of my country. And how he thinks Ireland is a tragedy. Ireland's troubles are not a tragedy. They are the crimes his country has done mine. That he does to me, by standing there.[72]

By describing the troubles in Northern Ireland as a tragedy, Chichester, the liberal intellectual, is accepting them as inevitable. On the other hand, in retaliating that the situation is *not* a tragedy and that it is the English who are responsible for Ireland's "tribal wars", the woman is able to make Chichester the scapegoat for British imperialism, and he is consequently executed. Brenton is suggesting therefore that the humanist can never provide the solution to Ireland's problem for, like Captain Thompson in *The Churchill Play*, he is incapable of taking radical measures and therefore simply attempts to rearrange and make more palatable the present situation.

   While employing myth and history in the construction of his play, Brenton also successfully deconstructs both of these in order to reveal their purpose and effect as demonstrated in English attitudes and behaviour in relation to Northern Ireland. To emphasise the significance of this process Brenton concludes *The Romans* with a scene that acts as a kind of coda to the play's earlier myth-making. In this scene one of the Celtic cooks whose Roman mistress has been previously killed by her steward, and who has now decided that he will become a poet, improvises the utopian myth of King Arthur:

Actually, he was a King who never was.

His government was the people of Britain. His peace was as common as rain or sun. His law was as natural as grass growing in a meadow.

And there never was a Government, or a peace, or a law like that. . . .

And when he was dead, the King who never was and the government that never was—were mourned. And remembered. Bitterly.

And thought of as a golden age, lost and yet to come.[73]

The second cook is left to give the king "any old name". He casually chooses "Arthur".[74] Another myth has been created before our very eyes. It has no more truth in it than any other and has simply been invented to satisfy the particular needs of the moment. Brenton revealed to Philip Oakes precisely what he had in mind at this point in the play: "I believe that Arthur was invented some evening in a ditch for a good historical purpose", he suggested. "He was needed. He gave voice to the aspirations of a defeated people; the once and future King. I dislike all Nationalistic myths. This is a peace play. It's about the survival of individuals, none of them exemplary."[75] Brenton has indeed woven a complex web of myth, history and personal opinion in which a number of private individuals attempt to survive as the epic events of history are enacted elsewhere. For them myth can be a comfort but is more commonly an articulation of fear or a weapon of oppression. The play forcefully demonstrates how potent these myths can be.

Some four years later, in *Bloody Poetry* (1984) which he wrote for the Foco Novo theatre company and which was first performed at the Leicester Haymarket Theatre, Brenton's approach to history had changed. Gone was the iconoclasm, the demystification and the epic sweep which, in various permutations, had characterised his earlier treatment of history. Gone also were the Situationist *coups de thé-âtre*, to be replaced by a more private study which encompassed both an exploration, implied by the play's title, of the role of the radical artist and of the possibility of creating that utopia which many of the characters in his earlier plays had believed in but not achieved. Written in the wake of Margaret Thatcher's second election victory which reinstated a government whose professed aim had been, from the outset, to terminate the post-war era of British socialism, the play reflected the changed political climate in which Brenton now found himself. For the time being the Left had been effectively discredited and the revolutionary fervour of the 1970s now already seemed a distant part of history. In the play a political writer is similarly distanced from the political activity which he seeks to support. Deprived of the latter and left only to construct *private* utopias, the politically committed artist, the play reveals, will remain an isolated voice accomplishing, in *public* terms, little or nothing.

Bloody Poetry portrays Shelley and Byron, who with their mistresses Mary Godwin (soon to become Mary Shelley) and her stepsister, Claire Clairmont, attempted to create a private utopia in Switzerland and Italy in the years between 1816 and 1822. Brenton has expressed his admiration for the group's attempt to discover a new way of living, even though that attempt, in common with that of many of the "hippy" communes of the 1960s and 1970s which the play's situation is undoubtedly intended to resemble, ended in grief and failure. The biographical and personal nature of the material makes it ideally suited to individualistic psychological or romantic treatment, but Brenton, while dramatising the private concerns and relationships of the group, is careful to avoid either personal psychology or romanticism. Indeed this rejection of the personal is clearly stated in one of Brenton's *Sonnets of Love and Opposition*, written with reference to Shelley himself:

Shelley said to me, when
I asked for a tip, "Write first
For a new world, only second
of the world within—Always of
Men, women, nature and society.[76]

Clearly aware of the potential tendency of an audience to focus upon the personal aspects of the situation, Brenton attempts, at the commencement of the play, to endistance his characters by providing them with a clear awareness of the mythic status that history will bestow upon their present travels. In the second scene, which is preceded only by a short monologue delivered by Shelley, Claire parodies the descriptions that will be self-consciously recorded in their own diaries or recalled, romanticised, by some later biographer: "The two poets meet on a beach. Lights blaze off the water, behind them. In their exile, they embrace. It will be like a statue. And I have been the lover of one, and am the lover of the other." She goes on to claim joyously that "all of us, we will become magnificent. The men and women of the future will thank us. We are their great experiment. We will find out how to live and love, without fear." Mary's response is to dispel the vision cynically with the words, "If the money does not run out".[77] The actual meeting between Shelley and Byron, which is enacted later in the scene, in fact turns out to be awkward and combative, and the working out of the "experiment" which the play goes on to portray is characterised by individual selfishness and cruelty on the part of the two poets. Nevertheless, rather than simply exploring the psychological and emotional forces at work within the group's peculiar configuration of personal inter-relationships, Brenton places their private, libertarian behaviour within a public context by emphasising that their activities were a contemporary source of public gossip and scandal. This public context is evoked primarily by the presence of Dr. Polidori, Byron's personal physician and official literary recorder of his travels in Europe. Polidori, who is jealous and therefore censorious of their fame and lifestyle, attempts to describe the group's activities in a manner that will enhance his own reputation both as a writer and a confidant. Reference is also made in the play to the prurient contemporary journalistic pre-occupation, particularly on the part of the *Daily Mail*, with the poets' libertarianism. As today, such gutter journalism was then employed either to draw attention away from any political criticism levelled by the artist or to denigrate his political commitment. Speaking of the Peterloo Massacre about which he has written, Shelley declares in exasperation, "the world is catching fire, the oppressors have bloodied their hands! But what excites the educated classes? The behaviour of the rich and famous in bed".[78] Earlier Claire has quoted from a "review" published in *The Daily Mail* which by means of a laborious simile refers to Shelley's life-style in order to deprecate his poetry: "Mr. Shelley is a bad poet. Like a bad tennis player, his verses forever smash into the net and fall to the ground. But Mr. Shelley is lucky. Two beautiful girls crouch on the sidelines, waiting to pick up his balls."[79]

The political signficance of the group is provided partly by the biographical fact that Mary's father and Claire's step-father was William Godwin, the libertarian Socialist and author of *Enquiry Concerning Political Justice* and partly by reference both to Shelley's *The Mask of Anarchy* and to Byron's anarchistic political views. The play's irony is of course that, although in terms of their life-style the group are rejecting English Establishment values, in doing so they are marooned in their utopia from the sometimes violent political activity taking place in England. Byron is, in contrast to Shelley, portrayed as an active rather than intellectual revolutionary. He recognises that the writer cannot change the world by himself and for his work to have any real purpose it must have an actual revolution to support or celebrate:

BYRON: A war. If only there were a war in England, not that endless—slow, sullen defeat. Why don't the bastards take up arms against such a government? Then we poets would be of some use, we'd do the songs, the banners, the shouts, but no. Sullen silence.[80]

At the close of the play their "voluptuous flight" and their attempt to be "Good, great, and joyous, beautiful and free"[81] fails and the group falls asunder. On the death of their daughter in Italy, Mary berates Shelley for the "pointless cruelty of all your schemes. . . . The endless—hopeless—schemes, and dreams, and . . . ".[82] She goes on to associate ironically what she sees to be the private and public failures of Shelley's recent life. When he reveals that he has written *The Mask of Anarchy* she declares that it will not, for political reasons, be published in England and scoffs, "The great revolutionary, English poem—unpublishable! Bury it in your daughter's coffin, poet",[83] the title of poet now being used to denote irrelevancy and failure and thereby becoming the ultimate insult.

Both Brenton and Hare's solo and combined historical plays successfully offered a novel and radical approach to historical drama. In these works the portrayal of private experience was employed to gain audience empathy, while Situationist deconstructive techniques were occasionally applied to promote new ways of seeing and epic sweeps of history were evoked to convey the possibility of change. As we have seen, this theatrical approach was clearly influenced by the interests of the contemporary Left, in that it combined Situationist disruption of the surface reality with Marxist theories concerning the interaction of public and private experience in the formation of individual character and the views of the New Left regarding the individual's place within socialism. Thus, "whether the criteria by which we have brought up are right; [sic] whether what each of us experiences uniquely really is what makes us valuable; whether every man should really be his own cocktail; or whether our criteria could and should be collective, and if they were, whether we would be any happier"[84] were the questions that lay behind much of both Hare and Brenton's historical drama.

Along with Edward Bond and David Edgar, during the 1970s and early 1980s Brenton and Hare were to establish radical historical drama within Britain's institutional theatres, the National and the Royal Shakespeare. Part of their success arguably may be attributed to the fact that, while they assaulted, on Brenton's part sometimes with considerable loathing, the Capitalist values of the Establishment as represented in its version of history, both were unwilling to propagandise for any alternative ideology. This, I am sure, was evidence neither of political cowardice nor of that career opportunism which would prompt them to eschew any political stance that might prove unacceptable to their predominantly middle-class audiences. Their attitude would appear rather to reflect a constitutional unpreparedness on the part of both dramatists to believe that, as Hare himself has concluded, "a few gim-crack mottoes of the Left will sort out the deep problems of reaction in Modern England".[85]

Edward Bond's Historical Allegories

One dramatist who, during the 1970s, set out consciously to develop a form of historical drama peculiarly suited to the political circumstances of contemporary Britain was Edward Bond. In 1978, with *The Woman*, it seemed that he had achieved his goal. Bond belonged to the generation that preceded that of Brenton and Hare and, by 1978, had a career stretching back some sixteen years to 1962. *The Woman*, of which he was also the director, was, however, the first of his plays to be performed by an institutional theatre, in this case the National, his work having for the most part been previously produced at the Royal Court. As had Brenton and Hare, in a preview interview he too justified his presence, as an extremely outspoken left-wing writer and director, within what John McGrath had described as the bastion of Establishment culture. Like Brenton and Hare he claimed an affinity with the large stages offered by the National. Plays set in small rooms he considered reflected a bourgeois mentality, whereas as a socialist, his own preference was for almost bare, open stages and exterior settings. "We need to set our scenes in public places where history is formed, classes clash and whole societies move. Otherwise we're not writing about the events that most affect us and shape our future", he asserted, and he went on to observe that the Olivier stage of the National Theatre was "ideally suited to this sort of theatre". Its effect was to call for "broad unfidgety acting that moves from image to image, each image graphically analysing the story".[1] This he saw as the expression of the public level of the play. Its private level, which he had grown to consider to be equally important to the communication of political dialectic, could then be established: "When the audience's attention has been won in this way it's possible to do very small, subtle things", he maintained, concluding that "this combination of large and small, far and near is the visual language of politics."[2] As far as his own play *The Woman* was concerned, it also needed about forty actors to perform almost a hundred parts. This was a size of cast available only to a large institutional theatre such as the National.

By this point in his career, history had become both a major target and an important tool in Bond's analysis of the nature of capitalist society and in his attempt to outline an alternative way of living. His concern with history was primarily intellectual and was centred upon historical issues rather than events. Like Arden's, Bond's plays of the 1970s were also to display an increasingly analytical and specific political awareness. This had evolved from the intuitive perception of the social iniquities of modern capitalism, which had produced the sheer anger revealed in early plays such as *Saved* (1965), into the sharper analysis of capitalism's inherent flaws. This process had been accompanied, from *Bingo* (1973) onwards, by various attempts on Bond's part to suggest and inspire alternative ways of organizing society. His first history play, *Early Morning*, belonged to the initial phase described above. It represented an *assault* upon history, and in its emotionally charged tone, its surrealistic structure, its attack upon the icons of an authoritarian, Capitalist society and its yearning for freedom and change as represented in the character of Arthur, it could be seen to reflect the anarchistic impulses of its period. In *Early Morning* for the first time Bond was to explore freely the stage's potential for visual imagery and the effect of the selective use of properties on a bare stage. These features were to characterise Bond's later historical drama whose narrative moves from one visual image to the next, each signified and extended by the verbal imagery that accompanies it, and each being a function of the concerns of the work itself rather than referring to universal forces or ideas outside the play. Thus Shakespeare's garden in *Bingo* has only symbolic meaning within the play itself, where it reflects Shakespeare's self-exile from the world and his emotional isolation from his family. The precision with which these images are communicated and the overall epic structure of the plays of which they are a part undoubtedly owes much to the example of Brecht, whose economical technique Bond had emulated in 1968 in *Narrow Road to the Deep North* in response to the critical incomprehension that had greeted the anarchic style of *Early Morning*.

In the 1960s and early 1970s "violence" and "aggression" were Bond's most favoured words in his prefatory analyses of capitalism and its consequences. However, with the advance of the 1970s and the sharpening of his political awareness, the concept of "culture" was gradually to take over as a major theme of Bond's public utterances. These references to "culture" may be seen to reveal Bond's now more acute identification of the mechanics of capitalism and of the social implications of its various assumptions. In 1975, in the preface to *The Fool*, he defined culture as "the rational creation of human nature, the implementation of rationality in all human activity, economic, political, social, public and private". The task of culture, he suggested, was to "show how we can live and how we ought to live so that there is a future for us".[3] Capitalism, according to Bond, is irrational and has no culture. It merely possesses an organisation and a technology. Consequently it employs myths, such as those concerning the innate evil within human nature, in order to justify its authoritarian treatment of human beings and thereby maintain its supremacy. He concluded, therefore, that the artist's role in society was to contribute to the creation of a rational culture, and it was with these things in mind that, from 1973 onwards, in *Bingo* (1973), *The Fool* (1975) and *The Woman* (1978), he was to turn to historical themes.

In these plays he "tried to deal with society at three important stages of cultural development". The past often works as a myth on the present", he maintained; "It is like a burden on our back and from time to time we have to rearrange it so that it becomes comfortable and we can go on with our journey."[4] The three stages were: in *Bingo*, the beginnings of the enclosure movement which may be viewed as the commencement of the evolution of British society from feudalism to capitalism; in *The Fool*, the start, after 1815, of the Industrial Revolution; and in *The Woman*, the establishment in the aftermath of a war of an exploitive, materialistic and affluent state which is devoid of spiritual values. In a more positive vein than that exhibited in the earlier two plays, *The Woman* also implies the possibility of a successful armed insurrection which would displace a materialistic and exploitive regime. In these plays history is used to illustrate that capitalist values are indivisibly linked to the creation of material wealth and that "when livelihood and dignity depend on money, human values are replaced by money values". The lesson Bond intends to impart to his audience is that although it may be argued that the physical cruelty and material poverty of the past have been replaced in most Western capitalist societies by relative prosperity for the majority of their citizens, in fact the quality of human life has not improved, for "a consumer society depends on its members being avaricious, ostentatious, gluttonous, envious, wasteful, selfish and inhuman. Officially we teach morality but if we all became 'good' the economy would collapse".[5]

Bingo, the first of these three plays, in common with all Bond's forays into history, represents a "vision" and is in no sense intended to be understood as objective historical truth. "I'm not really interested in Shakespeare's true biography in the way a historian might be",[6] stated Bond categorically in his introduction to the play. Instead he was more concerned with the ideological assumptions contained within the accepted mythology surrounding Shakespeare, the cultural icon. By altering those basic assumptions he aimed to produce an alternative view of Shakespeare whose discrepancy would provoke a re-evaluation of the values embodied in the accepted mythology. The anachronistic title, "Bingo", with its association of easy money is intended both to emphasise the economic rather than aesthetic concerns represented in Bond's version of the Shakespeare myth and, in common with his earlier use of anachronism, to affiliate past and present.

In *Bingo* stage imagery takes precedence over plot in its epic structure of "Scenes of Money and Death". Part 1 of the play is set in the open air, a location consistently associated by Bond with socio-political rather than personal concerns. The predominant image of this part of the play is of Shakespeare, spatially isolated, in his garden at New Place in Stratford, the garden itself being divided from the outside world by a hedge. A dramatist intent upon Naturalism would, of course, have embarked from here upon a psychological study, perhaps of the artist's *weltschmerz*. Although focusing the whole play upon this isolated figure, Bond, however, communicates little concerning Shakespeare's individual psychology and nothing about his writing. Instead, the first part of the play is motivated by the intrusion into his space, both physical and mental, of the outside world. The intruders are a young woman vagrant, Shakespeare's old gardener, the gardener's wife who is also his family's servant, the latters' son (all victims of the economic system to which we learn Shakespeare gives passive support), Shakespeare's own daughter Judith, and a landlord, Combe. On the private level we learn that Shakespeare recognises no emotional ties, even to his family. On the public level we see that he has also isolated himself from the barbarities of the world beyond his garden hedge. In the final scene of Part 1 which is set, significantly, on a hill *outside* the town, Shakespeare is, however, forced to face up to the reality of the wider world of which he is also a part. The nature of this world is signified most clearly by the figure of the young female vagrant who, having being convicted of arson, has been hung from the gibbet. It is a world of exploitation in which the kind of enclosures proposed by Combe will produce even more vagrants who will in their turn be punished for attempting to survive. Combe has

earlier justified that process of enclosure which will produce this iniquitous situation by citing a myth that conveniently suits his own purposes: "Men are donkeys, they need carrots and sticks. . . . That's why
we can get rid of bad farmers who *grow* starvation in their fields like
a crop, and create seven hundred poor in a town of less than two
thousand."[7] The potential victims, in an attempt to halt the
enclosures, are indeed sometimes provoked to violence, thereby
appearing to confirm the myth that force is needed to control them.

Part 2 contains two interior scenes. The first is set in a tavern and
portrays Shakespeare's drinking session with Ben Jonson. The
second, which is also the play's final scene and during which Shakespeare dies, is set in his bedroom at New Place. By their nature each
of these scenes forces its characters into close physical proximity.
This is utilised by Bond to intensify the demands made upon Shakespeare, first by Jonson who wants to borrow money, and then by his
daughter Judith who, in the harrowing final scene of the play, breaks
into Shakespeare's room. As he lies dying on the floor, having taken
poison, Judith rifles through his possessions in a frantic search for his
will. In both these scenes the desire for money and material possessions takes precedence over family concern or friendship. Indeed,
along with Combe, Judith and Jonson are used by Bond to represent
varieties of that aggression, greed and insensitivity which Bond
attributes to capitalism.

By installing him in the garden of New Place, from the beginning
of the play Bond associates Shakespeare not with literature but primarily with property. As the first scene develops Bond also focuses
upon Shakespeare's involvement in the plans put forward by Combe
and others to enclose the Welcombe Estate in Stratford. In return for
financial guarantees concerning his own income from rents for land
that he owns on the estate, Shakespeare agrees not to side with the
town council against Combe's enclosures. He is nevertheless keen to
point out that any action that he may or may not take is based not
upon support for the principle of enclosure but results purely from
self-interest. Shakespeare's belief that in this crude manner he can
opt out of any responsibility for the consequences brought about by
the economic system with which he has chosen to associate himself
has, however, by the close of the play, undergone a change, a change
that begins when he is confronted by the body of the young woman
hanging from the gibbet. At the end of the play he has begun to
acknowledge that the economic system by which he lives permits only
a minority of people to prosper, and they only at the expense of the
majority. With the image of the gibbet in his mind he is finally also
forced to admit that, as a liberal, humanitarian artist, he "howled

when they suffered, but they were whipped and hanged so that I could be free".[8] He further realises that, however humane it may be to howl, his drama has done nothing to halt or even alleviate the real suffering and barbarity of the age. He describes how, on his way to the theatre, he passed beneath displays of severed human heads, and how his lines were spoken onstage accompanied by the nearby sounds of bear-baiting. Thus Bond ingeniously introduces the theme of the "corrupt seer" who lives in a "barbarous civilisation"[9] similar to our own.

What Bond is not saying is that Shakespeare's plays were incapable of confronting or altering his society but that, by using the income from his writing to purchase New Place and presumably to invest in the Welcombe Estate, Shakespeare had made his art part of that iniquitous economic system of which enclosures were a feature. Any opposition to the further development of this economic system would inevitably affect Shakespeare's own financial security and therefore he attempts to avoid the issue. Towards the close of the play, however, he returns repeatedly to the question, "Was anything done",[10] this repetition being used by Bond to emphasise Shakespeare's ultimate admission of his culpability for the exploitation and death of others, a culpability that in Bond's opinion should not be excused by the fact that he had written a few humanitarian plays. He concluded that, faced with this realisation, suicide was for Shakespeare the only morally admissible choice. "If he didn't end in the way shown in the play", wrote Bond contentiously, "then he was a reactionary blimp or some other fool. The only more charitable account is that he was unaware or senile."[11]

As a whole, the play ingeniously combines the few public and private facts known about Shakespeare's life to create a metaphor which is used to explore the role of the artist in a capitalist society. In contrast to Bax and Rubenstein's romantic biographical treatment of the bard's life, by portraying Shakespeare for the most part as unemotional and apparently unconcerned with the lives of others, Bond keeps the audience detached from his character in order that it may view more critically the play's metaphoric implications. Nevertheless, Bond's iconoclastic suggestion that Shakespeare "supported and benefited from the Goneril-society—with its prisons, workhouses, whipping, starvation, mutilation, pulpit-hysteria and all the rest of it"[12] also emotively provokes the audience to reassess the myth surrounding Shakespeare and, in their inevitable attempt to reinstate their icon, perhaps to ask themselves whether politically even today anything has been or should be changed.

Although in *The Fool* (1975) Bond was again to focus upon an individual artist, this time the nineteenth-century peasant–poet John Clare, he was now to widen that focus in order both to accommodate reference to the contemporary literary establishment and to provide a more detailed illustration of the politico-economic system in which Clare lived. Unlike Shakespeare, Clare does not profit from this economic system but instead is portrayed by Bond in a Situationist manner as one of its commodities. Each of the "Scenes of Bread and Love" which make up the play is used to illustrate the place of the artist and his product within a capitalist society. The play opens in a rural community in Northamptonshire in the years after 1815 when, with the renewed enclosure of common land and the beginnings of the Industrial Revolution, capitalism was entering a period of consolidation. The performance of the Mummers' Play during the first scene effectively establishes the master/servant hierarchy of the period. It also contrasts the traditional community values represented by the play with the nature of the new society that is being formed by the Industrial Revolution. This new society is hailed with enthusiasm by the Parson who is thereby identified with the gentry rather than the people, and the local aristocrat, Lord Milton, takes care to remind the labourers that society is subject to economic "laws" which are inescapable, but whose downside will affect them most of all. "The war made us all prosperous but prices have fallen with the peace. Wages must follow. Not because I say so. That is a law of economic science. Wages follow prices or civil institutions break down."[13]

We soon learn that the lower-class community that performs the mummers' play is being threatened by new enclosures. Like the labourers in *Bingo*, those menaced react spontaneously and violently to protect what they consider to be their common rights. In this case the reaction takes the form of the robbery of the haves by the have-nots. "You call us thief when we took silver", the farmworker Darkie tells the Parson as he and his fellows strip him and steal his possessions, "You took us flesh".[14] Violence in the play is not, however, confined to the lower classes. Institutionalised violence, perpetrated by armed game-keepers, the militia and the hangman, is also employed by the upper classes to maintain their authority. The difference between the two, as illustrated by Bond, is that the violence of the poor is defensive, whereas that of the rich is exploitive.

This brutal and exploitive public world has been firmly established by Bond before he actually reveals that Clare is a poet. In the first four scenes of the play Clare is simply portrayed as one of the group of farmworkers, being only individualised, somewhat romantically, in terms of his lively sexual appetite which is illustrated by his fondling of Patty, his playing with himself and his making love to Mary, all within the play's first scene. As the play progresses Clare is given a private dimension. He is alienated by his art from his lower-class social background whose values are dictated by the fight to stay alive and are portrayed by Clare's eventual wife, Patty, who prefers *bread* to poetry. Clare is adopted as a poet by fashionable upper-class society, represented by the figures of Mrs Emerson and the Admiral, whose support continues only as long as he accords with their romantic view of the poet as one who is decorative and morally or politically inoffensive. It is their fellow members of the upper class who purchase Clare's books, and it is they therefore who have the economic power to make or break him. Indeed it is the eventual unwillingness of that class to buy his works which ultimately leads to his financial ruin. Now alienated from both the upper and the lower classes, Clare descends into madness and, at the close of the play, lonely and insane, dies in a mental hospital. All Clare's personal problems are therefore attributed by Bond not to any inherent personality defect but to the social and economic iniquities of capitalism. The major problem faced by the poet is that, in a class-riven society where there is no accepted place for him amongst his own people, the upper class treat him as just another commodity which they are quick to abandon as soon as it no longer pleases them.

It is the fifth scene of *The Fool* which most effectively crystallizes the relationship between the play's two major elements—the brutal, money-orientated society and the working-class artist. The setting is a London park where Clare is first introduced by Mrs Emerson to his other patron, the Admiral, and to the brother and sister, Charles and Mary Lamb. Clare learns that, although he is a writer, Charles Lamb is forced to work as a clerk in order to survive—another reference to the "bread" element of the play's subtitle. Lamb also brings his art into close contact with money by surreptitiously writing poetry on "the back of bills and promissory notes when the Governor's out of the office".[15] Both Charles and Mary are shown to be victims of their society—a fate soon to be shared by Clare himself. Charles has taken to drink to escape the anomalies that make up his life, while his sister is gripped by a madness that takes the form of a consumerist fetish for buying huge and unnecessary quantities of food which are simply left to rot—yet another image of "bread"—employed this time to signify its status within a consumerist society. Again Bond portrays his characters' problems as emanating not from personal weakness but from external forces. Charles is suffering in consequence of society's low estimation of his calling and the difficulty of surviving as an artist in such an uncongenial social climate. He is nevertheless still able to recognise that "Clare tells the truth",[16] a dangerous virtue in a society that views the role of the artist as being merely decorative.

While these aspects are being explored through the dialogue spoken in the downstage area, upstage there is a bare-knuckle boxing-match. This simultaneous staging technique, also employed by Bond in other plays, conveys forcefully the nature of a society based upon the brutal exploitation of the working class. The boxing match is intended by Bond as an image of the nature of Capitalism for in this "sport" poor men, like the baited bears of Shakespeare's day, are urged to violence for the entertainment and financial gain of their superiors. It is such a society that, in the play, maintains its aura of respectability by purchasing as commodities such works of art as the poetry of John Clare or Charles Lamb and in doing so also takes possession of the poets themselves for as long as they are fashionable.

Although Bond portrays John Clare and Charles and Mary Lamb as the victims of an uncultured, capitalist economic system, there is in the play also a hint of optimism. This is conveyed primarily in the visionary sequence in which Clare, having escaped from the asylum, meets his idealised lost love, Mary, and the labourer Darkie, who has earlier been hanged at Ely for his part in the resistance to the enclosures. Clare fights with Darkie and is knocked out. Mary offers Darkie bread, which he is unable to swallow because of the damage inflicted to his neck by the hanging. As a result of this vision Clare realises that had he allied himself with the forces that they represent—caring love and political activism—his poetry might have been employed for political change. "I'd hev teach him how to eat", he says, "I am a poet an' I teach men how to eat. Then she on't goo in rags. He on't blind. An' I—on't go mad in a madhouse."[17] The message embodied in Clare's vision is that art must ally itself with a truth that can only be discovered amongst the lower orders of society and which, as Lamb has suggested earlier, is "often ugly" and "shelters in the gutter". As Lamb warns, however, truth leads to wisdom but wisdom may itself prove to be dangerous. It is therefore tempting for the artist to avoid it for:

The Goddess of Wisdom is a bird of prey, the owl. But the fools have hunted *her* and put her in a cage. If you try to let her out she savages your hand. Only a wise man tries to do that—or another sort of fool.[18]

Clare is portrayed by Bond as just another sort of fool. He is the foolish seer who, in consequence of this gift, is alienated and destroyed by a society that is not willing to acknowledge his truths.[19] By the close of the play Clare has become a "shrivelled puppet" driven mad by his alienation. He ends his life in a world of industrialisation and railways, a world in which his village community has been absorbed into a nearby expanding town which has destroyed its culture. Society's other victim, Charles Lamb, has finally died of drink. In the play's final scene Bond nevertheless leaves his audience with the call of wisdom's owl and a flash of brilliant light, together intended to signify that, as Clare's historical period is transformed into our own, truth and wisdom are still attainable.

As mentioned at the beginning of this chapter, 1978 was to bring *The Woman*, the most ambitious of Bond's three historical allegories, to the stage of the National Theatre. The subtitle, suggesting an epic approach similar to that of *Bingo* and *The Fool*, was "Scenes of War and Freedom". In *The Woman*, however, Bond's political views were to be more clearly formulated than in either of the two previous plays. Nevertheless, as Hay and Roberts point out in their book, *Bond: A Study of His Plays*, the play's dramatic structure, with its dramatisation of the process of historical change in terms of the experience of a central character, closely resembles that already employed by Bond in *Lear*.[20] In *The Woman* the central character is Hecuba, the Trojan Queen, who like Lear progresses from political blindness to actual physical blindness and from physical blindness to political enlightenment. As in *Lear*, the enlightenment is brought about by personal experience of the irrational human violence that results from the intrinsic injustice of the political structure of which the central character is initially a part.

In both *Lear* and *The Woman* this profound personal experience provokes the central character to undertake an individual revolutionary act. In *Lear* this amounts to little more than a gesture, whereas in *The Woman* it takes the form of the slaying of Heros, the representative of the old irrational order, by the proletarian miner who has been inspired and organised by the blind but newly politicised Hecuba. With Marxist confidence this act is presented by Bond as a "logical development of history".[21] In terms of the play's allegory, revolutionary action is therefore shown to be neither the sole responsibility of the intellectual nor of the worker. If necessary the two must join together in violent revolution in order to eliminate that more pervasive violence which was, in Bond's opinion, both domestically and internationally synonymous with capitalism. The spade wielded by Lear is replaced in *The Woman* by a weapon of war. "I have represented history", wrote Bond, "as a woman with a sword under her skirt",[22] thereby marking a significant change in his view both of history and of violence. In spite of her evident centrality in the play Hecuba is not, however, intended by Bond to be perceived as an exceptional person. "I also wish to make it clear that the woman and the miner are not superhuman archetypes", wrote Bond in an essay in *Plays Three*. "They are shown as individuals struggling to take decisions, who are no wiser, stronger or persistent than others may be. Society can be changed only because there are many people like them—and that is the only way in which they can represent the large forces working through centuries: they are ordinary people who change the world."[23]

The play's allegory may be interpreted as follows: In the first part of the play Bond reworks the Homeric myth of the Trojan Wars to portray a society that is locked into myth, not out of religious belief but as a means of perpetuating its political and economic structure. The myth is centred upon the aesthetically uninspiring statue of the Goddess of Good Fortune which Bond portrays, instead of Helen, as the prize stolen from the Greeks by the Trojans which has provoked the long-drawn-out Trojan war. The statue has brought the Trojans bad luck, and Heros, one of the Greek commanders, recognises the inherent flaw in the Greeks' superstitious belief that without the statue *they* are deprived of good fortune, which therefore means logically that they will *never* have the good fortune to recover it. He nevertheless employs sophistry to explain the problem away. Because the Trojans are holding the Goddess against her will, he *reasons* irrationally, "They fight but they can't win—the Goddess of Good Fortune will punish them by giving us victory".[24] Here in the opening minutes of the play Bond thereby reveals a society that refuses to recognise truth and whose irrationality has within it the seeds of its own destruction. It is this inevitability that the play's mythic/historical references are used to illustrate.

Into this situation Bond introduces Ismene, Heros' wife. She, in an attempt to break the stalemate that has overtaken the war, gives herself as a hostage to the Trojans so that they may be assured that if they return the statue they will not then by slaughtered by the Greeks. In so doing, Ismene attempts to replace the Goddess of Good Fortune by the Goddess of Good Sense, an act that is, however, viewed by the Trojans as blasphemy and by the Greeks as treason. As a result of a rebellion within Troy the statue is thrown out of the city. The Greeks nevertheless follow their usual practice of rape, pillage and destruction and leave Troy, taking with them the statue and the Trojan Queen, Hecuba, who, having been confronted by the horror of human violence, has blinded herself. Ismene, who has set human rationality against the irrationality represented by Heros' mythology, is silenced by being immured in the remains of the walls of Troy.

Part 2 of *The Woman* takes place on a remote island whose primitive community of gatherers has become a safe haven for Hecuba and Ismene. The latter, after her ordeal, is now partly mad. Having escaped from her immurement when the wall was opened by her

Greek guards in order to steal the jewellery which she had intentionally worn to appeal to their greed, Ismene crept aboard the ship on which Hecuba was being taken to Greece. During a storm which struck the Greek fleet as it was returning to Athens, the two women were cast ashore on the island by a huge waterspout and have since lived in safety. The chaos of war which dominated the first part of the play is now replaced by an altogether calmer pace. This, however, is disturbed by the arrival of the old Greek, Nestor, who has been sent by Heros to search for the statue which was lost during the same storm that released Hecuba and Ismene. Next to appear is the Dark Man, a physically deformed miner who has escaped from slavery in the silver mines which are the source of Athens' growing power and influence. Finally arrives Heros, who is so obsessed with the statue that he is prepared to destroy the island's community if it is not recovered.

As Bond has stated, in the play's allegorical scheme "is a man Heros, who stands for the classical values of beauty and order, and he is opposed by a miner who stands for a new order, for a new proletarian direction of history. There's a conflict between them and the miner wins."[25] The action of the second part illustrates that, in spite of its material plenty, Athens remains unjust and continues to rely upon its myths to endow it with moral and spiritual respectability— hence Heros' obsessive desire to recover the statue. It is Heros' obsession which is used by Hecuba to defeat him. Although she has discovered that the eye which she believed had escaped her self-blinding has also become useless, she convinces Heros that she is yet able to see and capitalizes on his superstition by telling him that, in a vision, the goddess has promised to permit her discovery if Heros wins a running race against the obviously decrepit miner. As might be expected Heros does indeed win the race but is told by Hecuba that he has been enchanted (as in Bond's terms he has been politically throughout his life) and that during the race he stopped to sleep thereby allowing the miner to win. Thrown into confusion and unable to obtain help from his superstitious faith, he is killed at Hecuba's behest by the miner. Nestor, having been alienated by Heros' authoritarian obsession, leaves the island without exacting revenge. Having saved the island from Heros, Hecuba is subsequently killed by a waterspout, the natural force which, by rescuing her from the shipwreck, has altered history. The storm image recurs a number of times in the play and foreshadows change. At the end of the first scene Hecuba refers to an approaching storm each of whose raindrops bears a "human face".[26] This reference is followed immediately by the arrival of the Dark Man and is thereby associated with the *natural* inevitability of a proletarian revolution. The play ends optimistically with an alliance between Ismene, the truth-teller, whose mind has now cleared, and the proletarian activist, the miner. Whereas Lear's activism marked only the potential beginning of a process of change, Hecuba's alliance of truth and revolutionary action actually wins freedom and offers an opportunity to create a new, more rational society.

By means of the play's allegorical structure Bond has subverted a myth which in his view embodied the irrationality of Western capitalist society. In so doing he has demonstrated how such myths, which are fictions whose primary function is to communicate and perpetuate specific social or moral values and which are a vital part of the capitalist superstructure, must be replaced by *history* which, in his terminology, refers to the truthful retelling of the past. According to Bond in his introduction to the play, unlike capitalism, socialism needs no such myths for it is in itself a rational interpretation and understanding of men, society and history.

Of *The Woman*, the critic John Peter wrote, "you might weep for Hecuba; but would you weep for an archetype?"[27] Although in the three plays discussed above, Bond successfully places a single central character within a wider politico-economic context and illustrates how the behaviour of the former is influenced by the structure of the latter, his allegorical approach and his lack of humour tend somewhat to deprive his characters of the warmth of humanity. This, as Peter suggests, is particularly true of *The Woman*, whose dialectical credentials may be excellent but whose humanity is somewhat lacking. Indeed even the common people of the play are treated as a faceless mass whose lives are affected by wars and revolutions waged by other more bigoted or far-seeing individuals. Bond himself has claimed that, "if socialist writers can't create characters who are agents of history but who ring true as individuals, then perhaps there could be no fully socialist literature: we would not be able to portray the weapons of history and the tools of reason".[28] It must be admitted, however, that within the allegorical scheme of *The Woman* Bond is himself less than successful in communicating those private feelings of frustration, anger or despair which he, along with dramatists such as Brenton and Hare, considered to be the inevitable adjunct to capitalism.

The Woman's Place

Not until after 1968 did the radical historical drama which had evolved in Britain in the years after 1956 pay any serious attention to women. Indeed, as central characters, women were somewhat less apparent in the historical drama pre-1968 than they had been in the biographical historical drama of the 1920s and 1930s which had often focused romantically upon great women of British history, from Queen Elizabeth I and Mary, Queen of Scots to Elizabeth Barrett Browning and Florence Nightingale. In the more democratic post-1956 historical drama neither the lives nor the loves of monarchs were generally considered by left-wing writers to be suitable dramatic subjects. A notable exception was Edward Bond who, as illustrated in the previous chapter, in *Early Morning* and *The Woman*, centred his attention upon aristocratic women. Although in *Early Morning* Queen Victoria is lampooned both as a ruler and as a woman, over a decade later in the allegorical world of *The Woman*, Hecuba and Ismene are portrayed as being superior to the play's male characters in that they possess the ability to think and to act rationally. It is they who prepare the ground for a new, more equitable society. The play's conclusion with an alliance between the still child-like Ismene and the lustful Dark Man—an alliance that may produce a new, more rational society—while optimistic, is nonetheless merely a reiteration of earlier sexual stereotyping.

An early but, for some time, isolated example of the portrayal by one of the predominantly male dramatists of the 1960s of an ordinary woman who was neither merely the adjunct of a man nor only a bystander at historical events was Arnold Wesker's Sarah Kahn in *Chicken Soup with Barley*. Even here, however, although Sarah like Gorky's "mother" is certainly a political activist, unlike Gorky's character she is seen solely in the traditional female setting of the home and is cast primarily as a wife and mother. Also, in consequence of her husband, Harry's, physical decline she is forced to become the "man/leader" of the family and is therefore not realised purely in female terms. Nevertheless, as a combination of mother and committed socialist she is a fitting dramatic embodiment of that caring socialism for which the play calls. Although Wesker portrays her in part as the traditional Jewish matriarch, her political commitment and activism do demonstrate that ordinary women can and should take part in politics, for it is *political* decisions taken elsewhere which, as we see in the play, affect their private lives. Unfortunately, even such characters as Sarah Kahn were rare in the male-written historical drama of the period, and women dramatists tended to locate their female characters outside the domestic setting in order to portray them as being capable of operating in a public context as effectively as men.

As Angela Neustatter points out in *Hyenas in Petticoats*, a review of twenty years of feminism:

In Britain and America, the Women's Liberation Movement grew out of the student protest activities where women, exposed to political analysis, and the process of looking at power and its meanings within society, began to ask questions about their personal situations, about their subordinated status which they had previously accepted as immutable.[1]

Within the British, European and American protest movements of 1968 young men and women, dressed alike in jeans and sweaters and facing lines of police or National Guardsmen, appeared to have achieved what Neustatter calls "the model of genderless unity". As she goes on to reveal, however, all was not as it seemed. For example, the black American civil rights leader "Stokely Carmichael in his endlessly quoted homily made plain how little the revolutionary male perceived his sister as equal: 'The only position of women (in the Civil Rights movement) is prone.'"[2] In 1988, in her history of the women's movement compiled for B.B.C. Radio 4, Margaret Warters recalled, "Women barely rate a mention in all the memories of fighting on the streets during the Sixties. But women were taking the same risks, in the US, in the South working with the blacks in the Civil Rights movement, in London in the anti-war movement".[3] While their protest was certainly as significant and, in many ways, much more fundamental than anything favoured by the male-dominated groups of the 1960s and 1970s, women were to gain little support for their aims within the male-dominated pacifist, anarchist, or Marxist movements themselves and were forced to make their independent way in the face of male opposition from both Right and Left.

While male left-wing historical dramatists of the 1970s were, for the most part, as little interested as their colleagues of the previous two decades in altering the representation of women, male theatre managers (with the notable exception of the American Ed Berman, who staged the first Women's Theatre Festival at his Almost Free Theatre in Soho in 1973) equally saw little reason to encourage feminist theatre, historical or otherwise. In 1974 Pam Gems' *Queen Christina* was rejected by two male directors of the Royal Court Theatre, London, on the grounds that it was, "too sprawly, too expensive to do and anyway, it would appeal more to women". Gems recalls that, "that got to me. I mean, would they ever have said 'We can't do this play, it will appeal to men'?"[4] In common with much of the new historical drama of the 1970s it was first produced by the Royal Shakespeare Company and finally reached the stage of The Other Place in October 1977. This biographical historical drama dealt with the life of the seventeenth-century Swedish queen, Christina. On one level it was intended by Gems to counter the Hollywood myth created in the Greta Garbo movie that portrayed the same character, to replace Garbo's "shining, pale, intellectual beauty" with the harsh reality of a "dark, plain woman with a crippled shoulder."[5] On another level it offered a feminist parable concerning a princess who, in the absence of a male heir, is brought up as a boy in order that she will acquire the "appropriate" masculine qualities to rule a nation. Having adopted male behaviour and become Queen, she is then pressured to act as a woman by providing an heir. Whereas Garbo's Christina romantically gives up her throne for the love of a man, Gems' character refuses to revert to a female role for, as a man, she now despises women as hysterical and silly. She abdicates and travels around Europe in a futile attempt to discover a new way of life and later comes to regret that she has not experienced motherhood. She learns, therefore, what it means to be both male and female and realises that by being forced to mix gender roles which society normally insists must remain separate, her life has ultimately been destroyed. Although structurally the play is not very coherent, its examination of what it actually means to be male or female was a topic of some importance to political feminists of the 1970s.

With the growth of the feminist movement during the 1970s and the increase in women's theatre activity after the Women's Theatre Festival of 1973, some attempts were made, particularly by women writers and women members of socialist and feminist theatre groups outside the male preserve of the established theatre, to examine history from the viewpoint of ordinary members of their own sex. In common with the feminist movement as a whole, they employed history to examine "the social and sexual divisions within our society by analysing them from the point of view of women". The result was "a radical analysis of the repressive aspects of sexuality and the family, initiating a reassessment of the social roles of men and women, and a more open attitude to sexuality—homosexuality as well as heterosexuality".[6] A good example of this appeared in 1976, when the feminist theatre group Monstrous Regiment focused upon working-class women in SCUM—Death, Destruction and Dirty Washing. The setting was a laundry in Paris during the period of the 1870 Commune and portrayed the part played by women in the uprising. Susan Todd described the Company's aim as being, "a desire to convey a kind of passionate sense of the joyousnss of women's solidarity. A joyous quality, within the framework of a set of larger political events of quite wide significance within the socialist tradition as a whole".[7]

The members of the company also wanted to convey the potential for a change both in women's social roles and in their perception of themselves, a change that they felt had been emotionally and politically experienced by the women of the Commune. This perception is communicated in the play by having the women-workers take over the laundry, an action that not only demands the ejection of their female boss but also necessitates the establishment of a new system of management by the women themselves. Historically the women would have been distant both from the decision-making process and from any violence, so, in order to relate their private experience to the wider political events taking place elsewhere, the Company contrived the somewhat unlikely presence in the laundry of an aristocratic lady who delivered a soliloquy concerning events taking place at Versailles. This dislocating device, although the outcome of dramatic necessity, they nevertheless soon realised also effectively conveyed the "real gap between the arena in which political decisions were made and the experience and the challenges and the struggles of the people whom those political decisions affected".[8]

Unusually, female sexuality and social alienation were examined by the male writer Steve Gooch in the provocatively entitled The Women Pirates Ann Bonney and Mary Read which was directed by the ubiquitous Ron Daniels for the Royal Shakespeare Company and opened in August 1978. In the play Gooch attempted to offer a more positive and active portrayal of women who found themselves, through no fault of their own, to be outsiders from their society. On one level the play celebrates the tenacity of two eighteenth-century women, Mary Read and Ann Bonney, both of whom began as it were outside the law, in that their births were illegitimate. Mary Read, having, as a child, been passed off as a boy by her mother in order to obtain money from her mother-in-law, adopts the life of a man, firstly joining the army fighting in the Netherlands and then, in order to avoid the outcome of her discovery as a woman, throwing her lot in with a pirate crew who later capture her. Basically, however, Mary longs to be an ordinary wife and mother. Her contemporary, Ann Bonney, is the daughter of an immigrant Irish plantation-owner of Charleston, Carolina. She is both sexually and pugilistically aggressive and, without disguising her gender, she joins with a pirate crew to avoid the boredom of a wealthy but dull life as the wife of a plantation owner. The play's contemporary relevance is underlined, as in Gooch's earlier *Will Wat, If Not, What Will?* (1972), by the insertion, between the realistically chronicled scenes, of songs which draw the audience's attention from the play's action to the issues it raises. Foremost of these is that, more than two hundred years later, even within the most avowedly liberal groups in modern society, male stereotyping of women still exists. "The 'no-women' rule of the otherwise democratic pirate-crews", wrote Gooch in an introduction to the play, "afforded an interesting parallel with tendency towards sexism of some of today's 'alternative' institutions."[9] Angela Neustatter offers a telling description of this state of affairs:

. . . the "hippy" woman who travelled the Eastern trail with her man, wore similar clothes, appeared to live on equal terms and united with him in a disdain for the world of establishment values. But inside the communes and shared homes the status quo was seen to be remarkably traditional. Women would care for the children, cook the meals, wash the clothes and generally tend their men, who often enough, less traditionally, would not even be going out to work.[10]

This was a contradiction also to be referred to by David Edgar in his own historical survey of the revolutionary political movement of the 1970s, *Maydays*.

In *The Women Pirates* women and others seeking to establish alternative roles or social structures within present society are repeatedly exhorted by songs to band together to obtain strength through unity. As the final lines of one of these songs suggests, feminism is also associated with Socialism and, it would seem, separatism:

ANN: You can argue with me sister,
    But we do fight the same fight.
    And now that we're together,
    They'll have to see we're right.

MARY: I will argue with you sister,
    So we do fight the same fight.
    For now that we're together,
    We have to get it right.

BOTH: Women! In a men's world.
    Poor! Amongst the rich.
    In: a dog eats dog world,
    Who thinks: about the bitch?[11]

The capitalist system is seen to be at the heart of women's exploitation. In addition, however, women are further exploited by men. Therefore, as an article in the feminist magazine *Shrew* maintained, the fellowship and separate development of women may be a necessary prerequisite for their liberation:

Sisterhood is an attempt at redefining our relations with each other. Instead of seeing women in terms of stereotypes and therefore denying them their true nature, we learn to see women and act towards them as full personalities. Learning ourselves to see and treat women as the equals of men. . . . Men divide women from each other. As lover, husband and father to her children, a man is central to a woman's life while her own sex is peripheral, incidental. We need to be liberated not only from men and their domination of our environment but also be be liberated in relation to other women.[12]

Although this was only an aspect of Gooch's theme, for a male dramatist even to countenance the argument for separatism was contentious and may partly have provoked the virulent response that the play received from some male critics.

Ironically, owing to a quirk of English law, when the pirate community of which Ann and Mary were a part was caught and tried they alone escaped hanging. The reason for this anomaly was that both were pregnant and at that time the English criminal code did not permit innocent life to be forfeited. Therefore, while they attempted to avoid the gender-based restrictions imposed by their society, the two were to survive in consequence of sexual discrimination!

As suggested above, unfortunately the play was well received by neither audiences nor critics, and the Royal Shakespeare Company was forced to abandon the production at the end of August rather than, as had been planned, to keep it in the company's repertory until well into November. Irving Wardle was one critic who disliked the play. He described it in *The Times* as "an incoherent feminist extravaganza" which exhibited "a confusion between the desire to recreate past events objectively, and the desire to shape them into a historical reflection of the female gay movement".[13] Although Wardle's refer-

ence to the female gay movement was probably provoked by the perceived threat of female separatism referred to above and his
dismissive use of the word "feminist" is simply patronising, it must
nevertheless be admitted that as a whole the play fails, largely
because in it Gooch attempts too much. Unfortunately, however, the
result is little more than a swashbuckling yarn rather than, as was
obviously intended, an analysis and indictment of a male society that
could not cope with women who would not conform to its stereotypes.

As Pam Gems had attempted to free Queen Christina from a
romantic male view of women, so the poet Liz Lochhead sought in her
first play *Blood and Ice* to replace Mary Shelly as wife of the poet
Shelley and daughter of Mary Wollstonecraft (the author of *The Vin-
dication of the Rights of Women*) and William Godwin the libertarian,
with Mary Shelley as mother and a poet in her own right. The action
of the play, with its abrupt shifts of time and place, consists in part of
the dramatisation of Mary's own perception of the historical events
that took place between the years 1816 and 1822 in Switzerland and
Italy and involved Shelley, Byron and her half-sister Clare Clare-
mont, and of extracts drawn from Mary's own novel *Frankenstein*
which she narrates as if they were taking shape at that very moment
within her imagination.

The play initially saw the light of day in 1981 under the title of
Mary and the Monster. It was performed in the studio of the Belgrade
Theatre, Coventry, and received poor reviews from the critics.
Rewritten in something like its present form, it was then performed
during the Edinburgh Festival of 1982 at the Traverse Theatre. Here
it received a much better critical response but, still dissatisfied with
her play, in 1983 Lochhead was once again to amend it in preparation
for what proved to be an abortive production by students of RADA.
The play was ultimately produced in what appears to be its final form
by a small fringe theatre group called Pepper's Ghost at New Merlin's
Cave, a North London public house, in February 1984. Howard Brenton's *Bloody Poetry* was, coincidentally, to be performed by Foco Novo
at the Leicester Haymarket Theatre in October of the same year. It is
interesting to compare the two plays, which cover largely the same
period and events. Whereas Brenton focuses primarily upon the political side of Shelley's writing and of Byron's life and takes measures to
avoid reference to their personal psychology, in *Blood and Ice* the
action of the play is a projection of Mary's consciousness, the aim
being to link the events of her personal life as a woman with the ob-
sessions exhibited in her novel *Frankenstein*. The structure of *Bloody
Poetry* is basically linear, a thought pattern that some consider to
be typically male. *Blood and Ice*, on the other hand, exhibits the kind
of lateral structure of inter-linked images that is often seen as

characteristic of female thought processes. These contrasting structures might, however, be more appropriately explained by the fact
that while Brenton is concerned to produce a play that deals with
political and intellectual issues, Lochhead, as a poet as well as a
woman, is more concerned with the emotional and imagistic. That
their individual choice of approach may be considered to reflect gender preference is, I believe, open to dispute.

Significantly, whereas the word "bloody" in the title of Brenton's
play is associated with revolutionary violence, in Lochhead's it is
linked with such personal experiences as Mary's miscarriage after
which the "dark river"[14] of blood which threatened to kill her was
staunched only by Shelley immersing her in a bath of ice. Thus birth
and death are conjoined in her biological experience and are later
expressed in the creation of Frankenstein's monster. Images of blood
and ice reoccur throughout the play. Blood and ice are associated
with the conflict of emotion and reason in Mary's relationship with
Shelley and with male–female relationships in general. The cold
rationality of the pampered intellectual, Mary Wollstonecraft, is contrasted with her husband's hot "rutting",[15] while Shelley's insistence
that he and Mary establish a new way for men and women to live
together based on a cool, detached view of sexual relationships is
countered by Byron, the libertine, with the words ". . . there is something . . . hideously unnatural in such a cold-blooded put-together
passion, is there not? I cannot believe it can have been a pretty thing
in practice."[16] Blood gives life to Frankenstein's monster, while the
icy waste of the North Pole is the context for the scientist's hunt for
his escaped creation and the place where he meets the book's narrator, Captain Walton, who is himself seeking "a new and temperate
region of wonder where men and women might live".[17] These considerations are united at the close of the play in Mary's long monologue
during which she identifies herself in succession as a mother, as
Frankenstein, as a female monster who is "tied to the monster bed for
ever",[18] and as Captain Walton the idealist who, because he could not
endure the cold, abandoned his quest for a place where "Men and
Women Might Live in Freedom",[19] and scuttled back to his warm fire-
side. The play's music-like structure of inter-related recurrent motifs
is ultimately completed when, in the final words of the play, Mary
links the reference to blood and ice with her love for Shelley: "The ice
cannot stop you if your hot hearts say it shall not! . . . Oh Shelley"[20]—
reason and love are no match for passion and jealousy.

With its structure of poetic imagery and its personal/biological
exploration of Mary Shelley as lover, mother and writer, *Blood and
Ice* stands, then, in complete contrast to Brenton's much more literal
and male-focused exploration of the political features of that short

period when the poets and their mistresses attempted to live out their dreams of a new way of living. In each case, however, history is employed yet again to explore concerns of the present, in this case not of politics but of gender.

Among women dramatists of the 1970s and early 1980s, it was Caryl Churchill who most frequently and effectively employed history to analyse the social and sexual divisions inherent in her society. In *Vinegar Tom*, written in collaboration with Monstrous Regiment in 1976, and *Light Shining in Buckinghamshire*, written in the same year—this time in collaboration with Joint Stock—Churchill employed history to emphasise the oppression of women, particularly those who do not conform to male-constituted patterns of social behaviour. In *Vinegar Tom*, seventeenth-century accusations of witchcraft against old, poor, single and sexually unconventional women were used by Churchill as a context for speculation upon the apparently timeless nature of male prejudices concerning women. The phenomenom of the witchhunt was, the play suggests, merely an extreme demonstration of such prejudices. The play, however, is only loosely set in the seventeenth century and can hardly be described either as historical drama or as a history play. Her next play, *Light Shining in Buckinghamshire*, more closely follows documentary evidence drawn from its historical period. Its twenty-one scenes reveal, substantially from the perspective of a number of fictional lower-class characters and vagrants, how the millenium, which was expected by many to be the outcome of the English Civil War, failed to materialise and how the new rulers, under Cromwell, stifled the democratic aspirations of the Diggers and Levellers. The oppression of women is but part of this story and is represented particularly by the behaviour and treatment of two social outsiders, Margaret Brotherton, a vagrant whose harsh handling by the parish authorities is similar to that experienced by the young woman in Bond's *Bingo*, and Hoskins, a vagrant female preacher who at the end of the play identifies herself with the Ranters "whose ecstatic and anarchic belief in economic and sexual freedom was", according to Churchill, "the last desperate burst of revolutionary feeling before the restoration".[21] The play has obvious relevance both to the contemporary debate concerning sexual stereotyping and to the speculation amongst left-wing groups about the possibility and conduct of political revolution.

In *Top Girls* (1982) Churchill theatrically manipulates history in an extremely novel way in order to examine and challenge the values represented by the successful contemporary Thatcherite career woman and to set those values against the reality of the lives of her ordinary and apparently less "successful" sisters. The historical elements are confined to the play's first scene. This scene takes place in a modern restaurant where the fictional character Marlene is holding a dinner to celebrate her promotion to the managing directorship of the "Top Girls" employment agency. The novel aspect of this dinner is that Marlene's guests are all notable women drawn from history, myth and literature. There is a nineteenth-century traveller, Isabella Bird; a thirteenth-century Japanese emperor's courtesan, Lady Nijo, who was subsequently to become a Buddhist nun; Dull Gret, a figure from a Brueghel painting in which she is portrayed in armour, at the head of a crowd of women, routing the devils of hell; Pope Joan who, disguised as a man, was said to have been Pope during the ninth century; and Patient Griselda, the obedient wife who suffers at the hands of her husband in the Clerk's Tale of Chaucer's *Canterbury Tales*. Churchill's aim in portraying these characters is to reveal that, while their achievements were above average, each of them has been formed in the process to adopt male behaviour, to conform to male stereotypes of women or has felt guilty for not doing so, and has generally suffered at the hands of men. The scene also establishes their combined experience as a reflection of what Marlene has also had to give up to achieve success in a man's world. It also provides a background for her later behaviour towards her sister Joyce, who has adopted Marlene's illegitimate young daughter, is separated from her husband and lives in some financial hardship. In the second part of the play we also meet women who are members or are clients of the "Top Girls" agency. They, in their own words, repeat views and behaviour communicated by the historical figures of the first scene, thereby illustrating that, even today, for women little has changed. They are still expected to be subservient to men. In the initial production at the Royal Court this link between past and present was reinforced by having the actresses double between the historical and modern roles.

Although *Top Girls* features only female characters, in practice gender proves to be a less significant issue than that of cultural conditioning. While, as their various period costumes emphasise, each of the historical characters has had to adapt to her own male-dominated society, the nature of that adaptation has varied according to the cultural setting in which each of them existed. Thus, although their overlapping or simultaneous dialogue may, on one hand, convey a sense of the commonality of female experience, on the other it also represents the women's isolation within their own experience and their inability to find common cause with those of their own gender. The latter is reinforced in the second part of the play where even the name of the "Top Girls" employment agency emphasises a divisive hierarchical structure in which there must inevitably be winners and losers. As the agency interviews also reveal, although Marlene herself has reached a high position in that hierarchy, nothing has really changed for women in general. Each of the interviewees is offered work that is really no different in kind from that with which she is already familiar. Marlene, like her antecedents, is playing life's game by male rules. Angela Neustatter's description of Margaret Thatcher may, I am sure, not coincidentally be applied to Marlene herself. "Mrs Thatcher displays the characteristics feminists have seen and struggled against so long in men—a deep contempt for women. She gives the impression of aligning herself with male perspectives, behaviour, power structures. If she can be called a feminist by dint of what she has achieved it makes a mockery of a word which embraces in its meaning support for other women."[22]

In the second part of *Top Girls* through the relationship of Marlene and her sister Joyce, Churchill examines, on a private level, the general issues that have been established in the first part of the play. Their heated arguments reveal that unless, like Marlene, women become totally self-centred and ruthless, they are inhibited by society's social and political structures either from reaching positions of real power or even from realising their individual potential. At the close of the play this dichotomy is expressed in terms of the contrast between Marlene's individualist politics and Joyce's socialism. Marlene identifies herself with Margaret Thatcher—"She's a tough lady, Maggie. I'd give her a job"[23]—while Joyce, who recognises correctly that Marlene's bourgeois individualism which masquerades as feminism has no relevance for the majority of women and will reform nothing, argues for those less fortunate, such as Marlene's own daughter Angie.

MARLENE: I don't mean anything personal. I don't believe in class. Anyone can do anything if they've got what it takes.

JOYCE: And if they haven't?

MARLENE: If they're stupid lazy or frightened, I'm not going to help them get a job, why should I?

JOYCE: What about Angie?

MARLENE: What about Angie?

JOYCE: She's stupid, lazy and frightened, so what about her?

MARLENE: You run her down too much. She'll be all right.

JOYCE: I don't expect so, no. I expect her children will say what a wasted life she had. If she has children. Because nothing's changed and it won't with them in.[24]

To emphasise even more powerfully the private feelings of those such as Angie who are never likely themselves to become "Top Girls",

Churchill closes the play with Angie's repetition to Marlene of the single word "frightening".[25]

In *Top Girls* the historical elements are the foundation for a play with multiple levels of meaning whose structure allows themes generated in the first scene to resonate and expand in the remainder of the play and, in so doing, comment upon the present.

A woman who was also forced to hide her gender in order to follow her calling was the nineteenth-century traveller and writer, Isabelle Eberhardt [1877–1907], portrayed in Timberlake Wertenbaker's *New Anatomies* (1981). This short play explores the pressures and effects upon women of having to adopt male behaviour if they are to survive in areas normally dominated by men. It is structurally somewhat uneven but nevertheless offers a number of additional perspectives on a similar topic to that covered rather more effectively in the following year by Caryl Churchill in *Top Girls*. Wertenbaker poses questions that were becoming increasingly relevant in a period when women were beginning to penetrate hitherto traditional male bastions and reach the highest levels in their chosen professions and in which was coined the term "power-dressing" to describe the smart formal business clothing adopted by some women executives.

In scenes based upon events drawn from the curious life of Isabelle Eberhardt, Wertenbaker questions assumptions concerning the roles allocated to men and women in Western European society. Eberhardt, born in Geneva in 1877, was the daughter of a drunken Russian Anarchist and his unworldy wife, Anna. In her 20s she journeyed to French North Africa and, to the dismay of the French authorities, travelled through the desert dressed as an Arab tribesman. She died in a flash-flood in the desert village of Ain-Sefra in 1904.

Although there are a number of male characters, Wertenbaker intended the play to be performed by a cast of five women, a circumstance that, in consequence of cross-dressing both by the actresses and the characters whom they portray, makes the audience constantly aware of the play's central concern, that of sexual stereotyping. At the opening of the play the audience is introduced to Isabelle herself, a character who bears none of the attributes of a conventional heroine. She is 27 years old and "is dressed in a tattered Arab cloak, has no teeth and almost no hair".[26] Drunk and foul-mouthed, she begins to relate the story of her life to her companion Severine. The dramatisation of her story which follows is preceded by a song sung by a Victorian ingénue dressed in frills—a figure obviously intended, in contrast to the Isabelle whom we have just encountered, to represent the Victorian stereotype of young womanhood. Thenceforward the structure of the play consists of an historical narrative which

focuses upon various images of imprisonment and liberation, for Isabelle Eberhardt instinctively realised that she could only find personal
freedom and knowledge by escaping from her background and
environment.

As children in Switzerland, Isabelle and her brother play at escaping to the freedom of the desert. Even here Wertenbaker questions
gender assumptions. Isabelle is much more active and dominating
than her 16-year-old brother, who is described as "frail and feminine".[27] Their elder sister Natalie represents those bourgeois values
which dictate that a woman becomes "a mother who teaches her
children how to behave and looks after the house, cooks meals" and,
unlike her own mother, "doesn't let her children eat out of a slop
bucket".[28] After the death of her parents Isabelle decides to flee from
the "barred horizons"[29] and Swiss-clock orderliness of Geneva and
persuades her unwilling sister to accompany her to Algiers to visit
their brother who has himself run away to join the French Foreign
Legion. Under French colonialism however, even Algeria proves to
have its social restrictions, particularly for women. Isabelle's brother
turns out to have abandoned their dream of freedom to be an army
clerk, to marry a conventional bourgeois girl and to live by the rules
of white colonial society. When Isabelle angrily suggests to him that,
for all that he has seen of the desert, he might as well have stayed in
Switzerland, he replies, "I did see it. It's not how we dreamt of it. It's
dangerous, uncomfortable, and most of it isn't even sand", to which
she responds characteristically, "Freedom".[30] In theatrical terms
rather too conveniently, at this moment Natalie returns from town
with an armful of local costumes which she has been given by the
Arabs, whom she regards as stupid, and which she intends to take
home to sell in Switzerland. When Antoine's conventionally feminine
wife tries on one of the costumes she is disgusted to discover from
Isabelle that she is in fact wearing male attire. To Isabelle, however,
the jellaba or long cloak worn by men offers a route to personal freedom by liberating her from the restraints imposed upon her by Western society.

In the remainder of the play Wertenbaker examines how beneficial
for women has been the adoption in various contexts of male characteristics. Isabelle, disguised in her jellaba, finds acceptance amongst
the nomadic Arabs who, when challenged by a French officer who
does not think it proper that she should travel in the desert, reply
that although they are aware of her gender they are prepared to
accept any identity that she chooses to assume. Having been deported
from Algeria by the French as a potential trouble-maker, in a Paris
salon Isabelle meets other women who have for various reasons
adopted male dress. In this scene the central issues of the play are at

their most explicit. Of the assembled women, one, Verda Miles, is a
male impersonator, another, Lydia, is a writer and another, Severine,
is a journalist. Their cross-dressing is, however, merely an acknowledgement of male supremacy and a betrayal of their own gender. For
Verda, dressing as a man allows her to play hundreds of exciting
roles. It is, she says "much more interesting, much more challenging
to play men".[31] Lydia finds that wearing male garb when writing
removes the distractions conventionally associated with her sex.
"When I am dressed as a woman, like this", she tells the others, "I
find I am most concerned with the silky sound of my skirt rustling on
the floor, or I spend hours watching the lace fall over my wrist, white
against white."[32] Severine offers the much more basic reason that "I
can take my girl-friends to coffee-bars without having men pester
us".[33] Of them all only Isabelle has, however, really traversed the
gender gap. When she is beyond Western eyes, as Si Mahmoud, she
can live in the desert as a man. Towards the end of the scene Lydia
(who is wearing a skirt because some German diplomats attending
the salon are "very sticky about these things"[34]) predicts that the next
century may herald a new regime for women, "a revolution greater
even than the French revolution" in which "we'll defrock women".[35]
The context implies that such a development may prove to be a "cos-
metic" one rather than a genuine move towards sexual equality.

The play's final scenes cover Isabelle's return to the desert. She has
been employed by the American wife of the Marquis de Mores to
uncover information regarding his mysterious death in North Africa.
Although she is accepted into the Arabic Quadra brotherhood, an
attempt is made upon her life by a Muslim, probably at the instiga-
tion of the French. At the trial of her would-be assassin she is accused
of having a perverted nature and ordered to stay out of the desert.
Male influence once again inhibits female freedom, and to underscore
this Wertenbaker evokes yet another image of imprisonment:
"Fenced out. Always!" says Isabelle despondently. "Fenced in, Isabelle, all of us",[36] replies Severine. The play's penultimate scene is a
continuation of its first in which Isabelle has returned, ill and
exhausted, to report to the liberal French Colonel Lyautey who has
given her permission to travel in the desert. During the short final
scene we learn that she has been washed away in the flood, leaving
behind only some journals.

In 1981 women did not appear to have moved a great deal closer to
their "new anatomies" (new structures of gender) than had Isabelle
Eberhardt almost eighty years earlier. It was still necessary to play by
male rules. Nevertheless, Wertenbaker's play, although structurally
uneven in terms of its scenic arrangement and emphases, does challenge its audience to examine its own assumptions and provides a

useful departure point for the consideration of how men and women can find new ways of living equitably together.

Although I make no claim to have referred to all of the plays written during the 1970s and early 1980s in which history was used to explore feminist concerns, those that have been cited may serve to illustrate factors common to all. Primary amongst these was their employment of history as a means of de-naturalising the role of women in society. By offering an analytical, feminist and often socialist perspective on the past, their dramatists set out to reveal that the treatment of women in a male society was often the result not only of sexual stereotyping or ingrained superstition but also of economic pressure. The implication of such analyses was that society's treatment of women was based not upon biological reality but upon current male prejudices, expectations and assumptions which were generally endorsed by women themselves. In this manner history could be used to prompt audiences to "see anew", to become aware that, in matters of gender as in politics, change is forever possible.

Fact Plus Fiction Equals "Faction"

Like Howard Brenton and David Hare, to whose generation he belongs, David Edgar also graduated from the Fringe to the Institutional Theatre. He has written a number of history plays,[1] but his major contribution to the historical drama of the 1970s has been in his employment of what he himself has termed "faction"—a combination of fact and fiction—in his plays *Destiny* and *Maydays*. In both plays he was concerned with the present and future of British society, employing the recent past both to illustrate the forces that had produced the current state of Britain and to alert his audience to the dangers that threatened its future. In 1976 Ron Daniels introduced Edgar to the world of the institutional theatre by directing *Destiny* at the Royal Shakespeare Company's small Stratford theatre, The Other Place, from where it was later transferred to the Aldwych Theatre, London. Daniels, it should be remembered, had worked, as an actor, on the first documentaries produced by the Victoria Theatre, Stoke-on-Trent, and perhaps in consequence of this experience appears to have developed a particular interest in "history from below". He was also to direct Edgar's *Maydays* for the Royal Shakespeare Company at the Barbican in 1983. *Destiny* is essentially a history play with the type of interaction of private lives and public events already seen in Brenton and Hare's *Brassneck* (1973), but here much more emphasis is placed upon its factual elements which are the result of meticulous research. Its factually based subject matter is dramatised within a specific historical time-frame which stretches from the ending of Britain's colonial rule in India in 1947 to a by-election in the West Midlands in 1976. The particular significance of the events that occupy this time-frame, as in Brenton and Hare's history plays, is revealed through the experience of a number of fictional characters whose behaviour is likewise portrayed as being motivated by external events rather than by individual temperament.

In *Destiny* Edgar illustrates the steady growth of fascism in post-war Britain, placing the process within a public political context by setting a number of the play's scenes at specific points in British post-war history. These include the moment of India's Independence in 1947, after which the British army returned home; the 20th of April 1968, which was the anniversary of Hitler's birth and, probably coincidentally, the day on which Enoch Powell delivered his controversial "River of Blood" speech in which, in the wake of the assassination of Martin Luther King on the 4th of April 1968, the subsequent outbreak of race riots in many American cities and with a second Race Relations Bill imminent, Powell predicted that the presence in Britain of large numbers of coloured immigrants would here also lead to civil strife; and, finally, the General Election of 1970, which was lost by Labour. Within the context of these and some fictional events, Edgar sets out to reveal the private reasons that impel individual men and women to turn to fascism. While his motivation for writing *Destiny* was a deep-seated antipathy to fascism, Edgar's treatment of the private levels of the play is such that, instead of delivering a propagandist polemic that would characterise fascists as black-shirted, jack-booted cranks, he reveals that their influence is in fact apparent at all levels of society and that, particularly at moments of economic difficulty or social tension, their ideology may prove to be highly seductive. The play's primary message, for indeed Edgar's aim here is certainly to educate his audience, is that the threat posed by fascism should in no way be underestimated.

At the beginning of the play, in six fairly short scenes, Edgar effectively establishes a number of character "types" through whose subsequent political activities he will expose the nature of fascism, point out those most susceptible to its influence, reveal its potential victims, and illustrate how, since the war, fascist organisations have attempted to dissociate themselves from the militarism and barbarity of the Hitler Reich. Four characters are introduced in the play's first scene, which is set in a British army barracks in India as the British army is preparing to leave after independence. The stage is dominated by a huge, dark painting of the suppression of the Indian Mutiny which clearly, but in the context ironically, represents an imperialist assertion of racial superiority that, in a post-colonial period, may find other modes of expression. Those present in the scene are Turner, an army sergeant, Khera, a Sikh servant, Colonel

Chandler, the C.O., and Major Rolfe. In the remaining five scenes of
Act 1 Edgar illustrates the political climate of Britain circa 1968. The
play's narrative flow is, however, disrupted in four of these otherwise
realistic scenes by an opening verse monologue which is addressed
directly to the audience by one of the above characters. In this manner each is clearly identified as being "typical" of some aspect of
his historical context. Firstly, the ex-Indian-army officer, Colonel
Chandler, tells how, after India's independence, he returned to
"Another England, / Rough and Raw"[2] and entered politics in order to
continue the old Tory tradition of service and benevolence to society
in general and one's social inferiors in particular. Both Chandler and
his values soon die, and his parliamentary seat passes to his young
nephew, Peter Crosby, who has himself no sense of political calling
and proves subsequently to be no match for the fascists. Secondly, we
are introduced in a similar manner to Major Rolfe, who also has
returned from India. He, unlike Chandler, is not a "gentleman" and
has no sense of belonging to any social or political group. This is for
him a constant source of resentment. He likewise returns to what he
considers to be an altered England, a country seen from his perspective as "seedy, drab, / Locked in the dreams of glories she once had", a
"flaccid spongers' state" in which "the knot of old school tiredness is
still tight round England's throat"[3] and where the political Right will
not act to counter the country's obvious decline. Similar feelings of
resentment are also voiced by Turner, who has returned to England
to become a shop-keeper. His verse includes the lines,

Old certainties are scoffed at by the new sophisticates:
And big capital and labour wield an ever-bigger clout,
And it's him that's in the middle and it's him that's
      losing out—
Sergeant Turner, NCO:
Where's he going? Doesn't know.[4]

The final character to be re-introduced is Khera who, in 1958, has
arrived in Britain on a tide of immigration only to become the
scapegoat for the kind of resentment felt by Rolfe and Turner and
exploited by the fascists. Each character is therefore shown to be
motivated not by any quirk of individual psychology but by such
external influences as Britain's loss of empire, its apparent abandonment of idealism, the loosening of its previously rigid social hierarchy, the mass-immigration of the 1950s and the persistence of its
economic problems. In addition to these "types" Edgar also creates
characters who illustrate the ineffectiveness of those on the Left and
Right who oppose the fascists (Bob Clifton and Peter Crosby), or who

reveal the various strands and mutations of fascist policy and strategy (Cleaver, Drumont, Maxwell and Kershaw) which, it is Edgar's contention, are being employed insidiously to infiltrate all levels of British society. All these historical factors are systematically established in the first act in preparation for the second act's detailed fictional portrayal, in terms of the private lives of the various characters, of the workings of British fascism.

Although based on fact, *Destiny's* effectiveness either as a piece of theatre or as a play of ideas does not result from any attempt on Edgar's part to achieve documentary "objectivity" or to endistance his audience from its subject-matter. On the contrary, Edgar repeatedly sets out to engage the audience's emotional response. For example, on one occasion he permits the audience itself to be, for a few movements, seduced by fascist political tactics in order to reveal powerfully how easily one may be manipulated. The occasion appears in Act 2 at a public meeting during which the Fascist, Maxwell, interprets the stage audience's (and, I suspect, for a short period, the theatre audience's) individual social fears and prejudices as representing some grand conspiracy involving the Left, Jews and immigrants. As this conspiracy theory becomes gradually more ludicrous in its implausability the audience is intended by Edgar to become aware of how easily it has hitherto been manipulated and thereby to realise how effectively such tactics may be employed to penetrate the public consciousness. Such emotive dramatic techniques as this, in which audience involvement is followed by the revelation of the nature and implication of its involuntary participation, is typical of *Destiny* and was also to be claimed by Edgar in 1978 in "Ten Years of Political Theatre" to be one of the major features that distinguished the British political drama of the 1970s from that of Brecht.

History rather than fiction is briefly but specifically returned to at the close of play in order to furnish Edgar with an agitational conclusion. In the initial version of the play performed by the Royal Shakespeare Company, the play ended with the entrance, covered by a follow-spot, of an elderly man in a civilian suit who turns out to be Adolf Hitler. He addressed the following words to the audience: "Only one thing could have stopped our Movement: if our adversaries had understood its principle, and had smashed, with utmost brutality, the nucleus of our new movement. (*slight pause*) Hitler. Nuremberg. Third of September, 1933 (*blackout*)."[5] In 1986 in the third, revised, version of the play Edgar chose not to resurrect the figure of Hitler but instead simply to employ a disembodied voice uttering the same words in answer to Cleaver's question, "What on earth can stop us now?" Nevertheless, in both cases Edgar employs historical reference to evoke a chilling parallel between past and present.

With even more justification than *Destiny* can Edgar's later play *Maydays* (1983) be described as a history play. Throughout it we are made constantly aware of the effect upon the lives of its fictional characters of various significant moments drawn from the history of post-war socialism. In referring to socialism Edgar was not, however, interested in Britain's parliamentary politics but in the activities and aims of the extra-parliamentary forces of the Left and, to a lesser extent, of the Right. He illustrates how, since the war and, more particularly, since 1968, these forces have sought to change not only the government but also the whole political philosophy of Britain. It is an appropriate play with which to draw to a close this examination of radical historical drama. With Margaret Thatcher's new style of ultra-right conservatism then firmly established, Edgar's attempt to suggest why the Left appeared to have failed and why the Right seemed to be moving further and further towards authoritarianism will stand as a fitting *thematic* conclusion to that historical drama which had, for over twenty-five years, been closely associated with the concerns of the Left.

In *Maydays*, whose title evokes both a new beginning and a cry for help, Edgar's history of the post-war Left begins with a Communist Mayday rally taking place in England in 1945. Alone on the stage, the 17-year-old Jeremy Crowther proclaims to his audience that the working class is about to build its "New Jerusalem". Subsequent scenes portray the Russian suppression of the Hungarian uprising in 1956; the British and American movements that, from 1967, protested against U.S. military involvement in Vietnam; the internecine rivalries that developed during the 1970s amongst the various factions of the British Left and probably contributed to the parliamentary defeat suffered by Labour in 1979; and, finally, the propagandist exploitation of Soviet dissidents by the far-Right during the 1970s and 1980s.

As in *Destiny* Edgar constructs his post-war epic chronicle around a small number of fictional characters whom he introduces early in the play. Unlike in *Destiny*, however, a major feature of the portrayal of the characters in *Maydays* is that, in consequence of the political events experienced during the years covered by the play, each of these initially left-wing sympathisers becomes disillusioned with the Left and not only abandons his former political beliefs but also defects to the opposite side of the political spectrum. In *Maydays* there are three such characters. The oldest is Jeremy Crowther who is discovered addressing the Mayday rally at the opening of the play. He is initially a Communist who, in the early post-war years, looks back and wishes that he had been old enough to have fought in Spain with the International Brigade during the 1930s when the political values of the Left and Right were more clearly polarised and moral alternatives appeared more starkly drawn than in post-war Britain. The second major character is introduced to the audience in the context of the Hungarian Uprising of 1956. He is Pavel Lermontov, a Soviet army lieutenant who is later to become a dissident and defect to the West. There he is enlisted by the far-Right who, ironically considering its own authoritarian stance, attempt to use him as a weapon in their fight against the collectivism and tyranny that they claim to be endemic to left-wing politics. The third character is the youngest, Martin Glass, who, as the theatre critic James Fenton recognised in his review of the play in *The Sunday Times*, was rumoured to have been to some extent based on himself, his own career having followed, as he admitted, "certain parts of the trajectory"[6] travelled by Glass. Martin Glass progresses from anarchism, through the CND, American hippydom, and English Trotskyism into disillusionment and ultimately the New Right. In addition Edgar also introduces, rather more peripherally, other characters such as the American Anarchist and Vietnam War protestor, Clark Sullivan, and the American right-winger, Teddy Weiner, in order to further internationalise his theme and to suggest that the political struggles that took place in Britain during the 1960s and 1970s were not merely parochial but were part of a much wider international movement.

Unfortunately this attempt to be all-embracing makes for a long play which would perhaps have been better served by focusing solely upon the three central characters. Nevertheless, in spite of this, by again interweaving the political lives and experiences of various fictional characters who were historically "typical" of the evolution of left- or right-wing extra-parliamentary politics during the post-war years, Edgar was able plausibly and effectively to combine both the identification of public historical processes and the revelation of the private responses that are the mechanism of change.

In relation to the latter it is perhaps significant that Edgar sets more of the play's scenes in domestic environments than in either the exterior settings much favoured by Bond for communicating public concerns, or the political meetings, dramatised for example by Trevor Griffith, during which political views could be directly communicated to an audience. A prime example is the relatively long, Act 1, Scene 6, which is set in an old house in the Midlands during the politically mythic month of May 1968. It is characterised by a combination of the clutter of domesticity and political activism. On the one hand there is a washing-line full of nappies and on the other a duplicating machine used for printing political leaflets, a picture that would undoubtedly have struck nostalgic chords in the minds of some members of the play's initial audience. During this scene Cathy Weiner's short outbursts, firstly in response to Clark Sullivan's unceremonious abandonment of their relationship and then in response to the theft of her grapefruit by another of the residents of the house, illustrate with some humour the personal strain often experienced by members of the utopian communities of the late 1960s and early 1970s who found difficulty in totally abandoning, as the current dogma required, the concepts of personal, territorial and material possessions. This domestic picture is nonetheless not intended merely to evoke the warm glow of nostalgia nor to make fun of the beliefs of the recent past, nor even to elaborate upon the personalities of the play's characters. Rather, it is employed to offer an appropriately *human* setting which will stand in sharp contrast to the Leninist Socialist Vanguard leader, James Saunders', later advocacy of a tougher political line. In the light of the failure of the uprisings of May 1968, like Griffith's Kabak, Saunders advocates a centralist party "strong enough and hard and disciplined enough to provide at least the means whereby the masses can seize human history". Those who resist must be sacrificed like "human dust"[7] for the success of the revolution. This image of "human dust" attributed to Trotsky recurs at various points in the play as an expression of Edgar's central concern with the inevitable conflict between the needs and freedoms of the individual and the necessary requirements of a political movement as a whole. It is in consequence of the hard Left's unwillingness to recognise the validity of the claims of the individual that Martin Glass ultimately disassociates himself from socialism and moves towards individualism. At the close of Act 1, Scene 1, which is set in the autumn of 1978, Edgar uses a "voice-over" to express unambiguously the reasons for Martin's disillusionment with the Left. "And I looked from face to face, from 'Trotskyist' to 'Libertarian' to 'Democratic Socialist', and I realised that all these faces, from the harshest to the most benign, were set like flint against the way that human beings really are."[8] From a standpoint apparently shared by David Hare in his Cambridge lecture of 1978, Martin Glass also argues that political dogma concerning class and revolution has, during the 1970s, blinded the Left to the political realities of post-war Britain and has displaced any real concern for the aspirations of ordinary individuals.

In the play's final scenes Edgar illustrates that the Right, in spite of its emphasis upon individualism, also harbours a concept of "human dust". Trelawney, the Conservative M.P., suggests to Martin Glass that his belief "that the choir of humankind sounds best in unison"—in other words, as a collection of individuals singing together—should be replaced by the analogy of a choir singing in "harmony"[9]—that is, in an authoritarian *organised* manner in which each member has his or her own designated place. For his part the dissident, Lermontov, comes to realise that the desire of the far-Right to shift power from state bureaucracies to monopoly private owner-ship is merely to substitute right-wing authoritarianism for left-wing totalitarianism while the masses will remain oppressed, the "human dust" for whom nothing will change.

Having illustrated how in practice the Left was unable to build its New Jerusalem in the years following the Second World War, at the close of the play Edgar suggests that the spirit of individual protest is, however, by no means dead in either Eastern or Western Europe. In the final scene he portrays, in an overlapping sequence, the pro-tests initiated by the Women of Greenham Common against the installation of American Cruise missiles in Britain during the early 1980s. This is counterpointed and internationalised by scenes involv-ing a Soviet dissident's attempt to persuade a Moscow university pro-fessor to smuggle a manifesto out of Russia during one of his visits abroad.

The Women of Greenham Common have abandoned their private identities as a tactic in their public protest. In the absence of individ-ual identity no injunctions can be served to eject them from their camp outside the gates of the air-force base.

3RD WOMAN: We—in the sense of this—we have no names.

1ST WOMAN: No membership.

2ND WOMAN: And no committees.

3RD WOMAN: No printing press. No postal code. No phone.

2ND WOMAN: And I assure you—nobody "in charge".[10]

For strategic reasons they have revived the Anarchistic system of "non-organisation" which had been advocated in the late 1960s and early 1970s. In symbolic terms the absence of individual identity may, however, also be seen as Edgar's way of putting forward the contention that inherent in human nature is an instinct to resist oppression, a view supported by Amanda's reference in the same scene to "something in the nature of our species which resents, rejects and ultimately will resist a world that is demonstrably and in this case dramatically wrong and mad and unjust and unfair".[11] As James Fenton recognised, "the message at the end looks very much like "where there's life there's hope. It is a sentimental reduction of poli-tics to visible activism—anyone who stands up for anything against the odds is on the right lines".[12] Although I do not agree with the latter assertion, it is certainly true that at the close of play, having chronicled the reasons for the failure of post-war left-wing activism in Britain, as if to inject some spirit of hope into its final moments

Edgar turns to an instinctive reaction which is "in the nature of our species" and which, ironically for a history play, is therefore quite outside history. Nevertheless, in the play's defence it must be admitted that its theme and form were successfully unified. On the one hand, thematically, the play advocates the need to weigh the claims of the individual against the necessity for collective organisation, while formalistically, in its illustration of three characters' private journeys through an epic history of post-war political activism, it effectively dramatises the interplay between public events and private perception. In this, *Maydays* was a triumphant expression of a theme that had dominated radical historical drama since 1968; and, in that it also brought together most of the concerns voiced and acted upon by the radical Left during the post-war period—disillusionment with parliamentary socialism, anarchism, the New Left, the questioning of collectivism and the attempt to discover a form of socialism that would accommodate the claims of the individual, the failure of extra-parliamentary left-wing activism, the strengthening of the far-Right, the rise of the women's movement and, in theatrical terms, the attempt to establish a dramatic form that would encompass both private and public concerns—it stands as a fitting conclusion to my study of British alternative historical drama.

Afterword

As I have shown, the most characteristic feature of British historical drama after 1956 was that, in the hands of its writers, *all* history was to become *contemporary* history. One interest group after another was to employ history either to "educate" the general public or to unite, inspire or promote discussion amongst its members. Interpretation of the past became implicitly and often explicitly a revolutionary act, a rejection of the stultifying views of those who would maintain the status quo in politics, sexual relationships or gender stereotypes. Historical drama also clearly reflected the gradual hardening of left-wing politics over a quarter of a century. During that period the viewpoint of its dramatists ranged from the humanitarian socialism of the 1950s, emphasising the dignity of the working class, through the anarchism of the 1960s with its celebration of vitality and freedom into, after 1968, either grotesque iconoclasm inspired by situationism or political analyses based upon Marxism. Nevertheless, the dramatists were by no means comprehensive in their choice of subject matter and were to ignore whole areas of social, political and economic history. For example, while imperialism was repeatedly evoked as an issue, with the exceptions of Howard Brenton and the Ardens little interest was exhibited by the majority of dramatists in the plight of its *victims*, the indigenous population. For the most part imperialism was represented from a Marxist standpoint simply as an inevitable stage in the evolution of capitalism and was raised alongside its antecedent, enclosure, as an emblem of its intrinsic injustice. Racial issues, which were high in the public consciousness during the

1960s and 1970s, were barely touched upon in the historical drama and, as discussed earlier, women were mostly portrayed stereotypically by male dramatists in secondary roles as mothers, wives or lovers. It was not until the penetration of the theatre by the women's movement during the late 1970s and early 1980s that history was employed to draw attention to and to re-evaluate women's private, social and political roles.

During the Thatcher years of the 1980s, deprived of the fuel of left-wing political activism, radical historical drama lost its role in the political life of the nation. Its prevalence has, therefore, predictably been lost. Already, for example, the historical documentary established during the 1960s, politicised in the 1970s and characterised by its folksy ballads and its worthy but oppressed working-class characters, now appears as something of an anachronism. Nevertheless, in spite of these obvious symptoms of decline, the attempt to inter-relate the private experience of ordinary people with the public events of history will, I believe, continue. In spite of the present apparent dominance of capitalist values, human beings are not yet again being portrayed as individualists capable of carving out their own destiny by the sheer force of will, nor as mere puppets of inescapable historical forces. This may not be too surprising when one considers that those dramatists discussed in the previous pages are only now reaching their middle age, are established in their careers, are still writing, and are unlikely to alter fundamentally their political stance, at least in the foreseeable future. Finally, as the earlier biographical drama to a great extent reflected the hierarchical class-structure of the society in which it was produced, so the populist outlook of the historical drama of the past three decades will, I think, only be replaced when British society undergoes a similarly significant social or political reorientation to that which has taken place in Britain since the Second World War. Nevertheless, the fall of Margaret Thatcher, the combination of closer politico-economic union within Western Europe and the gradual removal of communism from Eastern Europe by ordinary people who, in unison and often peacefully, have influenced the course of history, may re-vitalize those very questions concerning capitalism, collectivism and individual freedom which have been at the centre of British radical historical drama since 1956. Perhaps, therefore, in the coming post-Thatcher years, we may witness a renewed but less parochial British historical drama.

Notes

Introduction

1. Edward Bond, "Us, Our Drama and the National Theatre", *Plays and Players*, 26, No. 1 (Oct. 1978), p. 8.
2. Gareth Lloyd Evans, intro. to Gareth Lloyd Evans & Barbara Lloyd Evans (Eds.), *Plays in Review 1956–1980* (London: Batsford, 1985), p. 34.
3. Ibid., p. 36.
4. Trevor Griffiths, "In Defence of 'Occupations'", *Occupations* (London: Calder & Boyars, rev. 1980), p. 7.

Chapter 1

1. E. H. Carr, *What Is History?* (Harmondsworth: Penguin, 1964), p. 23.
2. Ibid.
3. Ibid., p. 131.
4. Edward Bond, *Early Morning*, in *Edward Bond, Plays: One* (London: Methuen, 1977), p. 136.
5. Eric Bentley, *The Theatre of Commitment* (London: Methuen, 1968), p. 208.
6. The cultural materialism of the "New Historicist" criticism which has developed in English literary studies during the 1980s has resulted in critical studies that "examine the implication of literary texts in history". See J. Dollimore & A. Sinfield, *Political Shakespeare* (Manchester: Manchester University Press, 1985).
7. Angus Calder, *The People's War* (London: Jonathan Cape, 1969, repr. St. Albans: Granada Publishing, 1982).

8. David Hare, "A Lecture Given at King's College Cambridge", 5th March 1978, publ. in David Hare, *Licking Hitler* (London: Faber & Faber, 1978), p. 66.

9. Ernest Mandel, *Introduction to Marxism* (London: Pluto Press, 1982), p. 183. (2nd rev. ed. of *From Class Society to Communism: An Introduction to Marxism*, London: Ink Links, 1977.)

10. See Bertolt Brecht (trans. Carl R. Mueller), *The Measures Taken*, in *The Measures Taken and Other Lehrstücke* (London: Eyre Methuen, 1977).

11. See Brecht "The Modern Theatre Is the Epic Theatre", in John Willett (trans.), *Brecht on Theatre* (London: Eyre Methuen, 1978), p. 37.

12. Hare, "A Lecture Given at Kings College, Cambridge", p. 66.

13. Arthur Marwick, *The Nature of History* (London: Macmillan, 2nd ed., 1981) p. 209.

14. Ibid., p. 208.

15. For a concise description of British "People's History" which first began to be written in the late eighteenth century, and of which Marxist history is merely a facet, see Raphael Samuel, "People's History" and Peter Burke, "People's History or Total History", both in Raphael Samuel (Ed.), *People's History and Socialist Theory* (London: Routledge & Kegan Paul, 1981).

16. Howard Brenton, *Gum and Goo*, in *Plays for Public Places* (London: Eyre Methuen, 1972), p. 13.

17. Peter Flannery, *Our Friends in the North* (London: Methuen, 1982), p. 63.

Chapter 2

1. Katherine Worth, *Revolutions in Modern English Drama* (London: G. Bell & Sons, 1972), p. 5.

2. A. W. Pollard, intro. to H. F. Rubinstein & Clifford Bax, *Shakespeare* (London: Benn Bros, 1921), unnumbered.

3. Reginald Berkeley, *The Lady with the Lamp* (London: Gollancz, 1929), p. 14.

4. Edwin Morgan, "That Uncertain Feeling", in C. Marowitz & S. Trussler (Eds.), *The Encore Reader* (London: Methuen, 1965), p. 53.

5. Robert Bolt, intro. to *Vivat! Vivat Regina!* (London: Heineman, 1971), p. xxii.

6. Hilary Spurling, *Plays and Players*, 18, No. 2 (Nov. 1970), p. 42.

7. Marowitz & Trussler, *The Encore Reader*, pp. 135–136.

8. Kenneth Tynan, *Right and Left* (London: Longmans Green, 1967), p. 27.

9. Ibid.

10. Brecht, "Theatre for Pleasure or Theatre for Instruction", in Willett, *Brecht on Theatre*, pp. 70–71.

11. Bertolt Brecht, "A Short Organum for the Theatre", in Willett, *Brecht on Theatre*, p. 190.

12. Ibid., p. 191.

13. Ibid., p. 190.

14. John Osborne, *Luther* (London: Faber & Faber, 1961), p. 46.

15. Simon Trussler, *The Plays of John Osborne: An Assessment* (London: Gollancz, 1969), p. 99.

16. Tynan, *Right and Left*, p. 77.

Chapter 3

1. Quoted from Ann Wolrige-Gordon, *Peter Howard: Life and Letters* (London, 1969), pp. 137–138 in David Childs, *Britain Since 1945* (London: Ernest Benn, 1979), p. 13.

2. Arnold Wesker, in C. Marowitz & S. Trussler (Eds.), *Theatre at Work* (London: Methuen, 1967), p. 83.

3. Childs, *Britain Since 1945*, p. 115.

4. Ibid., p. 91.

5. John Osborne, *Look Back in Anger* (London: Faber & Faber, 1957), p. 85.

6. Childs, *Britain Since 1945*, p. 106.

7. Wesker, in Marowitz & Trussler, *Theatre at Work*, p. 83.

8. Wesker, *Chicken Soup with Barley*, in *The Wesker Trilogy* (Harmondsworth: Penguin, 1964), p. 75.

9. Ibid., p. 41.

10. Ibid., p. 73.

11. Ibid., p. 62.

12. Ibid.

13. Ibid., p. 42.

14. Ibid., p. 43.

15. Wesker, *I'm Talking About Jerusalem*, in *The Wesker Trilogy* (Harmondsworth: Penguin, 1964), p. 187.

16. Ibid., p. 216.

17. Ibid., p. 214.

18. Wesker, *Chicken Soup with Barley*, p. 48. (Ronnie later refers to Dave and Ada as being in the Cotswolds, but in *I'm Talking About Jerusalem* they are indeed discovered in the fenlands of Norfolk.)

19. Wesker, *I'm Talking About Jerusalem*, p. 164.

20. Ewan MacColl, *Uranium 235*, in H. Goorney & Ewan MacColl, *Agit-Prop to Theatre Workship* (Manchester: Manchester University Press, 1986), p. 126.

21. Theatre Workshop, *Oh What a Lovely War* (London: Methuen, 1965), p. 77.

22. John McGrath, *A Good Night Out* (London: Eyre Methuen, 1981), p. 48.

23. Peter Cheeseman, interview quoted in G. A. Elvgren, "The Evolution of a Theatrical Style: A Study of the Interrelationship of Select Regional Playwrights, the Director, the Community, and the Round Stage at the Victoria Theatre, Stoke-on-Trent", Unpubl. Ph.D. Thesis, Florida State University, 1972, p. 220.

24. Alan Plater, intro. to *Close the Coalhouse Door* (London: Methuen, 1969), p. vii.

25. John Arden, "Telling a True Tale" (1960), in Marowitz & Trussler, *The Encore Reader*, p. 128.

26. Ibid., p. 125.

27. Arden, Introductory Note, in *Ironhand* (London: Methuen, 1965), p. 5.

28. Ibid.

29. Ibid.

30. Ibid., p. 156.

31. Ibid., p. 36.

32. Arden, in Marowitz & Trussler, *Theatre at Work*, p. 50.

33. Arden, *Armstrong's Last Goodnight* (London: Methuen, 1965), p. 25.

34. Arden, in Marowitz & Trussler, *Theatre at Work*, p. 52.

35. Arden, "Author's Notes", in *Left-Handed Liberty* (London: Methuen, 1965), p. xii.

36. Arden, in Marowitz & Trussler, *Theatre at Work*, p. 52.

37. Ibid.

38. Arden, *Left-Handed Liberty*, p. xii.

39. Ibid., p. 83.

40. Ibid., p. 91.

41. Ibid.

42. Ibid., p. 92.

43. Ibid., p. xii.

Chapter 4

1. D. McKie & C. Cooke, *The Decade of Disillusion: British Politics in the Sixties* (London: Macmillan, 1972), p. 1.

2. Raymond Williams, *The Long Revolution* (London: Chatto & Windus, 1961; Harmondsworth: Penguin, 1965), pp. 360–361.

3. McKie & Cooke, *The Decade of Disillusion*, p. 4.

4. H. Young, "Politics Outside the System", in McKie & Cooke, *The Decade of Disillusion*, p. 217.

5. Ibid., p. 215.

6. Ibid., p. 220.

7. Nicolas Walter, *About Anarchism* (London: Freedom Press 1969), p. 6.

8. Colin Ward, *Anarchy in Action* (London: Allen & Unwin, 1973), p. 13.

9. David Stafford, "Anarchists in Britain Today", in D. E. Apter & J. Joll, *Anarchism Today* (London: Macmillan, 1971), p. 85.

10. David Hare, interviewed in "Face to Face", BBC2 TV, 16th May 1989.

11. Richard Gombin, "The Ideology and Practice of Contestation Seen through Recent Events in France", in Apter & Joll, *Anarchism Today*, p. 21.

12. Howard Brenton, *Magnificence,* in *Howard Brenton, Plays: One* (London: Methuen, 1986), p. 96.

13. Brenton, "Petrol Bombs through the Proscenium Arch", *Theatre Quarterly*, V, No. 17 (1975), p. 10.

14. Gustav Landauer, quoted in Ward, *Anarchy in Action*, p. 19.

15. Edward Bond, Preface to *Lear* (London: Methuen, 1971), p. xii.

16. Ibid., p. 13.

17. Ward, *Anarchy in Action*, p. 13.

18. Colin McArthur, *Television and History* (London: British Film Institute, 1978), p. 4.

19. David Edgar, "Ten Years of Political Theatre", *Theatre Quarterly*, VIII, No. 32 (1979), p. 29.

20. Ibid., p. 27.

21. Hare, "A Lecture Given at King's College, Cambridge", p. 63.

22. Edgar, "Ten Years of Political Theatre", p. 31.

23. Hare, "A Lecture Given at King's College, Cambridge", p. 63.

24. McGrath, *A Good Night Out*, pp. 42–43.

25. Edgar, "Ten Years of Political Theatre", p. 32.

26. Ibid., p. 29.

27. Bond, "The Activist Papers", in *The Worlds with the Activist Papers* (London: Eyre Methuen, 1980), p. 131.

28. Ibid., p. 129.

29. John Arden & Margaretta D'Arcy, *The Hero Rises Up* (London: Methuen, 1969), p. 13.

30. Ibid., p. 14.

31. Ibid., p. 15.

32. Ibid., p. 21.

33. Ibid., p. 16.

34. Robert Cushman, *Plays and Players*, XVI, No. 4 (Jan. 1969), p. 52.

35. D. A. N. Jones, *The Listener*, 14th Nov. 1968, p. 660.

36. Benedict Nightingale, *New Statesman*, 15th Nov. 1968, p. 682.

37. D. A. N. Jones, *New Statesman*, 5th May 1967, p. 627.

38. Robert Cushman, *Plays and Players*, p. 52.

39. See "An Asymmetrical Authors' Preface", in Arden & D'Arcy, *The Hero Rises Up*, p. 5.

40. Arden & D'Arcy, *The Hero Rises Up*, p. 23.

41. Ibid., p. 96.

42. Ibid., p. 25.

43. Ibid., p. 16.

44. Ibid., p. 101.

45. See "An Asymmetrical Authors' Preface", in Arden & D'Arcy, *The Hero Rises Up*, p. 6.

Chapter 5

1. C. W. E. Bigsby, "Language of Crisis in British Theatre", in C. W. E. Bigsby (Ed.), *Contemporary English Drama*, Stratford-upon-Avon Studies 19 (London: Edward Arnold, 1981), p. 38.

2. Caryl Churchill, intro. to *Light Shining in Buckinghamshire*, in *Caryl Churchill, Plays: One* (London: Methuen, 1985), p. 183.

3. Trevor Griffiths, quoted in M. Poole & J. Wyver, *Powerplays: Trevor Griffiths in Television* (London: British Film Institute, 1984), p. 35.

4. Trevor Griffiths, *Occupations* (London: Faber & Faber, rev. 1980), p. 46.

5. Ibid.

6. Ibid., pp. 59–60.

7. See Griffiths, "In Defence of 'Occupations'", p. 11.

8. Griffiths, *Occupations*, p. 18.

9. Trevor Griffiths, *Absolute Beginners*, in *All Good Men and Absolute Beginners* (London: Faber & Faber, 1977), p. 87.

10. Ibid., p. 82.

11. Ibid., p. 107.

12. Ibid., p. 78.

13. Peter Weiss, "The Material and Models: Notes Towards a Definition of Documentary Theatre", *Theatre Quarterly*, 1, No. 1 (Jan.–March 1971), p. 42.

14. Ibid., p. 41.

15. Ibid., p. 42.

16. Steve Gooch, *Will Wat, If Not, Wat Will?* (London: Pluto Press, 1973), p. 7.

17. Ibid., p. 41.

18. Ibid., p. 76.

19. Ibid., p. 67.

20. Ibid.

21. Ibid., p. 74.

22. Ibid., p. 78.

23. John Mortimer, *The Observer*, quoted in Steve Gooch, *Will Wat, If Not, Wat Will?*.

24. Gooch, "Writers Note", in *Will Wat, If Not, Wat Will?*, unnumbered.

25. Dan Garret, "Documentary Drama: Its Roots and Development in Britain" (unpublished Ph.D. Thesis, University of Hull, 1977), p. 94.

26. John McGrath, Note to *The Cheviot, the Stag and the Black, Black Oil* (London: Methuen, 1981), p. 77.

27. Ibid.

28. See Edgar, "Ten Years of Political Theatre", p. 29.

29. McGrath, "Better a Bad Night in Bootle . . . ", *Theatre Quarterly* V, No. 19 (Sept.–Nov. 1975), p. 51.

30. McGrath, *The Cheviot, the Stag and the Black, Black Oil*, p. 2.

31. Ibid., p. 73.

32. Ibid., p. 29.

33. Ibid., p. 57.

34. Ibid., pp. 59–61.

35. Ibid., p. 65.

36. John McGrath, *The Game's a Bogey* (Edinburgh: EUSPB, 1975), p. 53.

37. John Arden, Preface to *Two Autobiographical Plays* (London: Methuen, 1971), p. 11.

38. Ibid., p. 17.

39. Albert Hunt, *Arden: A Study of His Plays* (London: Eyre Methuen, 1974), p. 153.

40. John Arden & Margaretta D'Arcy, *To Present the Pretence: Essays on Theatre and Its Public* (London: Eyre Methuen, 1977), p. 158.

41. John Arden & Margaretta D'Arcy, intro. to *The Non-Stop Connolly Show* Vol. 1. (London: Pluto Press, 1977), p. v.

42. Arden & D'Arcy, *To Present the Pretence*, pp. 95–96.

43. Arden & D'Arcy, intro. to *The Non-Stop Connolly Show*, vol. 1, p. v.

44. Ibid.

45. Ibid., p. vii.

46. Ibid.

47. Arden & D'Arcy *The Non-Stop Connolly Show*, vol. 2, p. 18.

48. Arden & D'Arcy, *The Non-Stop Connolly Show*, vol. 5, p. 106.

49. Paddy Marsh, "Easter at Liberty Hall: The Ardens' Non-Stop Connolly Show", *Theatre Quarterly*, V, No. 20 (Dec.–Feb. 1976), p. 141.

50. Churchill, intro. to *Light Shining in Buckinghamshire*, p. 183.

51. Red Ladder Theatre, intro. to *Taking Our Time* (London: Pluto Press, 1979), p. xii.

52. Peter Whelan, *Captain Swing* (London: Rex Collings, 1979).

53. McGrath, *A Good Night Out*, p. 90.

54. Marowitz & Trussler, *Theatre at Work*, p. 123.

55. William Gaskell, in Marowitz & Trussler, *Theatre at Work*, p. 132.

56. David Hare, intro to *The Asian Plays* (London: Faber & Faber, 1986), p. viii.

57. Ibid., p. ix.

58. David Hare, *Fanshen*, in *The Asian Plays*, p. 13.

59. Ibid., p. 78.

60. Ibid., p. 76.

61. Ibid., p. 14.

62. Ibid., p. 78.

63. Bond, "The Activist Papers", p. 129.

64. Edgar, "Ten Years of Political Theatre", p. 29.

Chapter 6

1. David Hare, interviewed in "Face to Face", BBC2 TV, 16th May 1989.

2. Ibid.

3. Edgar, "Ten Years of Political Theatre", p. 32.

4. Hare, "A Lecture Given at King's College, Cambridge", p. 66.

5. Howard Brenton & David Hare, *Brassneck* (London: Methuen, 1974), p. 12.

6. Ibid., p. 55.

7. Ibid., p. 85.

8. Ibid., p. 94.

9. Ibid., p. 99.

10. Ibid., p. 102.

11. Howard Brenton, *Measure for Measure*, in *Howard Brenton: Three Plays* (Sheffield: Sheffield Academic Press, 1989), p. 163.

12. Howard Brenton, *A Sky Blue Life*, in *Howard Brenton: Three Plays*, p. 26.

13. Ibid., p. 28.

14. Ibid., p. 29.
15. Ibid., p. 43.
16. Ibid., p. 44.
17. Ibid., p. 45.
18. Ibid., p. 46.
19. Ibid., p. 17.
20. Howard Brenton, *Wesley*, in *Plays for Public Places* (London: Methuen, 1972), p. 32.
21. Howard Brenton, *Hitler Dances* (London: Methuen, 1982), p. 73.
22. Ibid., p. 74.
23. Howard Brenton, *The Churchill Play,* in *Howard Brenton, Plays: One* (London: Methuen, 1986), p. 113.
24. Ibid., p. 119.
25. Calder, *The People's War*, p. 112.
26. Ibid.
27. Brenton, *The Churchill Play*, p. 163.
28. Ibid., p. 170.
29. Ibid., p. 164.
30. Ibid., p. 167.
31. Ibid., p. 170.
32. Calder, *The People's War*, pp. 21–22.
33. Brenton, *The Churchill Play*, p. 157.
34. Ibid., p. 174.
35. Ibid., p. 149.
36. Ibid., p. 175.
37. Ibid., p. 176.
38. Ibid.
39. Ibid., p. 177.
40. Howard Brenton, *Weapons of Happiness*, in *Howard Brenton, Plays: One*, p. 183.
41. Ibid., p. 201.
42. Ibid., p. 232.
43. Ibid., p. 244.
44. Ibid., p. 248.
45. Ibid., p. 249.
46. Howard Brenton, *Magnificence*, in *Howard Brenton, Plays: One*, p. 85.
47. See Brenton, "Petrol Bombs Through the Proscenium Arch", p. 10.
48. David Hare, interviewed in *The Sunday Times*, 16th Dec. 1984, p. 37.
49. Hare, intro to *The History Plays*, p. 15.
50. See Hare, "A Lecture Given at King's College, Cambridge", p. 60.
51. Hare, *Licking Hitler*, in *The History Plays*, p. 12.
52. Hare, "A Lecture Given at King's College, Cambridge", p. 67.
53. Hare, intro. to *The History Plays*, p. 15.
54. David Hare, *Plenty*, in *The History Plays*, p. 193.
55. Ibid., p. 133.
56. Ibid.
57. Ibid., p. 199.
58. Ibid., p. 204.

59. Ibid.

60. Ibid., p. 207.

61. Hare, "A Lecture Given at King's College, Cambridge", p. 70.

62. Catherine Itzin, *Stages in the Revolution* (London: Eyre Methuen, 1980), p. 337.

63. Howard Brenton, in Philip Oakes, "Caesar on the South Bank", *The Sunday Times*, 12th October 1980, p. 39.

64. Howard Brenton, *The Romans in Britain* (London: Eyre Methuen, 1980), p. 65. The line is in part a quotation from W. B. Yeats' *Long-legged Fly* (1936–39) in which there is also a reference to Caesar, whose "mind moves upon silence".

65. Philip Oakes, *The Sunday Times*, 12th October 1980, p. 39.

66. Brenton, *The Romans in Britain*, p. 19.

67. Ibid., p. 24.

68. Ibid., p. 51.

69. Ibid., p. 58.

70. Ibid., p. 78.

71. Ibid., p. 100.

72. Ibid., pp. 100–101.

73. Ibid., p. 105.

74. Ibid.

75. Brenton, in *The Sunday Times*, 12th October 1980, p. 39.

76. Howard Brenton, *Sonnet 30*, reproduced in *Bloody Poetry*, Royal Court Writers Series (London: Methuen, 1985), unnumbered.

77. Ibid., p. 12.

78. Ibid., p. 70.

79. Ibid., p. 14.

80. Ibid., p. 74.

81. Ibid., p. 79.

82. Ibid., p. 71.

83. Ibid., p. 72.

84. Hare, "A Lecture Given at King's College, Cambridge", p. 69.

85. Ibid., p. 63.

Chapter 7

1. Edward Bond, "Us, Our Drama and the National Theatre", p. 9.

2. Ibid.

3. Edward Bond, intro. to *The Fool*, in *Edward Bond, Plays: Three* (London: Methuen, 1987), p. 75.

4. Edward Bond, in a letter to Tony Coult, 28th July 1977, quoted in M. Hay & P. Roberts, *Bond: A Study of His Plays* (London: Eyre Methuen, 1980), p. 179.

5. Edward Bond, intro. to *Bingo*, in *Edward Bond, Plays: Three*, p. 7.

6. Ibid., p. 4.

7. Bond, *Bingo*, p. 20.

8. Ibid., pp. 62–63.

9. Ibid., p. 10.

10. Ibid., see pp. 59–65.

11. Ibid., p. 4.

12. Ibid., p. 6.

13. Edward Bond, *The Fool*, in *Edward Bond, Plays: Three*, p. 88.

14. Ibid., p. 106.

15. Ibid., p. 122.

16. Ibid., p. 121.

17. Ibid., p. 148.

18. Ibid., p. 121.

19. Ibid., p. 150.

20. See Hay & Roberts, *Bond: A Study of His Plays*, p. 240.

21. Bond, draft of an article for *Socialist Challenge*, August 1978, quoted in Hay & Roberts, *Bond: A Study of His Plays*, p. 239.

22. Ibid.

23. Edward Bond, "A Socialist Rhapsody", in *Edward Bond, Plays: Three*, p. 270.

24. Edward Bond, *The Woman*, in *Edward Bond, Plays: Three*, p. 176.

25. Edward Bond, in an unpublished interview with Tony Coult, August 1978, quoted in Hay & Roberts, *Bond: A Study of His Plays*, p. 239.

26. Bond, *The Woman*, p. 232.

27. John Peter, *The Sunday Times*, 13th August 1978, p. 35.

28. Bond, "A Socialist Rhapsody", p. 270.

Chapter 8

1. Angela Neustatter, *Hyenas in Petticoats: A Look at Twenty Years of Feminism* (London: Harrap, 1989), p. 14.

2. Ibid., p. 13.

3. Margaret Warters, quoted in Neustatter, *Hyenas in Petticoats*, p. 14.

4. Pam Gems, interview with Micheline Wandor, *Spare Rib*, Sept. 1977, quoted in Micheline Wandor, *Understudies: Theatre and Sexual Politics* (London: Eyre Methuen, 1981), p. 162.

5. Pam Gems, afterword to *Queen Christina*, in Mary Remnant (Ed.), *Plays by Women, 5* (London: Methuen, 1986), p. 47.

6. Micheline Wandor, *Understudies*, p. 7.

7. Susan Todd, from an unpublished lecture given at the King's College Cambridge Conference on Political Theatre, April 1978, quoted in Itzin, *Stages in the Revolution*, p. 274.

8. Micheline Wandor, from an unpublished lecture given at King's College, Cambridge, Conference on Political Theatre, April 1978. Quoted in Itzin, *Stages in the Revolution*, p. 275.

9. Steve Gooch, intro. to *The Women Pirates Ann Bonney and Mary Read* (London: Pluto Press, 1978), unnumbered.

10. Neustatter, *Hyenas in Petticoats*, pp. 12–13.

11. Gooch, *The Woman Pirates Ann Bonney and Mary Read*, pp. 49–50.

12. *Shrew*, quoted in Neustatter, *Hyenas in Petticoats*, p. 34.

13. Irving Wardle, *The Times*, 1st August 1978, p. 9.

14. Liz Lochhead, *Blood and Ice*, in Micheline Wandor (Ed.), *Plays by Women 4* (London: Methuen, 1985), p. 112.

15. Ibid., p. 107.

16. Ibid., p. 100.

17. Ibid., p. 103.

18. Ibid., p. 115.

19. Ibid.

20. Ibid., p. 116.

21. Churchill, intro. to *Light Shining in Buckinghamshire*, p. 183.

22. Neustatter, *Hyenas in Petticoats*, p. 236.

23. Caryl Churchill, *Top Girls* (London: Methuen, 1982), p. 84.

24. Ibid., p. 86.

25. Ibid., p. 87.

26. Timberlake Wertenbaker, *New Anatomies*, in *Introductions* (London: Faber & Faber, 1984), p. 299.

27. Ibid., p. 302.

28. Ibid., pp. 304–305.

29. Ibid., p. 309.

30. Ibid., p. 312.

31. Ibid., p. 325.

32. Ibid., p. 325.

33. Ibid., pp. 325–326.

34. Ibid., p. 327.

35. Ibid.

36. Ibid., p. 333.

Chapter 9

1. In addition to *Destiny* and *Maydays* are *Oh Fair Jerusalem* (1975) and *Entertaining Strangers*, the latter originally written in 1985 as a community play for performance by an amateur cast in Dorchester but subsequently presented in a revised version at the National Theatre in 1987.

2. David Edgar, *Destiny*, in *David Edgar, Plays: One* (London: Methuen, 1987), p. 323.

3. Ibid., p. 331.

4. Ibid., . 336.

5. Ibid., pp. 404–405.

6. James Fenton, *The Sunday Times*, 23rd October 1983, p. 39.

7. Edgar, *Maydays* (London: Methuen, 1984), pp. 45–46.

8. Ibid., p. 106.

9. Ibid., p. 120.

10. Ibid., p. 145.

11. Ibid., p. 146.

12. Fenton, *The Sunday Times*, 23rd October 1983, p. 39.

Bibliography

THE POST-WAR BRITISH THEATRE

Bentley, Eric. *The Theatre of Commitment*. London: Methuen, 1968.

Bigsby, C. W. E. "Language of Crisis in British Theatre", in C. W. E. Bigsby (Ed.), *Contemporary English Drama*. Stratford-upon-Avon Studies 19. London: Edward Arnold, 1981.

Bull, John. *New British Political Dramatists*. London: Macmillan, 1984.

Dollimore, J., & Sinfield A. *Political Shakespeare*. Manchester: Manchester University Press, 1985.

Garret, Dan. "Documentary Drama: Its Roots and Development in Britain." Unpublished Ph.D. Thesis, University of Hull, 1977.

Itzin, Catherine. *Stages in the Revolution: Political Theatre in Britain Since 1968*. London: Eyre Methuen, 1980.

Jameson, Frederic. *Marxism and Form*. Princeton, NJ: Princeton University Press, 1971.

Lloyd Evans, Gareth, & Lloyd Evans, Barbara (Eds.). *Plays in Review 1956–1980*. London: Batsford, 1985.

Marowitz, C., & Trussler, S. (Eds.). *The Encore Reader*. London: Methuen, 1965.

Marowitz, C., & Trussler, S. (Eds.). *Theatre at Work*. London: Methuen, 1967.

McArthur, Colin. *Television and History*. London: British Film Institute, 1978.

Taylor, John Russell. *Anger and After*. Harmondsworth: Penguin, rev. ed. 1963.

Tynan, Kenneth. *Right and Left*. London: Longmans Green, 1967.

Wandor, Micheline. *Understudies: Theatre and Sexual Politics*. London: Eyre Methuen, 1981.

Weiss, Peter, "The Material and Models: Notes Towards a Definition of Documentary Theatre." *Theatre Quarterly*, Vol. 1, No. 1 (Jan.–March 1971).
Worth, Katherine. *Revolutions in Modern English Drama*. London: G. Bell & Sons, 1972.

HISTORY AND POLITICS

Apter, D. E., & Joll J. *Anarchism Today*. London: Macmillan, 1971.
Calder, Angus. *The People's War*. London: Jonathan Cape 1969; repr. St. Albans: Granada Publishing, 1982.
Carr, E. H. *What Is History?* Harmondsworth: Penguin, 1964.
Childs, David. *Britain Since 1945*. London: Ernest Benn, 1979.
Hinton, William. *Fanshen: A Documentary of Revolution in a Chinese Village*. New York/London: Monthly Review Press, 1968.
Hobsbawm, E. J. E., & Rude, G. *Captain Swing*. London: Lawrence & Wishart, 1969.
Mandel, Ernest. *Introduction to Marxism*. London: Pluto Press, 1982 (2nd rev. ed. of *From Class Society to Communism: An Introduction to Marxism*, London: Ink Links, 1977).
Marwick, Arthur. *The Nature of History*, 2nd ed. London: Macmillan, 1981.
McKie, D., & Cooke C. *The Decade of Disillusion: British Politics in the Sixties*. London: Macmillan, 1972.
Neustatter, Angela. *Hyenas in Petticoats*. London: Harrap, 1989.
Samuel, Raphael (Ed.). *People's History and Socialist Theory*. London: Routledge & Kegan Paul, 1981.
Thompson, E. P. *The Making of the English Working Class*. London: Gollancz, 1963; Harmondsworth, Penguin, 1968.
Walter, Nicolas. *About Anarchism*. London: Freedom Press, 1969.
Ward, Colin. *Anarchy in Action*. London: Allen & Unwin, 1973.
Williams, Raymond. *The Long Revolution*. London: Chatto & Windus, 1961; Harmondsworth: Penguin, 1965.

PLAYS AND CRITICISM

Jim Allen

Perdition. London/New York: Ithaca Press, 1987.

John Arden

Armstrong's Last Goodnight. London: Methuen, 1965.
Ironhand. London: Methuen, 1965.
Left-Handed Liberty. London: Methuen, 1965.
Two Autobiographical Plays. London: Methuen, 1971.

John Arden & Margaretta D'Arcy

The Hero Rises Up. London: Methuen, 1969.
The Non-Stop Connolly Show (5 vols.). London: Pluto Press, 1977.

John Arden & Margaretta D'Arcy. *To Present the Pretence: Essays on Theatre and Its Public.* London: Eyre Methuen, 1977.
Robert Cushman. *Plays and Players*, XVI, No. 4., Jan. 1969.
Albert Hunt. *Arden: A Study of His Plays.* London: Eyre Methuen, 1974.
D. A. N. Jones. *New Statesman*, 5th May 1967, p. 627.
D. A. N. Jones. *The Listener*, 14th Nov. 1968, p. 660.
Paddy Marsh. "Easter at Liberty Hall: The Ardens' Non-Stop Connolly Show." *Theatre Quarterly*, V, No. 20, Dec.–Feb. 1976.
B. Nightingale. *New Statesman*, 15th Nov. 1968, p. 682.

Reginald Berkeley

The Lady with the Lamp. London: Gollancz, 1929.

Robert Bolt

A Man for All Seasons. London: Heineman, 1961.
Vivat! Vivat Regina! London: Heineman, 1971.

Edward Bond

Lear. London: Methuen, 1971.
Early Morning, in *Edward Bond, Plays: One.* London: Methuen, 1977.
The Fool / Bingo / The Woman, in *Edward Bond, Plays: Three.* London: Methuen, 1987.

"The Activist Papers", in *The Worlds with the Activist Papers.* London: Eyre Methuen, 1980.
"Us, Our Drama and the National Theatre." *Plays and Players*, 26, No. 1, Oct. 1978.
M. Hay & P. Roberts. *Bond: A Study of His Plays.* London: Eyre Methuen, 1980.

Bertolt Brecht

The Measures Taken (trans. Carl R. Mueller), in *The Measures Taken and Other Lehrstücke.* London: Eyre Methuen, 1977.
Brecht on Theatre (trans. John Willett). London: Eyre Methuen, 1978.
Galileo (trans. John Willett), in *Brecht: Plays Three.* London: Methuen, 1987.

Howard Brenton

Gum and Goo / Wesley / Scott of the Antarctic, in *Plays for Public Places.* London: Eyre Methuen, 1972.

The Romans in Britain. London: Eyre Methuen, 1980.
Hitler Dances. London: Methuen, 1982.
Bloody Poetry. London: Methuen, 1985.
Weapons of Happiness / Epsom Downs / Sore Throats, in Howard Brenton,
     Plays: One. London: Methuen, 1986.
A Sky Blue Life / How Beautiful with Badges / Measure for Measure, in *How-
     ard Brenton: Three Plays*. Sheffield: Sheffield Academic Press, 1989.
     "Petrol Bombs Through the Proscenium Arch." *Theatre Quarterly*, V, No.
          17, 1975.
     Philip Oakes, "Caesar on the South Bank", *The Sunday Times*, 12th Octo-
          ber 1980, p. 39.

Howard Brenton & David Hare

Brassneck. London: Methuen, 1974.

Caryl Churchill

Top Girls. London: Methuen, 1982.
Light Shining in Buckinghamshire, in *Caryl Churchill, Plays: One*. London:
     Methuen, 1985.

Alan Cullen

The Stirrings in Sheffield on Saturday Night. London: Eyre Methuen, 1974.

David Edgar

Maydays, rev. ed. London: Methuen, 1984.
Destiny / The Jail Diary of Abbie Sachs / Saigon Rose / O Fair Jerusalem, in
     David Edgar Plays: One. London: Methuen, 1987.
     "Ten Years of Political Theatre." *Theatre Quarterly*, VIII, No. 32, 1979.
     "Towards a Theatre of Dynamic Ambiguities." *Theatre Quarterly*, IX, No.
          33, 1979.

Peter Flannery

Our Friends in the North. London: Methuen, 1982.

Pam Gems

Queen Christina, in Mary Remnant (ed.), *Plays by Women 5*. London:
     Methuen, 1986.

Steve Gooch

Will Wat, If Not, Wat Will? London: Pluto Press, 1973.
The Women Pirates Ann Bonney and Mary Read. London: Pluto Press, 1978.

Trevor Griffiths

The Party. London: Faber & Faber, 1974.
Absolute Beginners, in *All Good Men and Absolute Beginners,* London: Faber
& Faber, 1977.
Occupations. London: Faber & Faber, rev. ed. 1980.

   Tom Nairn. *7 Days,* 3rd November 1971.
   M. Poole & J. Wyver. *Powerplays: Trevor Griffiths in Television.* London:
      British Film Institute, 1984.

David Hare

Plenty / Licking Hitler / Knuckle, in *The History Plays.* London: Faber &
   Faber, 1984.
Fansen / A Map of the World / Saigon, in *The Asian Plays.* London: Faber &
   Faber, 1986.

   "A Lecture Given at King's College, Cambridge", 5th March 1978, publ. in
      David Hare, *Licking Hitler,* London: Faber & Faber, 1978.
   Peter Ansorge, "David Hare: A War on Two Fronts." *Plays and Players,*
      April 1978.

Liz Lochhead

Blood and Ice, in Michelene Wandor (Ed.), *Plays by Women 4.* London: Methuen, 1985.

Ewan MacColl

Uranium 235, in H. Goorney & Ewan MacColl, *Agit-Prop to Theatre Workshop.* Manchester: Manchester University Press, 1986.

John McGrath

The Game's a Bogey. Edinburgh: EUSPB, 1975.
Little Red Hen. London: Pluto Press, 1977.
The Cheviot, the Stag and the Black, Black Oil. London: Methuen, 1981.
A Good Night Out: Popular Theatre: Audience, Class and Form. London:
   Eyre Methuen, 1981.

   "Better a Bad Night in Bootle, . . ." *Theatre Quarterly,* V, No. 19, Septem-
      ber–November 1975.
   "The Year of the Cheviot." *Plays and Players,* Feburary 1974.

Ronald Millar

Robert and Elizabeth. London: French, 1967.
Abelard and Heloise. London/New York: French, 1970.

John Osborne

The Entertainer. London: Faber and Faber, 1957.
Look Back in Anger. London: Faber & Faber, 1957.
Luther. London: Faber & Faber, 1961.
    Simon Trussler. *The Plays of John Osborne: An Assessment*. London: Gollancz, 1969.

Alan Plater

Close the Coalhouse Door. London: Methuen, 1969.

Terence Rattigan

Adventure Story. London: French, 1950.
Ross: A Dramatic Portrait. London: Hamish Hamilton, 1960.
A Bequest to the Nation. London: Hamish Hamilton, 1970.

Red Ladder Theatre

Taking Our Time. London: Pluto Press, 1979.

H. F. Rubinstein & Clifford Bax

Shakespeare. London: Benn Bros., 1921.

Peter Shaffer

The Royal Hunt of the Sun. London: Hamish Hamilton, 1965.

George Bernard Shaw

The Dark Lady of the Sonnets, in *The Complete Plays of Bernard Shaw*. London: Constable, 1931.
In Good King Charles's Golden Days. London: Reinhardt, The Bodley Head, 1974.
Saint Joan. London: Longman, 1983.
Caesar and Cleopatra. London: Longman, 1985.

Theatre Workshop

Oh What a Lovely War. London: Methuen, 1965.

   Howard Goorney. *The Theatre Workshop Story*. London: Eyre Methuen, 1981.

The Victoria Theatre, Stoke-on-Trent

The Knotty. London: Methuen, 1970.

   G. A. Elvgren. "The Evolution of a Theatrical Style: A Study of the Inter-relationship of Select Regional Playwrights, the Director, the Community, and the Round Stage at the Victoria Theatre, Stoke-on-Trent." Unpublished Ph.D. Thesis, Florida State University, 1972.

Timberlake Wertenbaker

New Anatomies, in *Introductions*. London: Faber & Faber, 1984.

Arnold Wesker

Chicken Soup with Barley / Roots / I'm Talking About Jerusalem, in *The Wesker Trilogy*. Harmondsworth: Penguin, 1964.

Peter Whelan

Captain Swing. London: Rex Collings, 1979.

Index

About the Author

D. KEITH PEACOCK is Lecturer in the Department of Drama at the University of Hull, England, where he specializes in modern British theatre. He has published numerous articles in major scholarly journals, including *Modern Drama* and *Theatre Research International*, and contributed to important reference books and essay collections on the subject, including the *International Dictionary of the Theatre*.